War, Journalism and History

War Correspondents in the Two World Wars

Edited by
Yvonne T. McEwen and Fiona A. Fisken

With a foreword by
Phillip Knightley

PETER LANG

Oxford · Bern · Berlin · Bruxelles · Frankfurt am Main · New York · Wien

Bibliographic information published by Die Deutsche Nationalbibliothek
Die Deutsche Nationalbibliothek lists this publication in the Deutsche National-
bibliografie;detailed bibliographic data is available on the Internet at http://dnb.d-nb.de.

A catalogue record for this book is available from the British Library.

Library of Congress Cataloging-in-Publication Data:

War, journalism and history : war correspondents in the two world wars /
[edited by] Yvonne T. McEwen and Fiona A. Fisken.
    p. cm.
 Includes bibliographical references and index.
 ISBN 978-3-0343-0789-5 (alk. paper)
 1. World War, 1914-1918--Journalists. 2. World War,
1939-1945--Journalists. 3. World War, 1914-1918--Press coverage. 4.
World War, 1939-1945--Press coverage. 5. War--Press
coverage--History--20th century. 6. War correspondents--History--20th
century. 7. War correspondents--Biography. I. McEwen, Yvonne. II.
Fisken, Fiona A., 1962-
 D631.W37 2012
 070.4'4994030922--dc23

                                    2012028110

ISBN 978-3-0343-0789-5

Cover design by Susan Halcro. Image: iStockphoto.

Peter Lang AG, International Academic Publishers, Bern 2012
Hochfeldstrasse 32, CH-3012 Bern, Switzerland
info@peterlang.com, www.peterlang.com, www.peterlang.net

Printed in Germany

War, Journalism and History

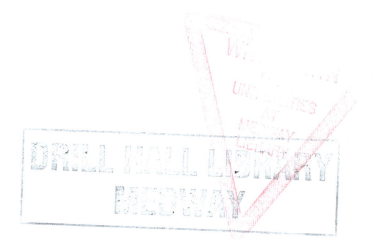

He has honor if he holds himself to an ideal of conduct though
it is inconvenient, unprofitable, or dangerous to do so
— WALTER LIPPMANN
Journalist (1889–1974)

*For the men, women and children who paid the price for
bringing us the truth about the obscenity of warfare.*

Contents

Acknowledgements

It is deeply regretted that Professor Jim McMillan, Director of the Centre for the Study of the Two World Wars, The University of Edinburgh, did not live to see the completion of this book. After a long but determined struggle with cancer he died on 22 February 2010. I am indebted to him for the encouragement he gave me when I first raised the idea of a conference and book examining the work of war corresponding in the two World Wars.

I am extremely grateful to all the contributors for their excellent submissions and the patience they have shown for the time it has taken for the book to come to fruition. However, I am more than delighted that national and international friendships have been established as a consequence of our collaborative efforts in producing this book on war correspondents.

Additionally, I would like to acknowledge the generosity of the Luard family for granting me permission to quote from the personal papers of E. K. Luard.

A very big debt of thanks goes to Professor Douglas Cairns who at the time of commissioning this book was Head of School at the School of History, Classics and Archaeology, The University of Edinburgh. His professional support and mentoring were invaluable to me and to the successful outcome of the war-correspondents' project. Thanks also to my Centre colleagues, Pauline McLean, Paul Addison, Jeremy Crang and David Stafford, who gave me great support, advice and encouragement.

The acknowledgments would be incomplete if I did not thank the staff at Peter Lang, particularly Lucy Melville and Holly Catling, for their hard work, and for having the vision to see the worth of this publication.

Finally, I could not have completed this book without the fantastic professional expertise of my co-editor Fiona Fisken. We met and worked together at Blackwell more than twenty-five years ago. Since then I have never faltered in my respect for her good judgement and wisdom. She has a wonderful capacity to face and solve professional and personal challenges and dilemmas. She is in one word, irreplaceable.

YVONNE MCEWEN

PHILLIP KNIGHTLEY

Foreword

The academics who took part in the War, Journalism and History Colloquium at the University of Edinburgh were delighted with the intellectual stimulation of the day's debate and the challenging new research and theories it produced. There was no reason for them to anticipate the historical significance of the occasion, for it is only now becoming apparent that the participants were describing and assessing a form of journalism that was already dying.

War journalism feels, like war, as if has been around forever. But it only really dates from the Crimean War of 1854 when William Howard Russell of *The Times* of London became the first civilian to send back to his newspaper reports of what was happening at the front. Until Russell came on the scene there were no reports at all or generals reported their own battles.

Russell's influence was enormous. For the first time a British army in the field was subjected to independent scrutiny and was found wanting. But Russell faced the problem that has haunted war correspondents ever since: how much could be told without endangering the war effort? As he wrote to his editor: 'Am I to tell these things, or hold my tongue?'.

The editor told him to go ahead and those reports he did not use in *The Times*, no doubt from apprehension that the newspaper would be accused of being unpatriotic, he circulated among Cabinet ministers, a process that eventually toppled the government.

The military was quick to realize the danger that this new form of reporting posed to its very existence and fought back, denying journalists access to the front lines, refusing information, interviews, guidance, support and courtesy. 'Out of my way, you drunken swabs', roared Lord Kitchener.

The military's methods became more sophisticated as it realized the war correspondents were here to stay and that it would have to coexist with them. Over the years it has tried censorship, appeals to the correspondents' patriotic instincts and, perhaps most successfully of all, recruiting the war correspondents into the overall war effort.

Owen Dudley Edwards, who was Reader in Commonwealth and American History at the University of Edinburgh, now Honorary Fellow, described in his presentation how Charles Masterman, head of the War Propaganda Bureau, organized a secret meeting of Britain's leading writers and journalists in 1914. They included Conan Doyle, Arnold Bennett, John Masefield, G. K. Chesterton, Sir Henry Newbolt, John Galsworthy, Thomas Hardy, Rudyard Kipling and H. G. Wells. Their recruitment into the war effort to write pamphlets, books and newspaper articles that promoted the government's view of the war was kept from the public until 1935.

The government was more direct with frontline correspondents. The six major ones were put into uniform and given honorary status of captains. They were provided with orderlies, lorries, cars, conducting officers and censors. When one of them asked General J. V. Charteris how much of an action he would be allowed to report, the General replied 'Say what you like, old man. But don't mention any places or people'.

They soon caught the mindset of the military they were supposed to be covering. One of them, Sir Philip Gibbs, wrote after the war: 'We identified absolutely with the Armies in the field [...] We wiped out of our minds all thought of personal scoops and all temptation to write one word which would make the task of officers and men more difficult or dangerous. There was no need for censorship of our dispatches. We were our own censors'.

The French were no better. Newspapers and reporters were subsumed into France's 'Union Sacree', that sacrosanct union of forces in France which conducted the nation's war. As described by Dr Tom Quinn, of University College Dublin, this system was so constricting that France's greatest journalist, Albert Londres, abandoned his attempts to cover the war and devoted himself to 'finding new measures of truth-telling'. He argued that censorship had an alienating effect on language and the nature of truth. So in a war-torn world where you could not believe what you read, the troops responded by printing their own newspapers in the trenches, and poets and novelists began to grapple with the task of finding new ways of presenting the truth about war. Londres posed the question that has concerned journalists ever since: 'How close can the war correspondent get to the pain, or to the truth? In a world of disintegrating narrative, what are the possibilities for the creation of a new narrative?'.

The search continued in the interwar years but the outbreak of the Second World War produced a major setback. The correspondents again became an integral part of the war effort and they were described by General Eisenhower as 'assimilated officers' or 'quasi staff officers'. A few were uncomfortable with the description. One, Charles Lynch, a Canadian who had been accredited to the British Army for Reuters, wrote, 'It is humiliating to look back at what we wrote during the war [...] We were a propaganda arm of our governments [...] We were cheerleaders. I suppose there wasn't an alternative at the time. It was total war. But, for God's sake, let's not glorify our role. It wasn't good journalism. It wasn't journalism at all'.

The debate was still going on fifty years later in Vietnam. American correspondent Michael Herr wrote that conventional journalism was the problem: it could no more reveal the Vietnam War than conventional fire power could win it.

British correspondent Gavin Young agreed. 'How can one depict the human facts of such a complete tragedy? What of the thoughts and feelings of the Vietnamese? How, if at all, have the Americans been changed by contact with the Vietnamese?' Young concluded, 'The Vietnamese War awaits its novelist'.

But news is meant to be instantaneous, especially with a twenty-four-hour a day continuous news cycle. It cannot wait for the reflections of the novelist. So the old dilemma remained – the military wanted to conceal all; the media wanted to reveal all.

The two sides thought about it and met to discuss it. At the meeting the BBC broadcaster, Sir Robin Day, said he doubted whether a democracy would ever be able to fight a war again, no matter how just, because of the way TV news would portray the horror of battle. The military took the warning seriously and the hunt began to find a way to manage the media in wartime. The United States led the way and the Department of Defense came up with a plan that it put into effect during the invasion of Iraq.

Its essence can be summed up in four points. Emphasize the dangers posed by the Iraqi regime. Dismiss and discredit those who cast doubt on these dangers. Do not get involved in appeals to logic but instead appeal to the public's hearts and minds, especially hearts. Drive home the message to the public: 'Trust us. We know more than we can tell you'. The Pentagon believed that this plan could not only shape opinion in the United States but all over the Western world. It was proved right.

A lot of thought went into controlling the correspondents. There had to be an appearance of openness and truthfulness. So briefings by officers trained to deal with the media were held at Central Command Headquarters. These briefings gave an official overall view of the war's progress. But correspondents clamoured for their own dynamic take on what was happening at the front and the freedom to report it. The difficulty was that every system that the Pentagon had tried for managing correspondents had aroused their ire precisely because the correspondents felt that they were being managed.

This time the military incorporated them into the national war effort by enlisting them and their organizations into the service of the country, exactly as it had done during the Second World War. In practice, this meant that the Pentagon offered media organizations, both American and foreign, the opportunity of 'embedding' a correspondent inside a specific military unit for the duration of the war.

The 'embeds' had honorary officer's rank and could wear uniform if they chose. Their unit provided them with accommodation, transport, food and protection. The 'embeds' accompanied the troops into action and could in theory write what they liked as long as it did not reveal information of value to the enemy.

But no matter how determined the correspondents were not to lose their journalistic objectivity and maintain their distance, once the war had started almost without exception they soon lost all distinction between warrior and reporter, and identified themselves with their unit, even to the extent of helping with the fighting. The relationship had come full circle and was back to World War One again. No wonder a disgruntled reader wrote to the editor of *The Guardian* newspaper saying, 'Despite scouring two national newspapers every day, listening to the radio, surfing the web and watching TV news, I have absolutely no clue how the war is going'.

It grew worse. One American critic described the lack of sustained TV reporting on Afghanistan as 'the most irresponsible behavior in all the annals of war journalism'. And when NATO attacked Colonel Gaddafi's forces in Libya, it flew 26,000 air missions and not one of them was covered on TV. This means more illustrations were published at the time of the fighting in the Crimean War, more than 150 years earlier. This is a sad commentary on today's status of modern war correspondents and raises the vital question: how much longer can they survive?

YVONNE MCEWEN

Introduction

News and gossip are sometimes indistinguishable. Particularly at times of national crisis, what the press does not provide, the rumour mill will readily invent. This was evidenced in the early days of news gathering when, during the American Civil War, the Editor of the *Chicago Tribune*, Wilbur Storey, instructed one of his correspondents to 'Telegraph fully all news you can get and when there is no news send rumors'. Oiling the wheels of the rumour mill is not just a wartime practice. However, as history demonstrates, the lack of credible information being dispatched from the fighting front to the home front inevitably lead to the creation of an information vacuum. Standing at the ready to fill the void were the war correspondents, the heroes, sometimes anti-heroes, of news reporting.

Arguably, it was the dispatches from the war in the Crimea by *The Times* correspondents, Thomas Chenery and William Howard Russell, that saw the beginning of an organized effort to report the activities on the fighting front to the home front. The correspondents wrote about the pitiful condition of the troops, the inadequacies of army leadership, and the appalling lack of medical and nursing care for the casualties. Writing during the Battle of the Alma, Chenery cynically observed the consequences of sending aged war veterans to care for the sick and wounded.

> At the commencement of this war a plan was invented, and carried out, by which a number of Chelsea pensioners were sent out as ambulance corps to attend to the sick. Whether it was a scheme for saving money by utilizing the poor old men or shortening the duration of their lives and pensions, it is difficult to say, but they have been found in practice rather to require nurses themselves than be able to nurse others [...] The man who conceived the idea that the hard work of a military hospital could be performed by worn-out and aged cripples must have had slight knowledge of warfare or have profited little by experience.[1]

ESERVED

The correspondents' dispatches infuriated the government and the military high command but the Editor of *The Times*, John Delane, advised them to 'continue as you have done, to tell the truth, and as much of it as you can'. The government eventually fell from power and the Secretary of State for War told Russell that it was his [Russell's] dispatches that were responsible for the collapse of the government. Emboldened by their ability to effect change, the press believed they had secured their role and a right to communicate to the masses how wars were being prosecuted.

Until the Crimean campaign, soldier–writers, with little mastery of war corresponding generally, wrote the dispatches from the front. This was the case in the Seven Years' War (1756–1763), and in the French Revolutionary and Napoleonic Wars (1792–1815).

It has been said that it was Marlborough's victories in Flanders in the 1700s that first whetted the British public's appetite for the latest news from the fighting front but there is strong evidence to support the view that it was the English Civil War, and the political strife that led up to it, that was the beginning of conflict corresponding in Britain.[2]

While the Crimea saw the establishment of war corresponding, its birth can be attributed to George Wilkins Kendal, one of ten full-time reporters who rode with the United States Army into Mexico in 1846 to cover the Mexican–American War. Kendall was a businessman and newspaper proprietor. In 1837, along with a friend, he founded the *New Orleans Picayune* and, throughout the period of the war with Mexico, he was both soldier and journalist. He was the first newsman to take advantage of the developments in transportation and technology, and the combined use of fast-moving ships and the newly established telegraph, gave him the lead in the collection and distribution of news. In the same conflict, Jane McManus Storms, writing under the pseudonym of Cora Montgomery for the *New York Sun*, went behind enemy lines in order to file her first-hand dispatches. She was the only woman to cover the conflict and was in all probability the first female war correspondent, therefore leading the way for women to report future conflicts.[3] Despite Arnold Bennett's acerbic critique on the standard of women's literary competence and their limited future in the field of journalism, not only did they become accomplished journalists but also during the First World War women were reporting on its social and economic effects, and some were reporting from the front. By the outbreak of the Second World War, they had won the right to become accredited war correspondents and women such as Margaret Bourke-White, Martha Gellhorn and Lee Miller became household names.[4]

Throughout the First World War, the press was the principal medium of news distribution, although war photography was well established and film was beginning to make its mark. The war brought with it an unprecedented rise in the sale of newspapers and journals, and their importance to the public would never again be matched. In the early days of the war the Recruiting Department of the War Office sought permission from Lord Northcliffe, the newspaper baron, for the use of his newspapers to aid recruitment. Unimpressed by the efforts of the War Office, Northcliffe wrote to the Prime Minister, H. H. Asquith, complaining that 'The chief hindrance to recruiting is that whereas the German public are supplied with the work of photographers, artists, cinematograph operators, and war correspondents, our people have nothing but the casualty lists and mutilated scraps with which it is impossible to arouse interest or follow the war intelligently'.[5]

Two years into the war, on 6 December 1916, David Lloyd George was invited by King George V to form a government in succession to Asquith's coalition War Ministry. Just two days before he was deposed, Asquith had reason to believe that Lloyd George had been 'trafficking with the press' for political gain.

The significance of his statement should be seen in the light of the persons Lloyd George held his first meeting with as Prime Minister. For it was not with his political advisers but two influential newspaper proprietors, Sir George Riddell (later Lord), owner of the *News of the World*, and Lord Burnham of the *Daily Telegraph*. Lloyd George understood that his success and the success of the government's direction of the war effort could only be achieved by keeping the press on board and the public placated.[6]

With the development of radio and film after 1918, the prominence of print journalism in the dissemination of information diminished in the Second World War. The distribution of news by various media was a potent force in shaping national morale. The public wanted to see the truth in print and to hear it on radio but, as the columns of *Hansard* can readily attest, British politicians, with their economy-of-truth philosophy, had different ideas. In this, there was perhaps more of a similarity between democratic and dictatorial regimes than leaders of the former would have cared to admit.

By 1940, Winston Churchill had come to believe that the spread of rumours was bad for national morale and instructed the Ministry of Information (MoI) that a wide campaign should be immediately put in hand against the dangers posed by rumours. In the early years of the war, the people of the United Kingdom and Northern Ireland were desperate for information but there was a widespread belief that their wartime news was being manipulated to produce either distortions or over-optimism. Furthermore, information regarding the developments and prosecution of the war was hard to obtain and this led, at times, to public suspicion of the government's war aims. The remit of the MoI was to prevent panics, allay apprehensions, remove misconception and generally keep up public morale. The British press, cynical about the role of the Ministry, and equally frustrated by the lack of information, referred to the MoI as the 'Ministry of Disinformation'.[7]

If there were lessons learned from the First World War about rumour control, newsgathering and distribution, by the time of the Second World War, they had either been forgotten or ignored.

The printed word alone did not assuage the public need for wartime information. Developments in film and cinematography ranked as informative contenders. During the Crimean campaign, Roger Fenton, a society photographer and one of the founding members of the Royal Photographic Society, was dispatched to the war zone. His remit was political, his patronage Royal, for he arrived in Balaclava with letters of introduction from Prince Albert. He was appointed to neutralize the damning literary images of the war coined from the pens of correspondents. In a war of confusion and catastrophe, his photographs created the illusion of military calm and control. Fenton deliberately avoided taking controversial photographs, namely human and animal detritus on the battlefield, the squalor of the troops living conditions, and the appalling facilities for the care of the sick and wounded. While sections of the press, particularly *The Times*, were accused of purveying untruths and were castigated by politicians and the military, Fenton's images were well received because he obligingly produced half the picture.[8]

Some five years later, The American Civil War proved to be a landmark in the history of photojournalism. With different mindsets and little political interference, the American Mathew Brady and the Scottish-born Alexander Gardiner were the first to bring the tragedies of the Civil War to the attention of the press and public alike. Despite the limitations of still photography in capturing the fast action of warfare, their photography captured the war in all its phases and locations, and was a remarkable accomplishment. Furthermore, Gardiner went on to produce *Photographic Sketch Book of the War* (1866),[9] which was the first published collection of Civil War photographs. It could be confidently argued that it was on the battlefields of the American Civil War that photojournalism in warfare was firmly established.[10]

As far as can be ascertained, the earliest moving pictures of warfare were produced during the Spanish–American War of 1898. Cinematography was in its infancy but short clips of images from the Boer War (1899–1902), the Russo–Japanese War (1904–1905) and the First Russian Revolution (1905) were made possible with pioneering developments in film making. By the outbreak of the First World War, front-line newsreel filming had achieved a degree of technical sophistication that allowed for lengthy film footage to be shown. Documentary films, such as *The Battle of the Somme* (1916), filmed by the cinematographers John Benjamin McDowell and Geoffrey Malins, lasted for over an hour. The main sources of newsreel information during the war years came from the *Pathe Gazette*, *Gaumont Graphic* and *Topical Budget*, which in 1917 was taken over by the War Office and run on propagandist lines as an outlet for official war films.

In the interwar years film production was prolific, and there was a corresponding rise in public attendance at the cinema. The quality of filmmaking, and the introduction of sound and colour, greatly improved the cinema experience. It was primarily from *British Movietone*, *Pathé* and *British Gaumont* newsreels that the cinema-going public obtained information about current events and the wider world. By the Second World War, film-makers nationally and internationally were using their skills to produce government propaganda documentaries, public-information and morale-boosting films.[11] Reporting of the war was no longer the sole prerogative of the newspaper industry. However, the technological developments in the collection of news did not safeguard its freedom for distribution. As experienced in the First World War, dissemination of news was still carried out under government control and censorship.

Nonetheless, in both wars there was a cadre of men and women who were prepared to take considerable personal and professional risks for the freedom of expression and information. This edited volume is an eclectic mix of lives and experiences of individual correspondents, and the mediums through which they reported war.

First World War

Stephen Badsey's chapter on the World War One cameraman John Benjamin McDowell begins this volume on war corresponding in the two World Wars. McDowell is simultaneously one of the most influential British wartime figures of the twentieth century and almost unknown as an individual. He was the hero of British front-line newsreel filming on the Western Front between 1916 and 1918. In 1916, although a film producer as much as a cameraman, he volunteered to serve with Geoffrey Malins on the Western Front and remained there as the doyen of British official cameramen for the rest of the war. McDowell was involved in filming all the major documentaries of that time, including the extremely influential *Battle of the Somme*. Additionally, he was the senior cameraman at British general headquarters from April 1918 onwards. The film images that McDowell produced had a popular reception around the world and he shaped public perceptions of the war on the Western Front. As Badsey explains, the role of McDowell and his fellow cameramen was to bring an impression of the war as experienced by the ordinary soldier to the people back home.

Jenny Macleod describes one of the most colourful if not controversial correspondents in World War One. Ellis Ashmead-Bartlett was a gifted and experienced war correspondent in the mould of the gentleman–adventurer. He witnessed at least ten different theatres of war, starting with the Greco–Turkish War in 1898. Most famously, he was the main British war correspondent at the Dardanelles in 1915 and was the first to publish a description of the Anzacs' dawn landings. As such, Ashmead-Bartlett has been credited with creating the Anzac legend but he also became its most trenchant critic. He gradually became disillusioned with the campaign and wrote to the British Prime Minister, H. H. Asquith, to condemn it, thereby breaking the censorship regulations and, arguably, hastening the abandonment of the doomed campaign. As Macleod observes, Ashmead-Bartlett had a cool nerve and an insouciant glamour. He was, however, dogged by ill health and died at the age of fifty. His obituary remarked that 'With the death of Mr Ellis Ashmead-Bartlett passes not only the greatest war correspondent of the twentieth century, but one of the most picturesque and romantic figures in the history of journalism'.

Tom Quinn, defines the *raison d'etre* of Albert Londres, who wanted to 'dip the pen into the wound' of France's brutal war experience. Londres was referred to as 'France's first war correspondent'. He forged his reputation early in World War One by being outspoken against the view of the war presented by the French press, which he believed to be hopelessly constricted, primarily, by its military and political masters. Unable to achieve the point of witness he needed, Londres abandoned the French war front to cover other theatres. At the request of the French government, in 1917, Londres took up residence close to the battlefields. Nonetheless, the reporting restrictions did not improve and he resigned in despair, turning his attention to matters outside the scope of French military and government censorship. Ultimately, the value of his witness would be to raise a voice of protest against the distorting impact of censorship on the reporting and perception of the war. As Quinn observes, censorship in wartime France had a profoundly alienating effect on many soldiers, reporters, and those who watched and listened from the home front. Londres is probably France's most celebrated twentieth century reporter.

Yvonne McEwen's chapter about Evelyn Kate Luard, Royal Red Cross and Bars, and twice Mentioned in Dispatches, describes a truly remarkable woman, a professionally trained nurse and an unofficial correspondent. A veteran of the Army Nursing Service in the South African War, when war was declared in 1914, she was mobilized for nursing duty on the Western Front and spent four-and-a-half years working in a variety of medical facilities on the Lines of Communication. Despite the severe professional and personal consequences of breaking the censorship rules, Luard managed to send unofficial dispatches to the home front. Frustrated and angered about what she was witnessing in the hospital trains, casualty clearing stations and field hospitals, in 1915, she published anonymously *Diary of a Nursing Sister on the Western Front*, presenting her diary entries from the autumn of 1914 to the summer of 1915. The publication details the struggle for life and hopeless deaths amongst the men of the British Expeditionary Force and the Allies. Luard's dispatches were bold and significant in their truthfulness about the human consequences of industrial warfare. Moreover, they are testament to the indomitability of the human spirit that sustains in and beyond the obscenity of war.

Second World War

Patrick S. Washburn examines the work of George Padmore and the Black American Press. Padmore was one of twenty-seven US blacks who were regularly assigned as war correspondents in the Second World War, and one of only two who served for four years (1941–1945). Hired by the *Pittsburgh Courier* and the *Chicago Defender*, weekly newspapers that were the largest and most influential black newspapers in the US, he wrote 575 bylined articles during the war. But Padmore was not a typical war correspondent as he was based in London for the duration of the war. His articles were read avidly and yet he wrote only about issues that involved or affected blacks. Thus, he focused on how black US soldiers were accepted in Britain and the extent to which they faced discrimination, rather than bombing attacks on British cities. Padmore wrote much about colonial rule in the British Empire, amongst other things, as well as about the effect on blacks of the war in Ethiopia, South Africa, the Belgian Congo, French West Africa, Liberia, India and the US. These stories were a mixture of how blacks from these countries were helping to win the war along with what their fortunes might be after it. In 2011, in appreciation of Padmore's work, the City of London named a street after him.

Steven Miner highlights the fact that Vasilii Grossman, unlike most Soviet war correspondents, had never been a journalist before his reporting of the Second World War – he was, rather, a moderately successful novelist. Born in the Ukraine and the son of Jewish parents, he rediscovered the importance of his Jewish identity following the Nazi invasion, the Holocaust and, later, the anti-Semitism of the post-war Stalinist Soviet state. Miner believes that Grossman found a sense of shared purpose among the front-line soldiers whose experiences he reported. He established a reputation as an outstanding reporter during the Battle of Stalingrad, singing the praises of the ordinary soldier on whose endeavours the Red Army depended. Although Grossman remained committed to the anti-Nazi cause, he was increasingly at odds with the Stalinist system because of the costs it imposed upon Soviet society. Along with the resurgence of Russian patriotism from 1943 came a revival of anti-Semitism. The Soviet authorities did not permit him to publish his pioneering documentation of the Holocaust, not least because it revealed that many non-Jewish Soviet citizens had collaborated in it. Grossman returned to the war repeatedly in his post-war fiction, coming to view the Stalinist and Hitlerian dictatorships as evil twins.

Phylomena Badsey moves away from the public perception of Vera Brittain as a young, World War One Voluntary Aid Detachment nurse and post-war author of the critically acclaimed autobiography *Testament of Youth*, and focuses on a more politically mature Brittain. By 1940, Brittain was middle aged, a Christian pacifist and a feminist. She remained, however, a patriot. She turned to reporting the effects of the Second World War on the British home front. The government allowed her broad latitude, in spite of her pacifist beliefs, and she published reports on the situation in air-raid shelters but also continued to criticize the Treaty of Versailles, which, she believed, had led to a Second World War. Brittain vehemently attacked Bomber Command and the policy of area bombing of German cities, and the loss of life and destruction of historic buildings that it involved, and was criticized by William Shirer and Franklin D. Roosevelt for doing so. She called for a negotiated peace, regarding war as the ultimate evil, and was castigated by George Orwell, in particular, for her published views. As Badsey observes, Brittain believed it was essential to challenge the ways in which the war was being waged while it was in progress and before victory was achieved.

Brian Hannon reminds us that Richard Dimbleby was one of the most prominent voices in bringing the dramatic sounds of the Second World War to millions of British radio listeners. He was the first journalist to record the sounds of battle when he reported from the Spanish border in 1939, the first radio reporter to fly on a Royal Air Force bombing raid, the first reporter to enter the Belsen concentration camp and the first Allied correspondent to arrive in the ruins of a defeated Berlin. Dimbleby helped to prepare the British Broadcasting Corporation's (BBC) nascent War Reporting Unit for its historic coverage of the D-Day landings. He was, however, a controversial character and he was recalled to London from North Africa in 1942 following accusations that he entertained military and government officials too lavishly. Executives within the BBC also claimed that those close relationships influenced Dimbleby to the extent that he filed excessively optimistic reports on the progress of British and Dominion forces. For all the criticism levelled at him, his reputation as the BBC's top correspondent remained undiminished. By the end of the war, Dimbleby had filed reports from some of the most important battlefields of Africa and Europe, and his name became a symbol of the BBC and synonymous with wartime journalism.

Jill Stephenson introduces us to Hans Ertl, champion skier, mountaineer, film-maker and all-round action man. Although documentary making in Nazi Germany is invariably linked with the work of Leni Riefenstahl, in the autumn of 1939, Ertl was drafted into the German army, and by 1940 he was reporting from the Western Front as cameraman and photographer. By 1941 Ertl was in North Africa and was the official photographer for Field Marshal Rommel. Ertl also worked on the Eastern Front, with Rommel again in Normandy in 1944 and by the end of the war he was filming in the Alps. Ertl represented himself as an apolitical patriot who supported his country's

cause. Certainly, he was no Nazi and clashed from time to time with his political masters in Berlin. The film that he shot of Rommel's exploits in North Africa was highly evocative and attracted particular popular interest when extracts from it were shown in German newsreels. His interest in the creative process was boundless. In his youth, Ertl had been obsessed with discovering ways to photograph movement and he pioneered underwater and ski-mountable cameras. After the war, he continued to make films while living in Germany and then in self-imposed exile, until his camera equipment was entirely lost in an accident in South America in 1962.

Integrity and wartime reporting

McDowell, Ashmead-Bartlett, Londres, Luard, Padmore, Grossman, Brittain, Dimbleby and Ertl share common traits. In disposition, they were all unstoppable mavericks. But is this true of all the men and women who report wars? In the absence of empirical evidence the answer would be purely speculative. However, for those men and women featured in this book it would appear that, for most, reporting the 'truth' of their witness to and experience of warfare was absolutely paramount. However, what is truth in warfare? The only certain truth about war reporting is that it is not a prescriptive practice, and the quality of dispatches is dependent on the skill, experience, conscience and bravery of the individual correspondent. Even the most committed correspondent's integrity can be challenged by *pro patria*. In reporting wars, patriotism can be a powerful force in the construction of truthful dispatches. As we understand it, in democratic societies, the function of the press is to gather and interpret news for public interest – its duty is to report it ethically. History demonstrates that in times of national crisis this ideal can be, and has been, challenged by governments, newspaper proprietors and individual correspondents who believe it is unpatriotic to do anything less than give full support to the war aims of the political and military administration.

Therefore, are we left with the disturbing belief that only the passage of time can authenticate whether our wartime journalism was a reliable and truthful witness to history in the making or, as illustrated in this book, will we always be dependent on mavericks?

Notes

1   A. D. Lambert & S. Badsey, *The Crimean War* (Stroud, Gloucestershire: Alan Sutton Publishing Ltd, 1994).

2   W. Steed, *The Press* (London: Penguin Books Ltd, 1938), 110–115.

3   M. S. Sweeney, *From the Front* (Washington, DC: National Geographic Society, 2004), 12, 13.

4   N. C. Sorel, *The Women Who Wrote the War* (New York, NY: Arcade Publishing, 1999).

5   C. Haste, *Keep the Home Fires Burning: Propaganda and the First World War* (London: Penguin Books, 1977), 83.

6   J. M. McEwen, 'The National Press during the First World War: Ownership and Circulation', *Journal of Contemporary History*, 17 (1982), 459.

7   I. McLaine, *Ministry of Morale* (London: George Allen and Unwin, 1979).

8   D. Anderson, *Glass Warriors: The Camera at War* (London: Collins, 2005), 1–14.

9   A. Gardner, *Gardner's Photographic Sketch Book of the War* (Washington, DC: Philp & Solomons, 1865–1866).

10   F. T. Miller (Ed.), *The Photographic History of the Civil War* (New York, NY: The Review of Reviews Company, 1911).

11   British Universities Film and Video Council, *News on Screen: The world's leading resource for the study of newsreels and cinemagazines* (London: British Universities Film and Video Council, 2011): available at http://bufvc.ac.uk/newsonscreen

STEPHEN BADSEY

J. B. McDowell and British Official Filming on the Western Front 1916–1918

At a curiously modest ceremony held on the Hohenzollern Bridge over the River Rhine in Cologne, Germany, in December 1918, Field Marshal Sir Douglas Haig, the victorious Commander-in-Chief of the British and British Empire forces that fought on the Western Front in the First World War, said farewell to his command, which had become the Army of Occupation of part of western Germany. Among those present were many of the official war correspondents who had served with Haig's headquarters, most of them the representatives of major British national newspapers, experienced professional reporters who had been given honorary rank and uniforms in return for an agreement between their organizations and the War Office regarding their behaviour and the terms of military censorship. Haig gave each of these men a small Union Jack flag, together with his handshake and his thanks. 'You have been the chroniclers of this war,' he told them, 'You have done fine work'.[1] Five senior British reporters also received knighthoods; and although at the time and ever since opinions have differed as to the value and accuracy of their reporting, there has been no dispute as to their importance in shaping wider British public opinion at home: the newspapers for which they wrote are habitually described as by far the dominant medium through which the British public gained its information about the war.[2]

The agreed conditions under which the reporters were allowed at British headquarters on the Western Front were drawn up to reflect the perceived importance of the London press in shaping public opinion, and so in maintaining support for the prosecution of the war. The broad rules for the war correspondents' conduct (some official but mostly part of an unofficial gentlemen's agreement) were that while they might describe the

experiences of the soldiers and their own impressions, they would not criticize either the war's higher direction or any politician or general directly. It
is a commonplace of the war that people on the home front are believed to
have had little perception of the realities of trench warfare, and this has in
turn promoted the belief that the war reporters produced a relentlessly and
falsely optimistic picture of the fighting. In fact, their pen-portraits of the
horrors of the trenches were on occasions so vivid that Haig's headquarters
was moved to complain. As the veteran reporter Philip Gibbs of the *Daily
Chronicle* made clear in his memoirs, his loyalties and those of his newspaper
were those of a patriot supporting his country's cause in the war, but this
sense of obligation did not prevent his describing the horrors of the worst
conditions of the trenches, any more than he would refuse to describe the
genuine elation of many soldiers at their victories. But from the origins of
the professional war correspondent in the first half of the nineteenth century, one of their most important functions had been not simply to report
the war in their newspapers but to act as unofficial and occasional channels
between the elites of the political and social establishment. While Gibbs's
published accounts of the Third Battle of Ypres (Passchendaele) in 1917
drew concern from Haig's staff as 'horror-mongering stuff', it was only
when back in London in a private conversation including Prime Minister
David Lloyd George that Gibbs felt free to tell 'the naked truth' about his
impressions of the battle and its conduct, a version of the truth that he
knew his newspaper neither would nor could publish, and which he and
other reporters accepted would damage the war effort should they ever
try to write it.[3] Although the front-line war correspondents were often
high-profile figures, both during the war and after it, they were in practice
highly constrained by the institutions and circumstances that surrounded
them in doing their jobs.

There were other British newsmen in uniform on the Hohenzollern
Bridge on the day that Haig bade farewell to the reporters, men who were
also civilian professionals that served at Haig's headquarters, but have for
many years remained unknown figures in the history of the war; and while
Haig distributed praise and flags, they were still working. These were the
cine-cameramen and still photographers of Haig's press section, led by
their doyen, Lieutenant J. B. McDowell. Almost completely unknown as

an individual, McDowell was certainly one of the most influential of war reporters, and in his way one of the most influential British wartime figures, of the twentieth century. For many years now, it has been most unlikely that anyone other than a specialist historian of the war would recognize the name of Philip Gibbs, or of his fellow war correspondents, such as H. Perry Robinson or William Beach Thomas, or be able to identify any of their writings on sight. However, although McDowell and his colleagues remain almost entirely anonymous figures, their film and photographs of the British Army on the Western Front are still almost instantly recognizable, largely through repeated use on television, and in newspapers and books. Whereas the war correspondents acted as conduits to elites as well as writing for a wider public, McDowell and his colleagues were able, within the constraints of the technological and practical limitations of their equipment as well as the institutional pressures and censorship that they faced, to bring an impression of the war on the Western Front to a much wider audience among the British working classes and around the world. Today, it is unlikely that any habitual television viewer, anywhere in the world, has not witnessed at least one scene filmed by J. B. McDowell.

What provided the outlet for the film shot by McDowell and his cameramen on the Western Front to reach such a large audience was the prodigious growth just before the First World War of the popular 'flea pit' cinema, eclipsing the music hall. The first practical cine-cameras were invented in about 1894, and exhibition of films as a novelty began within a year in Great Britain. The first purpose-built cinemas began to appear in the decade immediately before the First World War, and the growth in popularity of this new medium of entertainment was remarkable. Despite a wartime entertainment tax, which increased the price of cinema seats, it is an often-quoted figure that, of a British population of 43 million in 1917, there were approximately 20 million separate cinema attendances a week, a figure that probably reflects two or three cinema visits each week by most working-class families and by young adults.[4] This extraordinary growth meant that the wartime cinema-going audience far outnumbered the readership circulation for any newspaper.

Most of the programme of these early cinemas consisted of fictional films. But from the inception of cinema, short films of a newsworthy item known as 'topicals' were one of the mainstays of cinema, often distributed on the day that they were shot. The topicals were in turn superseded with the launch by British Pathé in 1911 of the first twice-weekly newsreel, containing compilations of topical scenes. The most common subjects for the topicals in Great Britain were sporting events usually taking place in London, such as the annual Football Association Cup Final, and royal pageants. It is a particular feature of British media history that, once a new media technology is available, it has often been taken up on a large scale because of a major public event, and the deliberate creation of impressive royal ceremonies from the end of the nineteenth century onwards provided just such occurrences: big boosts to the topicals and the newsreels came with the death of King Edward VII in 1910, resulting in his state funeral that year, and the coronation and Delhi Durbar of King George V a year later.[5]

One of the British film companies created before the First World War was the British and Colonial Kinematograph Company, based by 1914 in the Holborn district of London, and largely owned and managed for most of its existence by J. B. McDowell. Highly reminiscent of the 'dot. com' boom of the 1990s resulting from the establishment of the Internet and the World Wide Web, the whole basis of the film work of these early companies was novelty and rapid commercial exploitation, and once film had lost its commercial value it was usually thrown away, making the early history of the firm, usually known as 'British & Colonial' (or B&C), uncertain. British & Colonial produced its first known film, *Billie's Bugle*, in 1908, and soon branched out into short factual films and dramas as well as topicals. It was registered as a limited company in 1911, at which date its business premises were at 33 Endell Street, Holborn. McDowell's first job had been as an engineering apprentice at Woolwich Arsenal, and both he and Albert Bloomfield, his partner at British & Colonial, gave their professions as 'engineer' on the company documents; the two other company directors were William Frith, a solicitor, and Charles Stafford, a printer. McDowell was an accomplished cameraman, and the credits for the existing British & Colonial films list him as either a director or a director of photography.[6] By 1914, British & Colonial was regarded as one of the three top British production companies, along with Hepworth's, which under its founder Cecil Hepworth had been producing topicals from its studio in Walton-on-Thames since at least 1899, and the more recently founded London Film Company.

The main attractions at cinemas remained feature films and comedies, and partly because of the focus of the topicals on sport and pageantry, with the launch of more wide-ranging newsreels (which might include political and overseas items) coming only just before the First World War, the cinema was seen overwhelmingly as a form of working-class entertainment, at first either despised or neglected by the British war-making authorities. While it is debatable how much ordinary people learned about the world from the cinema, the depth and extent of the penetration of its films into working-class culture is a matter of record, and successive British governments took this increasingly to heart as the war continued. By 1918 the British propaganda organizations, most of them consolidated that year into a single Ministry of Information (MoI), had bought outright one of the twice-weekly newsreels, the *Topical Budget*, as *The War Office Official Topical Budget*, renamed later that year as *Pictorial News (Official)*. According to Lord Beaverbrook, the Minister of Information, 'The Topical Budget shown in every picture palace was the decisive factor in maintaining the moral[e] of the people during the black days of the early summer of 1918'. While this is surely an exaggeration, it is also a reflection of how greatly the newsreel films had come to be valued.[7] By 1918 the MoI even provided cinema vans with projectors that would take these official films out to the smallest villages, setting up a sheet as a screen in the village hall or even outdoors.

Much of the detail of the story of the MoI and its predecessors in the First World War has been lost to history, partly because of the very great speed with which the Ministry was wound up at the end of December 1918 and the loss of many of its papers. In recent years historians have performed heroic efforts in reconstructing the work of the MoI, and the organization and evolution of British propaganda in the war, including the immense significance of the official cine-cameramen.[8] The Imperial War Museum, which was established in London in 1917 for the purpose of preserving the artefacts and records of the British and Imperial war effort, automatically inherited in 1919 many of the Ministry's collections, including its official war films and photographs. But the technical problems of storing and viewing the official films meant that there was a hiatus of almost two years before work could begin on the Museum receiving and cataloguing them and, in the fast-moving world of cinema production, that break was fatal in terms of lost personal knowledge and interest. In 1950, when Rachael Low wrote the semi-official history of British film for the British Film Institute, McDowell and others who had filmed the Western Front were still alive, but they were not sought out and interviewed. Although praising the 'superb photographic quality' of their films, the book listed the cameramen only by name, criticizing their lack of 'a truly interpretive approach', and as being of only marginal importance to the development of British cinema, which was then felt to lie very much with feature-film production.[9] One of the official cine-cameramen, Geoffrey Malins, who served with the British in 1916–17 and then with the Canadians in 1917–18, staked his claim to fame in 1920 by publishing his memoirs, dramatically titled *How I Filmed the War*, which remain the most important published source on the official cine-cameramen and their work. Another, Bertram 'Billy' Brooks-Carrington, lived long enough to be interviewed by the film historian and producer Kevin Brownlow in the 1970s for his book on the early cinema, *The War, the West and the Wilderness*.[10] Since then, the story of British official filming on the Western Front has been researched and reconstructed by several historians, mostly working with the Imperial War Museum, and a broad story of how events unfolded has now come to be accepted.[11]

Following an initial War Office ban on any form of reporting of the fighting fronts at the start of the war, persistent lobbying and the recognized need for positive propaganda to support the war effort led in 1915 to reporters and cine-cameramen being allowed at British headquarters on the Western Front, followed by still photographers in early 1916. It is a constant source of surprise and disappointment that there is virtually no film of any of the fighting fronts for the first two years of the war, 1914–15. Despite positive support from the Permanent Secretary at the War Office, Sir Reginald Brade, it was only in November 1915 that the first two official cine-cameramen were assigned to British headquarters on the Western Front, sponsored by a consortium of newsreel firms known as the British Topical Committee for War Films, of which McDowell's British & Colonial was one. Apart from the technical details of military management, censorship and security associated with filming on the Western Front, a further significant problem was arranging a mutually acceptable method of payment by the film companies to the War Office for the films, the money going eventually to military charities. The first two cine-cameramen were Geoffrey Malins of Gaumont along with E. G. 'Teddy' Tong of Jury's Imperial Pictures, who wore uniform without rank badges and were counted as honorary officers while remaining technically civilians if they chose to do so. Their films were shot silent and in monochrome on cameras that were hand-cranked or sometimes powered by compressed air. The resulting film was edited and censored in London where the inter-titles (explanatory captions inserted between the filmed scenes) were written, and then sent back to headquarters in France for a final censorship check. In the cinema industry of the time almost anyone could do almost any job, and the cameramen routinely took part in the editing of their work, along with producers and others who joined in. The way that the films were shown depended on the resources of the individual cinema, but was usually with at least a piano accompaniment, sometimes with a full orchestra and sound effects, and with the image tinted and toned in a variety of colours.

The first official films taken by Malins and Tong, each only a few minutes long, were released to the public in January 1916. But the event for which the Army, the country and the cine-cameramen were all waiting was the forthcoming 'Big Push', the Battle of the Somme, which was set to begin in late June, marking the first major British offensive of the war involving the 'new armies' of the volunteers of 1914. In late June 1916 Teddy Tong fell ill, and J. B. McDowell of British & Colonial volunteered to come out and take his place, arriving just before the Somme offensive began, a decision which McDowell appears to have taken from entirely patriotic motives to keep filming on the Western Front alive, but which effectively meant the end of production at British & Colonial. The opening of the Somme offensive was a disaster for the British, with losses on the first day, 1 July 1916, of 57,000 men killed and wounded, the largest single day's loss of casualties in the British Army's history. In the course of filming that day, both cine-cameramen were in the front lines, and McDowell came under enemy machine-gun fire at least once and survived unharmed.

The story of the film shot by Malins and McDowell of the preliminary bombardment for the Battle of the Somme, the first day of attack, and the next few days of fighting while the Army recovered and took stock, has also now been well reconstructed by historians, both in terms of the filmed locations and the story of the resulting production.[12] Rather than break up the film shot by Malins and McDowell into short features, one of the members of the British Topical Committee for War Films, William F. Jury of Jury's Imperial Pictures, put aside his own business to work on the material and, in association with another film entrepreneur, Charles Urban, he produced a documentary over an hour in length, *The Battle of the Somme*. From its release in July 1916, this film broke box-office records throughout Great Britain. The most widely watched British film ever made, the most historically significant and, for its time, the biggest British money-making film ever, *The Battle of the Somme* has now become recognized as the essential starting point for any kind of historical discussion on what the British people of 1916 understood about the Western Front and of how it has been understood ever since.[13] The speed with which the film was shot and edited, and the almost casual response of the higher British authorities until they realized the quality and the success of the film, all speak of a genuine attempt to convey something of the truth about the battle, and the war, by the cine-cameramen and editors. Published responses, particularly in newspapers of the day, suggest that most people read into the film what they wished to read, from viewing it as a call to recruitment to being a pacifist tract; but the overwhelming majority found it both valuable to watch and essentially honest. The lack in 1916 of any means of public survey (such as scientific opinion polls) makes it hard to argue further. In July 2005 *The Battle of the Somme* was included in the UNESCO Memory of the World Register of cultural artefacts of global importance, the only British-made film contribution and one of the very few films to be included.

The unprecedented impact of *The Battle of the Somme* gave J. B. McDowell a brief moment in the spotlight in the newspapers, mainly in the cinema trade press, but no lasting fame; when he came to write his memoirs Malins did not even mention McDowell's name. McDowell left no personal records or papers; he never opened up his heart or his mind to a newspaper interviewer. His professional life story has been built up by highly diligent work locating the few existing fragments in official and unofficial records, including mentions in local newspapers and in the trade press. In the manner of some classical or mediaeval literary figure, we know McDowell almost entirely from his work. That this could happen in the modern age tells us much, both about the status of the cinema in the First World War, and of the changing priorities of historians within the last few decades, as the history of the working classes, the history of the media and entertainment, and the history of memory have all become more important subjects of study.

According to the available records and modern databases, J. B. McDowell was born in the first quarter of 1878 in Plumstead, London, making him thirty-eight years old when he first went out to the Western Front.[14] One of the problems that the cinema trade had in providing cine-cameramen for wartime service was that, after the introduction of conscription in January 1916, the War Office took the view that any fit man eligible to serve on the Western Front should do so in a fighting capacity, so that cine-cameramen had to be recruited from volunteers who were otherwise ineligible for various reasons. McDowell was old for front-line service but not over-age and, unlike several other cine-cameramen who served with him, he appears to have been quite physically fit; a photograph that appeared originally in the *Kinematograph and Lantern Weekly* on 13 July 1916, of McDowell posing in uniform beside his big hand-cranked Moy and Bastie camera, shows him wearing a wedding ring (and also a wristwatch, something of a status symbol in the First World War) and of course he had a reserved occupation with his own company to manage. This and other photographs show a man of medium height and build, with a medium-sized dark moustache – one of the most appealing things about McDowell is that he was so *ordinary*, a talented middle-aged businessman of humble origins who had made his mark through exploitation of the latest entertainment technology, and who was then thrust by the circumstances of war into a position of historical significance and was very modest about it.

McDowell's name at birth was recorded as Benjamin John, presumably an error because he always gave it as John Benjamin; he signed himself always as J. B. McDowell, and friends and colleagues habitually called him 'Mac'. He had become involved in the cinema business only a few years after the invention of the practical cine-camera. After his apprenticeship at Woolwich Arsenal, which began at age fifteen years (and as a consequence of which he never lost the habit of listing his profession as 'engineer', as in the British & Colonial company documents), in 1898 at age twenty he joined the British Mutoscope and Biograph Syndicate, for which he worked as a cameraman and as a projectionist, the first of a series of jobs for London-based cinema production companies. In 1906 he left to become chief cameraman for the Warwick Trading Company (apparently also acting as an electrician if the occasion required it); after a year he left again to become, briefly, chief cameraman at the Walturdaw Company (Walker, Turner and Dawson). In 1908 Albert Bloomfield, head of the Walturdaw Company darkroom staff, left to found British & Colonial and he was joined by McDowell (who may have already left the Company) no later than January 1910. British & Colonial's premises were in Twickenham at first, and as a small start-up firm it was reported as using McDowell's house as a darkroom. Within a year the company was flourishing, and began to justify its name by making publicity films for the Canadian Pacific Railway, the first of a series of projects around the Empire. Bloomfield, who also acted as a cameraman on occasion, ceased to be a director of British & Colonial in 1913, leaving McDowell effectively in charge. By this time the company had moved to larger premises more than once, finally settling in Holborn, and it was nothing unusual for McDowell to lead a team of five or six cameramen to cover an important event for one of their topicals, for which British & Colonial had a high reputation for getting the story out first. As the topicals began to be replaced by the newsreels, British & Colonial increasingly emphasized feature and costume dramas, still with McDowell as director or chief cameraman. In giving up his company's work in 1916 McDowell was making a considerable financial sacrifice.

It has been reasonably argued by historians that a large part of the phenomenal box-office success of *The Battle of the Somme* was simple curiosity on the part of many people on the home front to see what the battlefields and life for their soldiers in France actually looked like, an interest that lasted for about another year. One problem about which the cine-cameramen could do nothing was the size and cumbersome nature of their cameras, which effectively limited them to working just behind the lines, often with artillery crews or at supply and distribution points, or with field hospitals. Taking up a camera position in a front-line trench, at considerable personal risk, sometimes produced dramatic film but more often only a vague impression of the enemy trenches, while it was quite impossible to take a camera across no man's land during a battle to show the troops fighting. These technological limitations meant that issues of censorship very rarely applied to the cine-cameramen, who knew that even if they had filmed (for example) a badly dismembered corpse the film would never have been shown at any cinema in Britain; the same limitations also led to an emphasis on heavy guns, an empty sky, the wounded and troops waiting for an attack to begin; all the clichés of the Western Front experience as it has come to be recognized over the years began with these films.

For their successor to *The Battle of the Somme*, the British Topical Committee for War Films decided to retain the format of the big documentary. An official visit by King George V to the army in France in August 1916 was filmed by Malins and McDowell as *The King Visits His Armies in the Great Advance*, released in October. This was followed by their film of the rest of the Somme offensive, which lasted through until November, including the first use in September by the British of a new secret weapon, the first tanks, released in January 1917 as *The Battle of the Ancre and the Advance of the Tanks* (the River Ancre is a small tributary of the River Somme, which is itself some distance south of the main British battlefield of 1916). *The Battle of the Ancre and the Advance of the Tanks* was almost as great a popular and commercial success as *The Battle of the Somme*, by some measurements possibly greater, and it has its advocates among historians as the better film.

Between January and April 1917 the arrangement between the British Topical Committee for War Films and the War Office had been dissolved, to be replaced by a simpler arrangement, the War Office Topical Committee, consisting of Sir Reginald Brade as Permanent Secretary, the Conservative MP Sir Max Aitken (Lord Beaverbrook from January 1917), who as a Canadian himself was also head of the Canadian War Records Section in London and heavily involved in propaganda, and William F. Jury, who's Jury's Imperial Pictures studios became increasingly during the war the production house for British official propaganda films. This meant a considerable financial loss for Jury, whose studio's commercial work had to be abandoned for the duration of the war; his reward was exclusive rights to exploit the official films for two years after the war's end and a knighthood at Beaverbrook's insistence. A third full-length documentary shot on the Western Front between February and April 1917, *The German Retreat and the Battle of Arras*, released in June, was a commercial failure, probably because the cinema-going public had adjusted to what a film of the Western Front showed and to the fact that a big offensive did not mean a big advance or victory. Instead, as well as releasing a compilation serial called *Sons of Our Empire*, in May 1917 the War Office Cinema Committee came to an agreement with the Topical Film Company to use the *Topical Budget* newsreel as a vehicle for official film material, leading in September to the Committee buying the company outright for the duration of the war to produce the *War Office Official Topical Budget*.[15]

Meanwhile, McDowell stayed on the Western Front as the senior member, and increasingly the unofficial leader, of a small group of British and Empire official cameramen. Most of their material went into the *War Office Official Topical Budget* or into short films, and sometimes lack of documentation makes it hard to identify McDowell's work specifically. Because of Beaverbrook's position of dominance over British official filming, and eventually his appointment as Minister of Information, McDowell was sometimes directed to film Canadian, rather than British, troops. In May 1917 the officer responsible for the cameramen at headquarters, Lieutenant Colonel J. C. Faunthrope, wrote to Beaverbrook that 'As I understand you want a good Canadian film I put McDowell on to get it', and Beaverbrook appears to have offered McDowell the chance of a Canadian officer's commission at about the same date, which he declined.[16] Probably the most well known of McDowell's later films was that of the military funeral given to the German fighter ace Manfred von Richthofen 'The Red Baron', who crashed and died behind British lines in April 1918. Malins took repeated sick leave between September 1916 and June 1917, partly from the strain of working in the front lines but also to give him time to complete his memoirs in December 1916, although these were blocked from publication for the remainder of the war, chiefly because they contained what other officers and censoring officials judged to be inaccuracies and exaggerations. For filming the Battle of Arras in April 1917, McDowell was instead joined by Harold C. Raymond, one of Charles Urban's cine-cameramen, who arrived in March, and by the first Canadian official cameraman (Frederick) Oscar Bovill, a Londoner and experienced newsreel cine-cameraman who had joined the Canadians on the Western Front in July 1916. Material from the Australians was supplied by (George) Hubert Wilkins and Frank Hurley, both Australian nationals and well known as cinematographer–explorers before the war. Unlike the Canadians, the Australian and New Zealand forces on the Western Front employed their own nationals as cine-cameramen and still photographers, and kept their organizations distinct from that of the British. By July 1917 Malins appears to have been worn out, and although he was officially transferred to the Canadians, he was not employed on any more major filming projects on the Western Front; made a lieutenant in the British Army in 1918, in June he was discharged from the Army as a result of prolonged ill-health.

Both the problems with finding suitable people and the strain on cine-cameramen and stills photographers, who persistently had to put themselves at risk, remained considerable on the Western Front, and in addition to Raymond, who served until November 1917, only a small handful of associates joined McDowell, coming and going over the next two years. There were several cases of nervous or physical breakdown, or of men being gassed or slightly injured, but remarkably none of the cine-cameramen was killed, although in 1917 one of the still photographers, Armando Consolé (a Londoner of Italian origin), lost a leg to a German shell.[17] Brooks-Carrington joined the cine-cameramen in April 1917 but was invalided off the Western Front in June. Bovill was dismissed at the same time, apparently for poor camera-work, being replaced by Walter Buckstone of British Pathé. In July, Beaverbrook wrote to Sir Reginald Brade that 'The life of a cameraman in the field is a very strenuous one', so that men who were not completely fit and in good mental health were 'very likely to break down under the great strain which is imposed upon them, and besides, few are able to carry out their duties in the midst of shell fire'.[18] An additional cameraman, Frank Basil of British Pathé, who arrived in December 1917, was also considered to be unequal to the job. Walter Buckstone, also of British Pathé, who had left the Canadians in

December 1917, came back out for the British in May 1918; while the final addition to this small band of cameramen, Frederick Wilson, joined in the last few months before the Armistice of November 1918. For most of that part of the war for which filming the Western Front was allowed, from July 1916 until May 1918, McDowell never had more than one other cine-cameraman working with him.

Through all this, J. B. 'Mac' McDowell carried on, according to the records without a break of any length, although he did request short leave once or twice. In April 1918, the cine-cameramen had their status within the Army officially regularized by being required to accept commissions as lieutenants on the Special List (meaning without a parent regiment), somewhat reluctantly in McDowell's case. Along with his commission to lieutenant, he was almost immediately awarded the Order of the British Empire (as was Malins) and also the Military Cross [MC], the only British or Empire still or cine-cameraman to be decorated for bravery in this way.[19] The last survivor, Brooks-Carrington remembered that McDowell had taken up a filming position in a shell-hole in no man's land on the night prior to an attack, and when the troops swarmed over the trenches 'he got so enthused that he jumped out of the shell hole and shot them going into the Jerry trenches as well. He got the M.C. for that'.[20] McDowell was certainly a very brave man, and there are several mentions in the records of his being under shellfire. In May 1918, he was made responsible for the other cine-cameramen at headquarters and their overall direction, as well as the production, developing and printing of all films, on the grounds that he knew all sides of the business, including producing the films and what would appeal to the public.

It is sometimes forgotten in discussions of the British experience on the Western Front that the vast majority of men who fought there survived, and after the war simply got on with their lives. McDowell was one of these. After 1918, he seems to have preferred to continue work as a cine-cameraman, working for the newly re-privatized *Topical Budget* and founding McDowell's Commercial Films in 1922; British & Colonial was officially wound up in 1924. McDowell joined the Agfa Kine Film Department in 1926, working for the company for about a decade before apparently once more branching out on his own. He retired from the film business in 1949 and died in November 1954 in Pitsea, Essex, at seventy-six years old.

It is a common belief that the camera cannot lie, and an equally common criticism of that belief that as soon as the cameraman starts his work he must make choices, and those choices continue through the production process to an end-product that may not necessarily be the truth. The film images that McDowell produced, and which were produced by cameramen who served with and under him, had an enormous popular reception both in Great Britain and throughout the world. Like the war correspondents, the official cine-cameramen were subject to censorship and to political and commercial pressures, but unlike the war correspondents their first objective was to be with the troops and where the battle was taking place. While the importance of their work was acknowledged by King George V, by Prime Minister David Lloyd George and by many senior officers, including Field Marshal Sir Douglas Haig, they had no access to political or military elites. Rather, their constituency was the cinema-going working class, and it is not perhaps too much to describe them, with hindsight, as its heroes.

Notes

1   P. Gibbs, *The Pageant of the Years* (London: William Heinemann, 1946), 239. M. J. Farrar, *News from the Front: War Correspondents on the Western Front* (Sutton: Thrupp, 1998), 219–220. C. E. Montague, *Disenchantment* (London: Chatto & Windus, 1922 [1928]), 188–189.

2   A. Gregory, 'A clash of cultures: the British Press and the opening of the Great War', in T. R. E. Paddock (Ed.), *A Call to Arms: Propaganda, Public Opinion, and Newspapers in the Great War* (Westport, CT: Praeger, 2004), 15–49. G. R. Wilkinson, *Depictions and Images of War in Edwardian Newspapers 1899–1914* (London: Palgrave Macmillan, 2003).

3   P. Gibbs, 207–211. S. Badsey, *The British Army in Battle and its Image* (London: Continuum, 2009), 27–28.

4   R. Low, *The History of the British Film 1914–1918* (London: George Allen & Unwin, 1950), 23–25. N. Reeves, 'Film propaganda and its audience: the example of Britain's official films during the First World War', *Journal of Contemporary History*, 18 (1983), 463–492. N. Hiley, 'The British cinema auditorium', in K. Dibbets & B. Hogenkamp (Eds), *Film and the First World War* (Amsterdam: Amsterdam University Press, 1995), 160–170.

5   L. McKernan, *Topical Budget: The Great British News Film* (London: BFI Publishing, 1992), 4–5. D. Cannadine, 'The context, performance and meaning of ritual: the British monarchy and the invention of tradition, c. 1820–1977', in E. Hobsbawm & T. Ranger (Eds), *The Invention of Tradition* (Cambridge: Cambridge University Press, 1983), 128ff.

6   Information from The Centre for British Film and Television Studies: The London Project website http://londonfilm.bbk.ac.uk/view/business/?id=121 (accessed April 2009); and the Internet Movie Database website http://www.imdb.com/company/c00103011/ (accessed April 2009). See also G. Turvey, 'Ideological contradictions: the film topicals of the British and Colonial Kinematograph Company', *Early Popular Visual Culture*, 5(1) (2007), 41–56.

7   A. J. P. Taylor, *Beaverbrook* (London: Hamish Hamilton, 1972), 144.

8   M. L. Sanders & P. M. Taylor, *British Propaganda during the First World War* (London: Macmillan, 1982). G. Messinger, *British Propaganda and the State in the First World War* (Manchester: Manchester University Press, 1992). P. M. Taylor, *British Propaganda in the Twentieth Century: Selling Democracy* (Edinburgh: Edinburgh University Press, 1999).

9   R. Low.

10   G. Malins, *How I Filmed the War* (London: Imperial War Museum, 1993). [This reprint of the 1920 edition includes a foreword by Nicholas Hiley with much valuable information on Malins.] K. Brownlow, *The War, The West and the Wilderness* (London: Secker and Warburg, 1979), 66–68.

11   The pioneering work on this was carried out in particular by Nicholas Hiley, Nicholas Reeves and Roger B. N. Smither, and the present author was also involved; see N. Reeves, *Official British Film Propaganda During the First World War* (London: Croom Helm, 1986). S. Badsey, 107–136.

12   A. H. Fraser, A. Robertshaw & S. Roberts, *Ghosts on the Somme: Filming the Great Battle, July 1916* (London: Pen & Sword, 2009). S. Badsey, 107–136. N. Reeves, 157–168.

13   In 2005 there was an excellent DVD release of a digitized version of *The Battle of the Somme* by the Imperial War Museum in association with Dragon Digital, with alternative music soundtracks, and with viewing and historical notes from which some of the information cited above has been taken. A copy of these viewing

notes may be accessed from the website of *The Battle of the Somme:* www.iwm. org.uk/somme-film. Acknowledgement is owing to Roger B. N. Smither, Keeper of the Film and Video Archive at the Imperial War Museum, as the principal figure in the sustained campaign to achieve modern recognition for the film.

14 Information about McDowell taken from various sources, including the database of the British Film Institute http://ftvdb.bfi.org.uk/sift/individual/13082; and the database of the British Universities Film and Video Council http://public. bufvc.ac.uk/BUND/staff/detail.php?id=33056. Acknowledgement is owing to Dr Nicholas Hiley of the University of Kent for much of the research into McDowell's early life.

15 For details of these and all the British official films shot on the Western Front see R. Smither (Ed.), *Imperial War Museum Film Catalogue.* Vol. 1. *The First World War Archive* (Trowbridge: Flicks Books, 1994) [with an introduction by the present author].

16 House of Lords Record Office, London, UK: Papers of Lord Beaverbrook, Letter from Lord Beaverbrook to Sir Reginald Brade, 6 May 1917.

17 Personnel file of Armando Consolé, Imperial War Museum Department of Photographs, Ministry of Information files, IWM (Photo) Papers.

18 House of Lords Record Office: Papers of Lord Beaverbrook, Letter from Lord Beaverbrook to Sir Reginald Brade, 9 July 1917.

19 The author is grateful to William Spencer of the National Archives for confirming that it holds a record of McDowell's award of both the OBE and the MC; because of the circumstances of the award during the war there is no extant citation for the MC award.

20 Quoted in K. Brownlow, 68.

JENNY MACLEOD

Ellis Ashmead-Bartlett, War Correspondence and the First World War

Ellis Ashmead-Bartlett was the main British war correspondent during the Gallipoli campaign of 1915. Aged thirty-four at the time, his passport described him as 5 foot 10 inches tall, slim, with green eyes, an oval face, a high forehead and a small chin.[1] He was already highly experienced having witnessed at least ten different theatres of war dating back to the Greco–Turkish War in 1898. Then, as a seventeen-year-old guest of the Sultan, he had been taken prisoner by the Greeks. From that time until his death in 1931, as his obituary notes, 'he tasted everything in the way of excitement that an unstable world could offer. There seems never to have been a war or an earthquake or a massacre in any corner of the world but Ashmead-Bartlett was on hand'.[2] His first assignment as a war correspondent saw him covering the siege of Port Arthur during the Russo–Japanese War in 1904. He died in Lisbon whilst covering the Spanish Revolution. Perhaps his most famous exploit came when he attempted to circumvent the censorship arrangements at Gallipoli by smuggling his highly critical assessment of the campaign back to the Prime Minister and, it has been argued, thereby precipitating the demise of General Sir Ian Hamilton as Commander-in-Chief.

War corresponding is often a difficult and dangerous job that requires resourcefulness and courage. Ashmead-Bartlett typified the restless and, perhaps, reckless spirit that is common to many war correspondents. Yet the First World War saw the severe curtailment of the independent and adventurous element of the job. Ashmead-Bartlett thus witnessed the transformation of the war correspondent from that of a lone adventurer to the tamed creature of general headquarters.

'Vilely brought up':
Ashmead-Bartlett's character and motivation

Ashmead-Bartlett came from a well-connected but eccentric political family. His father, Sir Ellis Ashmead-Bartlett (1849–1902), was a Conservative MP and held the post of Civil Lord of the Admiralty in Lord Salisbury's governments. He was a vehement opponent of Liberal foreign policy and he promoted his political views through the weekly newspaper, *England*. The expense of this enterprise drained his finances and meant his wealth at death was £100. He and his wife had eight children but he also became embroiled in a scandal in 1889 when his affair with Blanche Hozier, mother of Clementine Churchill, came to light.[3] Sir Ellis Ashmead-Bartlett's (1849–1902) brother, William Lehman Ashmead Bartlett (1851–1921), who was also an MP, shared his political views and also had an unconventional private life. William made what Queen Victoria described as a 'mad marriage' to a woman thirty-seven years his senior. His wife, Angela Burdett Coutts, was the richest heiress in England and a noted philanthropist. He amalgamated his surname with hers, thereby saddling himself with a quadruple-barrelled name: William Lehman Ashmead Bartlett Burdett Coutts.[4]

Two of the younger Ellis Ashmead-Bartlett's colleagues in the war correspondents' camp at Gallipoli remarked upon the way in which his family had moulded his character. Charles Bean, the official Australia war correspondent, felt that his rebellious character was sealed by the time he was at public school.

> He is a chap with an exceedingly nice nature but vilely brought up in the sort of wild selfish third rate society that surrounded his father. [...] He hated his school days at Marlborough – and the compulsory cricket and football, and his schoolmasters – almost every one of them, and their families. The only part he looks back on with pleasure is his active rebellion – as when he and a friend exploded 10 lbs. of mine powder on a neighbouring hilltop during the solemn procession of the masters and their wives and families to chapel.[5]

Similarly, the veteran war correspondent, Henry W. Nevinson, identified his upbringing as the source of Ashmead-Bartlett's arrogance as well

as his dazzling wit. He wrote in his memoirs, 'association from boyhood
with the rich and great had given him a proud self-confidence and a self-
centred aspect of the world, but his scornful and often antagonizing wit
made him a difficult, though attractive, companion in a camp'.[6]

After the war, Ashmead-Bartlett followed in the footsteps of his father
and uncle, winning a seat in parliament at the third attempt when he became
Conservative MP for North Hammersmith in 1924. His time as a parlia-
mentarian was, however, brief and undistinguished because bankruptcy
forced him to resign his seat after just two years in the House. Nor was this
his first financial crisis, because just a few months before Ashmead-Bartlett
went out to Gallipoli he was declared bankrupt with debts of £4,314.[7] He
gave two reasons to the court for his dire financial straits, firstly, and dis-
armingly frankly, 'his failure was due to extravagance in living'.[8] But matters had also come to a head because 'he was without income at present
because war correspondents were not allowed at the front'. In fact, he had
been to the Western Front on two occasions as part of organized tours
in January and March 1915.[9] This restricted access to the front reflected
the War Office's early suspicion of journalists on the Western Front. The
Dardanelles campaign, however, was initially organized by the Admiralty
and Winston Churchill, the First Sea Lord, took a more enlightened view
in allowing journalists to work in this theatre. Ashmead-Bartlett was one
of the three men chosen to travel with the Mediterranean Expeditionary
Force as war correspondents in March 1915.

Despite the inevitable privations of life in-theatre, Ashmead-Bartlett
was wont to retain his high-living lifestyle as far as possible. During the
South African War, where he served as a junior officer in the Bedfordshire
Regiment, he took with him a mixed case of champagne, port and whisky.
When the order came through to leave behind all unnecessary baggage, he
and a fellow officer concealed it in the Company's ammunition cart late
one night. Unluckily for them both, the cache of alcohol was discovered
and promptly consumed by the men.[10] More agreeably, in the early weeks
of the Gallipoli campaign Ashmead-Bartlett stayed on a series of battle-
ships. This proved to be a most comfortable arrangement. On 29 April,
four nights after the first landings on the peninsula he was part of a 'very
convivial gathering' drinking port in the wardroom of *Implacable* – he

noted in his diary that the Captain, Tubby Lockyer, was 'a tremendous man for sitting up'.[11] But it was not without its dangers. In the rewritten diary entry relating to his last night on the *Majestic* when all concerned felt sure they would be torpedoed, Ashmead-Bartlett's trademark combination of luxurious living and insouciant bravery is apparent. He recalled that he shared 'a kind of farewell dinner in the Wardroom and I drank a bottle of champagne with the PMO [Principal Medical Officer]. The port also went round more times than usual and some of us sat up until 11 o'clock'. He collected a new life jacket,

> I then went down below, undressed and wrapped up all my notes and valuable papers in a waterproof coat, and placed them in my small handbag [...] I took my cigarette case and put £30 in notes in my pyjama pocket, went up on deck, lay down and was soon fast asleep.[12]

Later that night, the ship was indeed torpedoed with the loss of fifty men.[13] Ashmead-Bartlett survived and returned to London to replace his lost belongings but when he came back to the Eastern Mediterranean, he found less salubrious living conditions with all the correspondents herded into a single camp on the island of Imbros. Nonetheless, Ashmead-Bartlett continued to throw noisy champagne parties late into the night.[14] Perhaps incongruously in a war zone, he also continued his habit of sleeping in silk pyjamas, maintaining that they wore better than other alternatives.[15] Nevinson described the scene he created:

> he would issue from his elaborately furnished tent dressed in a flowing robe of yellow silk shot with crimson, and call for breakfast as though the Carlton were still his corporeal home. Always careful of food and drink, he liked to have everything fine and highly civilised about him, both for his own sake and for the notable guests whom he loved to entertain.[16]

Nor did Imbros mark the end of his association with the Navy's hospitality. One of the scenes captured by Ashmead-Bartlett on his cinematograph was the landings at Suvla Bay on 7 August. Remarkably, he shot these from on board the *Minneapolis* 'fortified by whiskies and sodas and a beautifully iced bottle of champagne'.[17]

Ashmead-Bartlett's continued extravagance, despite the parlous state of his finances, meant that money was a guiding motive for him. He was paid £2,000 a year as a war correspondent by the Newspaper Proprietors' Association, and asked for a raise part way through the campaign.[18] He also sought to supplement his income in other ways. He promised to obtain sketches for one editor,[19] and his cinematographic efforts were prompted by a deal struck in June 1915, which accorded him 45 per cent of any future profits from the ensuing film.[20] After he left Gallipoli for good he signed a deal for a lecture tour: twenty-five lectures for a fee of £100 per lecture, with an option on another seventy-five lectures.[21] Ill-health dogged those plans and a tour in America had to be aborted, but he was able to fulfil a similar contract for twenty-five two-hour lectures in Australia.[22] Whilst he was there, he sold his papers to the Mitchell Library in Sydney for between £200 and £300.[23] Furthermore, having secured a book deal with a handsome advance during the campaign,[24] he also published three books relating to the campaign. Two of them reprinted articles: *Ashmead-Bartlett's Despatches from the Dardanelles: An Epic of Heroism* was brought out swiftly and reprinted his despatches covering the period prior to the Suvla landings.[25] *Some of My Experiences in the Great War* also reproduced some of his journalistic work. This volume contained one chapter on Gallipoli describing general scenes on the beaches and in the trenches.[26] His third Gallipoli-related book, *The Uncensored Dardanelles* published in 1928, was a more considered piece that enabled him to express his views in full. When he initially envisaged this book he hoped that this period of reflection would bring 'a far greater sale than one which would merely be more or less of a rehash of what has already appeared in the Press'.[27]

Clearly though, a person does not become a war correspondent purely for the money; Ashmead-Bartlett would surely have earned a better income if he had capitalized on his training as a barrister. The excitement and fascination of observing important and dangerous events at close hand must instead have played its part in his career choice. For example, Ashmead-Bartlett, who had not previously worked closely with the Navy, was exhilarated by cruising just off the Dardanelles Straits soon after he first arrived. He wrote in his diary on 10 April 1915, 'it was thrilling work for a novice, like myself, to be really on a battleship and within such close proximity to the enemy'.[28] Nonetheless, the financial aspect of things must have heightened various concerns; to establish himself as the key interpreter of an important campaign was potentially a meal ticket for years to come. His entrepreneurial activities – the cinema film, the lectures, the book deals – indicate that he recognized this. It also meant, perhaps, that despite his mounting frustrations with the way in which his work was censored, he stuck with the campaign longer than he might otherwise have done. He found the censorship exasperating, for it ripped some of the best elements out of his carefully crafted despatches and, thereby, had the potential to endanger his relationship with his employers, the Newspaper Proprietors' Association. Nicholas Hiley has argued that General Sir Ian Hamilton and his censors failed to understand this commercial aspect of Ashmead-Bartlett's work. Hence, a better supply of accurate news rather than ever-tighter restrictions on his work may have mollified the rebellious journalist.[29] Indeed the requirement for interesting copy is illustrated by the criticisms Charles Bean faced towards the end of the campaign, when the Melbourne newspapers, the *Age* and the *Argus* ceased to print his despatches.[30] Thus, Ashmead-Bartlett's concern to secure his role as the pre-eminent commentator on Gallipoli and the requirements of his employer, mingled with professional pride and the duty he perceived to act as an independent critic, to inform his behaviour during the campaign.

With clipped wings: the transformation of war correspondent from adventurous competitor to descriptive writer

According to Ashmead-Bartlett's private reminiscences, prior to the First World War, the world of the war correspondent was a toughly competitive one. Each represented a private enterprise that would spend 'fabulous'[31] sums to secure a story ahead of its rivals – the most rapid available transport might be hired at great cost, as long as the correspondent managed to send the story home first, and thereby boost the sales and prestige of the newspaper.[32] He later wrote,

> The War Correspondent in the old days had to combine many qualities, hardiness, resourcefulness, and a certain measure of unscrupulousness. He must learn everything for himself (official information was almost unknown before the present war); he had to keep all his news to himself, he must grasp a situation at a glance, and very often when competition was excessively keen, he had to judge the finish of a battle without actually waiting to see the end.[33]

Ashmead-Bartlett carried these competitive habits with him at the start of the Gallipoli campaign. When it was suggested before the campaign got under way that he and the other British journalist, Lester Lawrence, should work separately, Ashmead-Bartlett was happy to acquiesce, noting in his diary, 'I much prefer to work alone, and not to give anybody else the benefit of my experiences'.[34] But then he began to worry that the novice war correspondent Lawrence was gathering and sending more material than he was.[35] Yet, Lawrence was to prove no match for Ashmead-Bartlett and was ultimately adjudged a 'useful but not a brilliant War Correspondent'.[36] Instead Ashmead-Bartlett was able to beat all his colleagues to the scoop of the campaign: his description of the landings was the first to be published, a full ten days before his Australian counterpart Charles Bean's appeared.[37] One theory to explain this happy state of affairs was that the post office in Alexandria interpreted his mark 'urgent' as an instruction to telegraph the article at urgent rates and extortionate cost.[38] Ashmead-Bartlett discovered he had the scoop on 16 May, when he found that the battleship *London* had lots of letters for him as well as copies of the newspapers containing his article on the landing of the Australians at Gallipoli: 'I spent most of the day reading them. They have in fact received a very good show in all the papers'.[39]

The competitiveness also went on between the newspapers themselves. Ashmead-Bartlett was sent to the Dardanelles as the official representative of the National Press Association, and Lester Lawrence was the representative of Reuters. Hiley explains that the Press Association and Reuters managed to exclude their commercial rivals from the allocation of war correspondents at Gallipoli, prompted in part by considerable financial difficulties resulting from falling advertising revenue. They also withheld Ashmead-Bartlett's reports from provincial newspapers to reinforce their competitive edge.[40] It was only in mid-July that Henry Nevinson was sent to Gallipoli to report for the provincial press, along with Herbert Russell, acting for Reuters, and Sydney Moseley, for the Central News.[41] The arrival of these extra war correspondents was, in part, an attempt by Hamilton to play upon the journalists' competitiveness as a means to control them. As he wrote to Churchill, 'it is much easier to deal with a dozen, who can be set one against the other, than with a single individual'.[42]

One crucial element in facilitating the correspondent's ability to gather news was freedom of movement. Ostensibly, the journalists covering the Gallipoli campaign were fortunate in this respect. Moseley later recounted Hamilton's welcome to the late arrivals.

> Against precedents in France and against the advice of some of his most trusted advisers, he had therefore issued orders that no restrictions whatever should be placed upon our movements. We were free to go anywhere, see anything, speak to anyone, write anything, and, if truthful, our articles would be passed, provided always it was not cowardly stuff, not stuff calculated to encourage enemies or depress friends.[43]

Yet, despite these fine promises, the removal of the journalists' camp to Imbros was a ploy to regulate their access to the front and, particularly, to impede the troublesome Ashmead-Bartlett. Nonetheless, the reliable Bean and his New Zealand counterpart Malcolm Ross were allowed to roam freely as before,[44] and the issue remained one that was negotiated between the parties to some extent. Thus, when in August, with the arrival of Major Delmé Radcliffe, another press officer, it seemed that the correspondents' freedom of movement might be curtailed even more, a deputation to Hamilton led by Nevinson secured a guarantee of freedom.[45]

Gallipoli remained unusual in this respect. The privatized competition between war correspondents that partially survived there, was tamed and militarized on the Western Front. Ashmead-Bartlett observed that the war correspondents in France and Belgium had formed a 'common brotherhood' where there was 'no rivalry' and 'no scoops'.[46] Their every need was provided for by the Army, from food and shelter to the provision of stories:

> they are informed of every intended movement and are told the correct spot from which to witness it [...] They are invariably shown the same thing so that every paper each morning has the same tale told in a different writer's language. Every word they write is carefully censored, not a note of criticism is ever allowed to creep in, and only successes gained over the enemy are ever allowed to be commented on.[47]

Henry Nevinson also found that correspondents on the Western Front led a comfortable life: 'the strain of a war correspondent's life was relaxed till it almost ceased'.[48] The war correspondents gathered their information in the company of a press officer, and then shared their material over lunch back at the chateau. The correspondents developed friendly bonds with their conducting officers. Keith Grieves has described the relationship as that of 'a kind of jailer and spy, eating, sleeping, walking and driving together'.[49] This virtual Stockholm Syndrome contributed significantly to the correspondents' patriotic disinclination to challenge the system. As the leading Western Front correspondent, Philip Gibbs, later wrote, 'We identified ourselves absolutely with the Armies in the field [...] We wiped out of our minds all thoughts of personal scoops and all temptation to write one word which would make the task of officers and men more difficult or dangerous. There was no need of censorship of our despatches. We were our own censors'.[50] Hence, in the subsequent estimation of one Gallipoli journalist, the task of being a war correspondent had changed out of all recognition. Sydney Moseley wrote,

> The traditional war correspondent became extinct after the South African War [...] And all the correspondents of the Great War were birds of a different feather. Their wings were so clipped by the authorities and the censors that they seldom fluttered to the front line. And their most magnificent flights were flights of rhetoric or pure fancy.
> I became a war correspondent myself and though I flapped my juvenile wings to some effect, I never fooled myself that I was, in fact, *reporting* the war. We were, of necessity, commentators and descriptive writers, not reporters.[51]

'To tell the world the blunders [...] on this blood-stained Peninsula': Ashmead-Bartlett's aims

There is at least one man, however, who fought to retain his right to report and to criticize the war. Ashmead-Bartlett had the ability to write about war in dramatic and vivid terms, and he was determined to go on doing so.[52] He preferred the grand overview of developments to the nitty-gritty details: he reputedly dismissed his meticulous Australian colleague's front-line research, saying, 'Oh, Bean – I think he almost counts the bullets!'.[53] For his part, Bean was highly critical of Bartlett's tendency to exaggerate and add extra colour to his articles. Bean wrote in his diary,

> I can't write about bayonet charges like some of the correspondents do. Ashmead-Bartlett makes it a little difficult for one by his exaggerations, and yet he's a lover of the truth. He gives the spirit of the thing: but if he were asked: 'Did a shout really go up from a thousand throats that the hill was ours?' he'd have to say 'No, it didn't' [...] Well, I can't write that it occurred if I know it did not.[54]

Whilst Ashmead-Bartlett was not above adding the occasional picturesque embellishment, and put a positive spin on events where it was feasible, he attempted to combine these with frank criticism and observations. The balance struck between these elements was the result of ongoing negotiations between the censors and the journalist.

Because the campaign was initially conceived as a naval attack, naval officers undertook to censor the journalists' despatches. Ashmead-Bartlett found Commodore Keyes to be a benevolent censor. However, as the army's involvement in censorship developed in tandem with the emergence of a joint campaign, Ashmead-Bartlett began to complain privately about the increasing restrictions placed upon him. On 30 April, after speaking to Captain Unwin, he wrote up an account of the River Clyde and the landings at V beach. He wrote in his diary, 'I was able to visualise the whole situation and thus to write a long account of these events, which was subsequently largely spoilt by the authorities at home, who insisted upon taking out the names of all the regiments, which is like trying to paint a picture with only one colour in it'.[55] The tensions became explicit in the aftermath of the second battle of Krithia between 6 and 8 May. The failure to capture this village and the high ground of Achi Baba signalled the end of the hope that the Gallipoli peninsula might be captured swiftly and cheaply. Yet, it seems that Bartlett was forced to conceal his true opinion in reporting the attempt to capture Krithia, a battle he described grandly in his despatch as the 'Battle of the Nations'.[56] It is apparent from his account that the battle involved much terrible and furious fighting, but the wounded and the dying are not described, nor are absolute exhaustion, the mutilating effect of gun fire, pain, suffering, confusion, fear – all things that were part of the battle. Even so, Ashmead-Bartlett's despatch on the battle was more informative and pessimistic than the Commander-in-Chief's official despatch – a fact that did not escape some newspapers at home. *Truth* noted:

> Mr Ashmead-Bartlett's illuminating despatches from the Dardanelles are admirable supplements to the meagre reports which reach us from Sir Ian Hamilton. We now know, what was anticipated in truth from the first, that the process of clearing the Gallipoli Peninsula of Turkish troops will be a slow one.[57]

Ashmead-Bartlett vented his frustration in his diary and his complaints became ever more scathing, after Krithia he wrote that this was a 'ridiculous [way] of conducting warfare'.[58] He later wrote in his book, 'It is heartrending work having to write what I know to be untrue, and in the end having to confine myself to giving a descriptive account of the useless slaughter of thousands of my fellow countrymen for the benefit of the public at home, when what I wish to do is to tell the world the blunders that are being daily committed on this blood-stained Peninsula'.[59] His mounting discontentment led him to draw up a frank memorandum about the campaign. On 26 May he was told that it was impossible to send it home, 'Then I knew', wrote Bartlett later in his diary, 'what was going on and became still further convinced that the truth was not known either in private or public circles at home'.[60]

Later that night, the sinking of the *Majestic* required Ashmead-Bartlett to return home to re-equip himself. Whilst he was in London, he not only arranged various lucrative publication deals but also he engaged in a vigorous round of breakfast, lunch and dinner meetings whereby he explained the situation in Gallipoli to a series of influential political and media figures. He was not a welcome figure upon his return to the peninsula, and he found his freedom of movement and expression ever more curtailed. By 18 July he was complaining in his diary,

> I thought there were limits to human stupidity but now I know there are none. The censorship has now passed beyond all reason. They won't let you give expression to the mildest opinions on any subjects. They apply it to taste style poetry and events of which the enemy are by now fully cognisant and which have already appeared in the press. The long article I wrote on Lancashire Landing has been returned without a single word being passed. The reason is that they state it makes the people on W beach look as if they were afraid. I wrote the article to please those on W beach and they were tickled to death with it? There are now at least four censors all of whom cut up your stuff. Maxwell starts it then Ward then General Braithwaite and finally Sir Ian Hamilton. All hold different views and feel it their duty to take out scraps. Thus only a few dry crumbs are left for the wretched public. The articles resemble chicken out of which a thick nutritious broth has been extracted.[61]

In September, at a stage when it was increasingly apparent that the campaign had failed, Ashmead-Bartlett's frustration culminated in a sensational attempt to step outside the constraints of censorship. He wrote another letter to H. H. Asquith about the campaign and persuaded the visiting Australian journalist Keith Murdoch to smuggle it to London. When this letter was seized from Murdoch by the military police, he wrote his own version and forwarded it to the British Cabinet and to his friend, Andrew Fisher, Prime Minister of Australia. Ashmead-Bartlett's actions resulted in his dismissal. At about the same time, Hamilton was also replaced as Commander-in-Chief.[62]

An independent critic for a nation-in-arms: Ashmead-Bartlett's significance

How important was Ashmead-Bartlett? It is likely that his subterfuge provided the occasion rather than the cause of Hamilton's recall and the beginning of the end of the campaign. Hamilton may have blamed Murdoch and Ashmead-Bartlett for his downfall, but in truth they were not lone critics, and the endgame of the campaign is more complex than their admittedly exciting part in it. As Kevin Fewster has pointed out, his letter did not evade security and censorship: it was intercepted, and it only made a significant impact because key political figures were already dissatisfied with the campaign.[63]

Ashmead-Bartlett has also been assigned a role in creating the Anzac legend for Australia and New Zealand[64] – this is undoubtedly true. Not only was he the first to report the landings on the peninsula, but also as the main representative of the British press during the campaign's most important phase his 'despatches were getting enormous "spreads" in all the papers,'[65] and, hence, he provided an influential early source of information on the campaign on both sides of the world. Yet he has rightly been overshadowed by Charles Bean in the long run owing to the Australian's long association with the Australian Imperial Force (AIF), and his Herculean efforts in writing and editing Australia's official history of the war. Perhaps instead we should rate Ashmead-Bartlett as a military critic. He certainly fancied himself in the role, arguing forcefully for an alternative operational approach in attacking at the neck of the peninsula. But his ideas have never been taken seriously and were perhaps only important in so far as they assisted his post-Gallipoli career posing as the great critic of the campaign who held the key to success.

Nonetheless, he remains a fascinating character in his own right, whose part in the Gallipoli campaign raises questions about the role of the war correspondent. The experienced Nevinson recognized the anomalous position of the war correspondent as a quasi civilian[66] who straddled two worlds. It is the appropriate loyalties of such a figure that are in question here. Another Gallipoli colleague, Moseley, with less finesse than Nevinson, believed himself to be the 'mouthpiece'[67] of the army. For him, the interests of the public had become synonymous with the interests of the army.

> I supported the censorship all the time I was in the Dardanelles as a war correspond-
> ent. For war is a madness which negatives all normal standards of conduct and belief.
> A nation at war surrenders all its liberties. If man can be conscripted for 'cannon
> fodder', it seems childish to object to any lesser compulsions.[68]

Yet Ashmead-Bartlett recognized that a nation at war meant that the rules of the game had to change. 'The fundamental error of the Government and the Military Authorities is the failure to realise the difference between the army as it existed before the war and the immense national army, in which the entire nation has a stake, which has been created since the war began' and hence 'the Government [must] take the nation more fully into its confidence'.[69] For him, the changed relationship between the armed forces and the nation meant that the old habits of the army had to be questioned. In one encounter, Hamilton's Chief of Staff told Ashmead-Bartlett that 'as a private individual I might hold what views I liked but that as a War Correspondent I had no right to any except those which were officially given me'.[70] On the contrary, Ashmead-Bartlett wrote in his diary that he 'was not prepared to be an official eyewitness but was determined to remain an independent critic who could not be got at in any one's interests'.[71] This may be the eternal dilemma of the war correspondent – are they official eyewitnesses or independent critics? In circumstances where lives and even national survival are at stake, the traditional journalistic commitment to transparency and truth-telling was subject to compromise in the eyes of many war correspondents. Driven by money, arrogance and principle, Ashmead-Bartlett disagreed.

Notes

1   Institute of Commonwealth Studies, London, UK: Ellis Ashmead-Bartlett
     papers, passport: ICS 84/1/2/14. National Library of Australia, Canberra, hold
     a microfilm of these papers (Ashmead-Bartlett papers Mfm M2582).

2   Institute of Commonwealth Studies: Campbell Dixon, 'The Man on the Spot' (1931): ICS 84/1/228.

3   J. P. Anderson, 'Bartlett, Sir Ellis Ashmead- (1849–1902), rev. H. C. G. Matthew', in *Oxford Dictionary of National Biography* (Oxford: Oxford University Press, 2004). Online edition, May 2006. http://www.oxforddnb.com/view/article/30627 (accessed 8 November 2007).

4   B. Holden Reid, 'Coutts, William Lehman Ashmead Bartlett Burdett- (1851–1921)', in *Oxford Dictionary of National Biography* (Oxford: Oxford University Press, 2004). Online edition, May 2006. http://www.oxforddnb.com/view/article/58663 (accessed 8 November 2007). E. Healey, 'Coutts, Angela Georgina Burdett-, suo jure Baroness Burdett-Coutts (1814–1906)', in *Oxford Dictionary of National Biography* (Oxford: Oxford University Press, 2004). Online edition, May 2006. http://www.oxforddnb.com/view/article/32175 (accessed 8 November 2007).

5   Australian War Memorial, Canberra: C. E. W. Bean papers, diary, 2 October 1915: AWM 38 3DRL 606, item 17.

6   H. W. Nevinson, *Last Changes, Last Chances* (London: Nisbet and Co. Ltd, 1928), 35.

7   *The Times*, 25 February 1915. For further details of his extravagant lifestyle, see N. P. Hiley, '"Enough Glory for All": Ellis Ashmead-Bartlett and Sir Ian Hamilton at the Dardanelles', *Journal of Strategic Studies*, 16(2) (1993), 245.

8   *The Times*, 25 February 1915.

9   N. P. Hiley (1993), 241.

10   Institute of Commonwealth Studies: 'Some reminiscences': ICS 84/C5/6, 6–8.

11   Mitchell Library, State Library of New South Wales, Sydney, Australia: Ashmead-Bartlett papers, diary, 29 April 1915: ML A1583, 50.

12   Mitchell Library: diary, 26 May 1915: ML A1583, 78–79.

13   Mitchell Library: 'Last days of the Majestic', 26 May 1915: ML A1584.

14   S. A. Moseley, *The Truth About a Journalist* (London: Pitman, 1935), 101.

15   S. A. Moseley (1935), 103.

16   H. W. Nevinson, 35.

17   Quoted in P. Dutton, '"More Vivid Than the Written Word": Ellis Ashmead Bartlett's Film *With the Dardanelles Expedition* (1915)', *Historical Journal of Film, Radio and Television*, 24(2) (2004), 211.

18   This is according to Hamilton cited in C. Mackenzie, *Gallipoli Memories* (London: Cassell & Co, 1929), 106. It tallies roughly with the £150 per month that he was receiving three years earlier. *The Times*, 25 February 1915. Mitchell Library: diary, 7 June 1915: ML A1583, 90.

19   Ashmead-Bartlett to the Editor of *The Sphere*, 11 July 1915. Bartlett promised
     to try and pick up some sketches, not to draw them himself. The editor had
     promised to pay 'what you think fair'. National Library of Australia: Editor of
     The Sphere to Ashmead-Bartlett, 7 May 1915: Mfm M2582, B/3/65.

20   Mitchell Library: diary, 12 June 1915: ML A1583, 103. This film became *Heroes
     of Gallipoli* (Australia, 1920). R. Smither (Ed.), *Imperial War Museum Film
     Catalogue*. Vol. I. *The First World War Archive* (Trowbridge: Flicks Books, 1994),
     373. See also P. Dutton, 205–222.

21   Mitchell Library: diary, 14 October 1915: ML A1583, 192. Henry Nevinson also
     undertook some lecturing in October 1915 but not it seems on the huge scale
     of Ashmead-Bartlett. National Archives, London, UK: General A. J. Murray,
     'Report on Press Representatives', 23 August 1916, P.R.O.: CAB 19/30.

22   National Library of Australia: agreement with J & N Tait, Melbourne, Australia
     and London, 4 December 1915: Mfm M2582 C1/5/41.

23   Mitchell Library: W. H. Ifould, Principal Librarian, Public Library of New
     South Wales to Messrs. Angus and Robertson Ltd., 5 April 1916: ML A1583, 6.

24   Mitchell Library: diary, 10 June 1915: ML A1583, 91.

25   E. Ashmead-Bartlett, *Ashmead-Bartlett's Despatches from the Dardanelles: An
     Epic of Heroism* (London: George Newnes, 1916). This is the copy held by the
     British Library; however, a review in the *Daily Telegraph* suggests that this book
     was first published around 13 September 1915. National Library of Australia:
     Mr Ashmead-Bartlett's Despatches. 'An Epic of Heroism', *Daily Telegraph*, 13
     September 1915: Mfm M2586.

26   E. Ashmead-Bartlett, *Some of My Experiences in the Great War* (London: George
     Newnes, 1918).

27   National Library of Australia: Ashmead-Bartlett to Hughes Massie (his agent),
     26 August 1915: Mfm M2582 B/3/124. This letter is discussing a deal with Sir
     George Hutchinson. Hutchinson & Co. were the eventual publishers of:
     E. Ashmead-Bartlett, *The Uncensored Dardanelles* (London: Hutchinson &
     Co, 1928).

28   Mitchell Library: diary, 10 April 1915: ML A1583, 20.

29   N. P. Hiley (1993), 249.

30   J. F. Williams, *Anzacs, the Media, and the Great War* (Sydney: University of New
     South Wales, 1999), 71.

31   Institute of Commonwealth Studies: 'Some Reminiscences': ICS 84/C5/6, 3.

32   Institute of Commonwealth Studies: 'Some Reminiscences': ICS 84/C5/6, 2.

33   Institute of Commonwealth Studies: 'Some Reminiscences': ICS 84/C5/6, 2.

34   Mitchell Library: diary, 5 April 1915: ML A1583, 16.

35   Mitchell Library: diary, 27 April 1915: ML A1583, 47.

36   National Archives, London, UK: CAB 19/30.

37   E. Ashmead-Bartlett (Dardanelles, 24, 26 & 27 April), 'Graphic story from the Dardanelles. Historic scenes. Army disembarked by moonlight. Dashing colonials. Capture of positions. Special cablegrams', *Daily Telegraph*, 7 May 1915. C. E. W. Bean, 'Gallipoli (one)', *Commonwealth of Australia Gazette* No. 39, Monday 17 May 1915. Australian War Memorial: AWM 38 3DRL 8039, item 1, 931–933.

38   K. Fewster, 'Ellis Ashmead-Bartlett and the making of the Anzac legend', *Journal of Australian Studies*, 10 (1982), 19. The British authorities in Alexandria held up Bean's account until 13 May.

39   Mitchell Library: diary, 16 May 1915: ML A1583, 65.

40   N. P. Hiley (1993), 244–245.

41   Mitchell Library: diary, 14 July 1915: ML A1583, 123.

42   Hamilton to Churchill, 26 June 1915. M. Gilbert, *Winston S. Churchill*. Vol. III. *Companion*. Part 2. *May 1915–December 1916* (London: Heinemann, 1972), 1060. Quoted in N. P. Hiley (1993), 240–264.

43   S. A. Moseley, *The Truth About the Dardanelles* (London: Cassell & Co, 1916), 13.

44   Australian War Memorial: C. E. W. Bean to GSO 1st Australian Division, 27 June 1915: AWM 38 3DRL 6673, item 270.

45   Mitchell Library: diary, 2 August 1915: ML A1583, 123. N. P. Hiley, *Making War: The British News Media and Government Control 1914–16* (PhD thesis, Open University, UK, 1985), 179–180.

46   Institute of Commonwealth Studies: 'Some Reminiscences': ICS 84/C5/6, 3. Ashmead-Bartlett worked as a correspondent with the French Army on the Western Front in 1916.

47   Institute of Commonwealth Studies: 'Some Reminiscences': ICS 84/C5/6, 4.

48   H. W. Nevinson quoted in A. V. John, *War, Journalism and the Shaping of the Twentieth Century: The Life and Times of Henry W. Nevinson* (London: I. B. Tauris, 2006), 157.

49   K. Grieves, 'War correspondents and conducting officers on the Western Front from 1915', in H. Cecil & P. Liddle (Eds), *Facing Armageddon* (London: Leo Cooper, 1996), 719.

50   P. Gibbs, *Adventures in Journalism* (London: Heinemann, 1923), 231. Cited in P. Knightley, *The First Casualty: The War Correspondent as Hero, Propagandist and Myth Maker from the Crimea to Vietnam* (London: Andre Deutsch, 1975), 81.

51   S. A. Moseley (1935), 89.

52   For a more detailed discussion of Ashmead-Bartlett's despatches from Gallipoli
      and his battles with the censors, see J. Macleod, *Reconsidering Gallipoli*, chapter
      3 (Manchester: Manchester University Press, 2004).

53   Quoted in K. Fewster, 30.

54   Australian War Memorial: C. E. W. Bean, diary, 26 September 1915: AWM 38
      3DRL 606, item 17.

55   Mitchell Library: 30 April 1915: ML A1583, 51.

56   *Daily Telegraph*, 19 May 1915. This description the Battle of Nations is probably
      a reference to the Battle of Leipzig in October 1813.

57   National Library of Australia: *Truth*, 26 May 1915: Mfm M2585.

58   Mitchell Library: diary, 8 May 1915: ML A1583, 59.

59   E. Ashmead-Bartlett (1928), 101.

60   Mitchell Library: diary, 26 May 1915: ML A1583, 77. Hiley notes that *The
      Uncensored Dardanelles* (pp. 269–277) contains an appendix that is supposed
      to be the 13 May memorandum, but is actually a later version, the original having
      been lost on 27 May 1915. N. P. Hiley (1985), 167 (footnote).

61   Mitchell Library: diary, 18 July 1915: ML A1583, 125.

62   For a long time it was thought that Nevinson had tipped off Hamilton about
      the smuggled letter, but recently, Nevinson's biographer has suggested that it
      was the navy's official photographer, Ernest Brooks, who had done so. Nicholas
      Hiley believes it may have been Malcolm Ross. A. V. John, 152. Bodleian Library,
      Modern Papers Reading Room, Oxford, UK: Henry Woodd Nevinson Papers,
      journal, 15 September 1916, MS Eng misc e. 620. N. P. Hiley (1985), 183 (footnote
      91).

63   K. Fewster, 24–25.

64   K. Fewster, 24–25.

65   S. A. Moseley (1935), 97.

66   H. W. Nevinson, 32. It is not entirely clear whether this is Nevinson's own phrase
      or his paraphrase of comments by Hamilton.

67   S. A. Moseley (1916), 1.

68   S. A. Moseley (1935), 100.

69   Institute of Commonwealth Studies: untitled document, *c.* October 1917: ICS
      84/C5/8.

70   Mitchell Library: diary, 30 June 1915: ML A1583, 114.

71   Mitchell Library: diary, 20 May 1915: ML A1583, 68.

TOM QUINN

Dipping the Pen into the Wound: Albert Londres – French War Correspondent

The First World War [...] acted as the site of Londres' apprenticeship as a proactive journalist. [...] His apprenticeship brought home to him his true vocation: to locate, describe and denounce alienations.[1]

— WALTER REDFERN

Albert Londres carried inside him, right until the end of his days, an abomination of injustice.[2]

— PAUL MOUSSET

If only one could tell all that one sees, and all that one knows.[3]

— ALBERT LONDRES

In the beginning

The Great War of 1914–18 made Albert Londres. The journalist, often described as France's first war correspondent and who gave his name to France's foremost prize for journalism, was born in 1884 in the town of Vichy. Londres' biographer, Pierre Assouline, describes the young Londres as 'being in no way remarkable'.[4] Undistinguished at school, Londres' first employment saw him trying to make a career for himself as an apprentice accountant in a mining firm based in Lyon. It was really not for him and, in the evenings, he balanced the mediocrity of his days by espousing a bohemian lifestyle, becoming part of a loosely anarchic poetic circle and seeking refuge in febrile dreams of a literary career. In 1904, after he had lost his employment, Londres escaped Lyon for the more liberating spaces of Paris.

The third decade of his life, which begun with the birth of his only child, Florise, and the loss soon after of his partner, Marcelle Laforest,[5] saw Londres determinedly pursuing his Muse. In 1904, he published his first volume of poetry but, living a garret existence in Paris, he felt constrained to seek more gainful employment. He found it in the world of newspapers. Place proved defining. Writing to the editor of the Paris office of Lyon newspaper *Le Salut Public*, Élie-Joseph Bois, who also hailed from Vichy, Londres boldly introduced himself. 'I come from the same region as you do. I am only twenty years old. My trade is the writing of verse. I want to create literature. Do you want to help me?'[6] The ploy worked and having exploited the connection with his birthplace, Londres began working in the editorial room of *Le Salut Public*, where he learned quickly and regretfully the supremacy of scissors and paste over the agility of pen but where, however, he appears to have spent most of his time indulging his inveterate instinct to write poetry.

Two years later, in 1906, Londres moved to the editorial staff of one of the big four Parisian newspapers, *Le Matin*, where he continued to pursue his would-be career as a poet. In 1910, this pursuit effectively ended with the publication of his fourth volume of poetry.[7] The time was ripe for a new beginning and, moulting from his poet skin, Londres began his amazing transformation into a reporter.

A reporter is born

'Life arranges things well', the French have a habit of saying.[8] Life, or fortune, certainly played a significant role in deciding the destiny of Albert Londres. One Sunday in 1912, when he was twenty-eight, a shipping accident occurred on the Escaut River, north of Paris. As there was no reporter on duty at *Le Matin* to cover the story, Londres was dispatched from Paris; later, his report on the accident was considered so satisfactory that he was promoted to the rank of parliamentary reporter.[9]

Following the outbreak of the Great War, in August 1914, Londres' newspaper, like many of the Paris dailies, moved with the French government to Bordeaux. Londres, however, wanting to be close to the action, stayed in its Paris office. In September 1914, *Le Matin* was again short of reporters; Londres was called upon and sent to Reims, which had just been liberated from the Germans. Londres was now not just close to the action, he was immersed in it. It was at Reims that the Great War made Londres, finally, definitively, a reporter. The death of the historic cathedral of Reims was, in a sense, Londres' apotheosis.

Death of a cathedral

As Londres arrived in Reims, accompanied by a photographer, Moreau, the Germans began fiercely to bombard the city. On 21 September, his sensational eyewitness account of the bombardment appeared in *Le Matin*. 'They have bombarded Reims', Londres began, 'and we saw it happen'. The train carrying them from Paris having halted because of the danger, the two men, journalist and photographer, entered the city on bicycles. Already in the distance one supreme object had taken hold of their attention.

> Reims was fifteen kilometres away. In the distance the cathedral displayed the majesty of her profile soaring above the plain where she sang her poem of stone. We could not take our eyes off her. We advanced. A companion nudged with his elbow: 'Look', he said, 'there's smoke'.
> [...]
> The fate of this building which for eight centuries had amazed the world now tore at our minds.[10]

As Londres entered the town, he witnessed the exodus of its citizens, women and children, and a regiment departing. Night was falling. Ineluctably, irresistibly, 'drawn by a movement of love, as if we could protect her', Londres and Moreau climbed to the porch of the cathedral. At the core of his article, is a poignant account of the suffering of the great cathedral as the shells shattered her.

> We could not prevent ourselves from walking around and around her. We sensed something bad was about to happen to her. As we had no lodging, we spent the night by her side.
>
> She was the best preserved cathedral in France. You would have to become Catholic for her alone. Her towers soared so high that they did not stop where her stone stopped. You watched them soar beyond themselves, rising all the way to the sky. Reims cathedral was not suppliant, like Chartres, nor on her knees like Notre Dame, nor powerful like the cathedral at Laon. She was the majesty of religion descended on this earth.
>
> And they were about to burn her.
>
> [...]
>
> A shell had just fallen on the cathedral square.
>
> [...]
>
> A second shell fell thirty seconds later. It lodged ten meters from the first [...] It was just the beginning. The guns were being adjusted. This time *they had her*. We lost count of the blows. They rained down relentlessly.
>
> We left the porch and entered the street, positioning ourselves opposite the cathedral, one hundred meters away.
>
> We watched the cathedral. Ten minutes later we saw her first stone fall. It was 19 September 1914, at 7.25 in the morning.

This founding article of Londres' career as a war correspondent contains in *résumé* nearly all of the features of his writing style and his *modus operandi* as a journalist. There is a resourcefulness, endeavour and the courage he showed in using the bicycle to get to his goal. There is his intensity, his emotion and his almost 'heroic' positioning of himself as observer. From his very first line, he places himself in the thick of the action and declares his own privileged position as witness. He uses the presence of others, such as Moreau, to bolster and confirm this position, and while it is the suffering of the cathedral which dominates his article, from start to finish he provides a supporting human – and a non-human – cast that adds rich colour to the breathless intensity of his description, which tumbles along with all the drama of a war novel. There are women, 'heads bare, heading for the fields, wanting to save their children from death'. A child twists frantically in the arms of its mother. 'A dog, gone mad, chases its tail, leaping to try to take an invisible sugar lump'. There are French soldiers on guard at the cathedral and inside, incredibly, as the shells fall on her, two hundred German wounded lying in the great nave.

It is all very literary but for all the interest and colour that the suffering human brings to his text, at Reims Londres discovered his forte – or his formula – as a war correspondent: describing the suffering of the non-human, particularly that of buildings. In general, in his war reporting, rather than dwelling on atrocities against the human, writes Walter Redfern, Londres 'concentrates on the massacre of buildings and countrysides'.[11] It has been suggested that Londres was more moved by the suffering of buildings than of people[12] but it is more likely that when it came to the suffering of humans he preferred to cover the tragic or horrific with a veil of reticence, a sort of *pudeur*. It may also be that throughout his career as a war correspondent he was drawn back mentally and in his writing to the founding moment when the burning edifice of Reims cathedral became the presiding symbol or *idée fixe* of Londres' own experience of war, as if the intensity of that initiating experience had left its mark on him and on his writing forever. Whatever the case – and we have seen that even his founding article is peopled with a host of human characters – Londres seems to have been lumbered with this perception of his war writing. As Walter Redfern writes:

> His instinct and his realism must have told him he could best bring the war home to civilian readers not by front-line reporting of armies locked in lethal combat [...] but by writing of the effects of war on the very fabric of French [...] life: its villages, towns and buildings, and their denizens, the human and non-human landscapes of war.
> [...]
> Where he excels is in passing on to readers something of the very feel of war: the noises, the smells, the catastrophic impact on the non-human world.[13]

In his Reims article, Londres instinctively and implicitly draws on the symbolic significance of Reims Cathedral, profoundly identified with Catholic – and with Royal – France in the mind of his reader,[14] to create a deeply resonant and poetic image of the war itself. Indeed, the focus on the cathedral allows it to do most of the work for Londres: it becomes a vector carrying complex layers of meaning and experience in simplified form to a readership at a remove not only from the theatre of war but also from an understanding of it. It is as if the years of servitude to his Muse had now found their true purpose in the reality of the historical moment. Out of the hard and pitiless act of war, Londres had pulled a memorable image filled with poetry. The would-be poet, at thirty years of age, had found a new vocation. Only it was more than a vocation: it was a destiny.

It could be argued that Londres' Reims article is one of the most successful pieces of war journalism ever. At *Le Matin*, the piece was considered of such significance that it was published using Londres' name, an unaccustomed practice.[15] The byline underlined Londres' authority as witness, his 'I was there' status but it also gave him lasting affirmation and identity as a reporter. Londres' article had an immediate impact on the public and on his fellow journalists, who recognized immediately the talent of the newcomer. Édouard Helsey, an established reporter at the time, wrote that Londres' article melded journalism, history and poetry into a terrible act of witness.[16] Walter Redfern describes it as 'a prose-poem, and an indictment of a war crime, an atrocity against the non-human.'[17]

The article was the making of Londres but it was much more than that. According to Thomas Ferenczi, it constituted one of three key moments in the course of the Great War where the nature of journalism in France was radically changed. With this article by Londres, Ferenczi maintains, the horizons of journalism were enlarged, and a new style of journalism and journalist had emerged in France.[18] In the destruction and flames of the Great War, declares Ferenczi, the narrow vision, preoccupations and sedentary traditions of the pre-war French press gave way to a new style of reporting spearheaded by an engaged and committed observer on the move. This new style of reporter often came with literary credentials – Ferenzci gives the examples of Francis Carco, Blaise Cendrars, Pierre MacOrlan and Joseph Kessel – but it was the failed poet, Albert Londres, who provided its essential, iconic, embodiment and it is his article on the burning of Reims Cathedral that is the key moment or true starting point of its development.

The reporter at war

As if by some alchemy, the flames of Reims Cathedral remodelled and remade Albert Londres. From now on Londres acts as an improvised correspondent and the war is his theatre of operations. Above all, he begins to move. During the next few months he will roam tirelessly across the major towns of the Western Front bogging down in stasis: Hazebrouck, Arras, Dunkirk, Ypres. By the end of 1914, his articles were appearing almost every day on the front page of *Le Matin*. His biographer, Pierre Assouline, writes that Londres 'expresses himself [at this time] with an assurance, a command, and a personality, all the more astonishing given that three months earlier, he was nothing'.[19]

At war, Londres saw himself as more than at mere reporter. Excited, as much as angered by the spectacle of war, he sees himself as a combatant whose weapon is his pen: to write is to fight. In a letter to his parents, he writes: 'Above all, tell yourselves, I am like the soldiers [...] I am bored only when I am far from the fighting. All the soldiers with whom I live and whom I see along the Front sing like madmen. At Arras, while waiting for shells to fall, the soldiers sang [...] and laughed'.[20]

Londres' description of the common soldier needs to be read with some prejudice, as the trend among reporters in general at this time was to enliven their reports of the infantry for public consumption, often portraying the simple soldier marching to sacrifice with a smile. On the other hand, Londres' identification with the soldier may represent unconscious psychological compensation for the fact that he himself had been declared unfit for military service; or it may simply represent the admiration of a man of words and the envy for the man of action. Of course, Londres would prove a man of action in his own right, as when he persuaded the French General Dossin to allow him and photographer, Moreau, to enter the closed town of Nieuport in Belgium, disguised as prisoners.[21] Indeed, this type of daring would characterize Londres' entire career as a reporter.

As the war progressed, Londres tirelessly followed the still-shifting line of the Western Front. Walter Redfern writes:

As a war correspondent, [Londres] strove always to reach the most advanced, the most dangerous positions, and he was ever ready to harness any means of locomotion (horse, ox-cart, bicycle, lifts in cars or boats, or Shank's pony) to get there. He suffered. He slept rough, ate no better than the *poilus*, and exposed himself to the constant risk of being killed, by shelling, sniping, or by disease.[22]

It seems as if Londres was now hooked on war or on the excitement of it. He seems driven to and by it. 'Londres went everywhere', Assouline tells us, 'everywhere where there was killing, where the dead were being gathered up, and where they were being buried. It was as if he had a nose for it'. In Furnes, in Flanders, Londres reported the last words of an eleven-year-old newspaper seller whose skull had been shattered by an exploding shell. The boy's papers swim in his blood, while an old woman rescues his scattered coins. '*Merci* [...]' is the boy's dying acknowledgement.[23] The passage shows how sensitive Londres remained to the effect of war on people.

At war with censorship

Londres' Reims article constituted a major scoop, not simply because it represented a leap forward in the reporting, and the public perception, of the war but because, from the very outset of it, reporting was being severely controlled and curtailed by the French military, who blamed press indiscretion in relation to troop movements for the defeat of France during the Franco–Prussian War over four decades earlier. This time things would be different. As early as 3 August, the French War Ministry had established a press bureau to censor all military information.[24] By 5 August a comprehensive law governing the reporting of war was in place. Less than three days after the appearance of Londres' article the vice was made even tighter, when the elderly French statesman and newspaper editor, the so-called 'Tiger' of French politics, Georges Clemenceau, launched a scathing attack in his *L'Homme libre* newspaper against the apparatus of censorship, which was already extending its scope beyond concerns with the purely military.[25]

Every sensible person recognises that censorship applies only to matters of a military nature. Beyond that it is and can only be an unacceptable abuse of power [...] Alas, our government does not see it that way. What has the censorship of military news got to do with that of a political article which may or may not please His Majesty the Government?[26]

A year later, *Le Temps* newspaper protested bitterly: 'Censorship has extended its preventative jurisdiction to all press articles [...] It has placed itself above the law [...] Not only are the rights of the Press and of the Nation in danger, but the future of Liberty itself in France'.[27] Ironically, when Clemenceau himself gained power in the autumn of 1917 he would, contrary to expectation, tighten rather than loosen the vice of censorship.

Through its *Section d'Information* (SI), the army wanted to ensure that it was the only source of information on the war. Journalists were dependent on the three communiqués issued daily by the SI for news about the war. Throughout the war, 'information on military matters [in France] was under the most severe control',[28] while the figure of the journalist very quickly became *persona non grata* at the front.[29] Journalists were not allowed to visit the front and civilian newspapers could not be distributed along it. The only newspaper available along the front was the official army bulletin *Bulletin des Armées de la République*. Ironically, soldiers began to create their own trench newspapers, some of which would in time enter the mainstream press, one or two even remaining there.[30] All the while, however, both the traditional press and its journalists were losing the trust and respect of the combatant. According to historian Marc Bloch, the written word itself would lose credibility in the course of the War.[31]

The situation regarding censorship was in general accepted by the newspapers, which can be faulted for excessive loyalism in their reporting of the war. Ultimately, however, the press would pay a great price for its role in constructing what Ferenczi calls the 'patriotic lie',[32] even where this was done with the best intentions. Witness, for example, Helsey's famous apology at the end of the war for his description – troublingly reminiscent of Londres in his letter to his parents – of soldiers laughing before the Battle of the Marne and for declaring the battle won before it had even begun. 'I wrote that they laughed and sang, those men I saw passing like shadows, falling from fatigue, bewildered by marching and fighting, none of which they could understand, tired of dying, broken, finished. Alas, I even fabricated the remarks of some soldiers'.[33] Helsey had wanted to spare the soldiers' families the distress of knowing the grim reality; but to the soldiers who knew that reality only too well, such misrepresentation confirmed that the French press was a lying one. The resulting divide between the front and rear was thus seen as being in great part because of the press.[34] By the third year of the war, Helsey wrote, the anger of the soldier towards the figure of the journalist had become 'very violent and nearly unanimous'.[35]

The rationale for censorship was clear: ensuring that sensitive information was kept safe from the enemy. As France's foreign minister, Aristide Briand, put it, while the French soldier was bravely defending France's frontiers, censorship would defend the morale of the home front;[36] in doing this the rule of censorship became increasingly far-reaching. One of its more important roles was to counter 'defeatism' and prevent the spread of pacifist ideas.[37] Censorship was thus used to create a favourable climate for the war itself, and newspapers played an important role in this. 'Reading a newspaper should no longer be a source of pessimism or discouragement but of perseverance and enthusiasm', the French General Pétain demanded.[38]

'You can only describe well what you know perfectly', wrote the most surprising of war correspondents, Baroness Horta.[39] But censorship ensured that the conditions of knowing perfectly and describing well were no longer in place. Above all, the horror of the war was simply occulted. The reality of censorship meant that the reality of the war was hidden from the French people who were being asked to support it. France was the only combatant country in which it was 'strictly forbidden' to publish lists of casualties.[40] It was only in 1920 that the extent of France's human losses was acknowledged publicly, and even then the figures proved unreliable.[41] The ultimate effect of press censorship was to ensure continued public support for the war and the continuation of the war itself. At the end of it all, the French press and its journalists would stand condemned. Witness French Great War veteran and writer Jean Guéhenno's startling accusation:

For four years, a journalism of the heroic, busied itself in leading unfortunate men to the edge of their graves while promising them every morning a good and comfortable death. The war only lasted because of those lies and that hypocrisy. The truth would have ended it.[42]

It was in this context of censorship that the nascent war correspondent Londres had to evolve and act; and very soon censorship was to become his greatest enemy.

All quiet on the Eastern Front

From late 1914, the war on the Western Front had ceased to be a war of movement and, as a result of military control and censorship, French reporters had also been bogging down in the world of journalistic inanition. Londres wanted movement, and he wanted freedom to report; he also wanted another scoop. He expected a dramatic change to come in the progress of the war but believed that it would not come in France but in the East, the Dardanelles. He pleaded with his editor to be sent there but to no avail. Instantly he resigned – in a gesture that was to become typical of him – and left *Le Matin*, accused of having 'contaminated [the newspaper] with the germ of literature'.[43]

By this time, however, Londres had forged a reputation for himself; and, before the day was out, he had received an offer from another one of the big four Parisian dailies, *Le Petit Journal*. At this time French newspapers, frustrated with a lack of news from the Western Front, were reducing their budgets at home, while multiplying their budgets abroad. In the course of the war, *Le Petit Parisien*, for example, would halve its budget in France, while multiplying its foreign budget eightfold.[44] In this context, Londres' proposal to go to the Eastern Front was readily accepted. Londres would spend the next two years covering the war outside of France.

Away from France while the greatest battle in its history and of the Great War was raging at Verdun, Londres – reduced very nearly to the status of tourist – moved restlessly across the Mediterranean and Balkans. There were forays to Gallipoli and Serbia but the expected turning point in the war never materialized. Eventually, in the company of some other reporters, including Helsey, Londres settled in a villa near Salonica, close to the newly arrived French Expeditionary Force. There the journalists started their own newspaper, *L'Écho de France*, with some success,[45] and there Londres began rising in arms against his greatest enemy: censorship.

Already at the beginning of the war, in France, Londres had been aware of nascent censorship and, now, as his articles were being increasingly censored, he launched attack after attack against the censor in letters and telegrams home. 'If only one could tell all that one sees, and all that one knows', he wrote, echoing Baroness Horta, 'readers would rush to read the newspapers. But it will have to wait [...] I am going to avenge myself on the censors who have launched an onslaught on me [...]'.[46] Together with Helsey, he wrote a report denouncing the censoring of their articles. They sent copies of this report to anyone they believe might be able to influence policy or opinion in France but to no avail.[47] Londres planned to avenge himself by publishing his restored articles in book form but that would have to wait until after the war.

At this time, while he vegetated in Salonica, stranger aspects of Londres began to emerge. Astonishingly, he instigated a fantastic plot to kill the British General Philips, whom he saw as protecting the pro-Germany Greek monarch, Constantine. The actual assassination was only averted at the last moment when news arrived that Constantine was to leave Athens.[48] At the same time, in his letters home, Londres began to suggest mysteriously to his parents that he was involved in activities, the nature of which he cannot reveal.[49] A couple of years later, this 'fantasist' Londres offered his services to the French Foreign Ministry, proposing to journey to Revolutionary Russia as a reporter, while carrying out spying activities there, recruiting saboteurs, and plotting the assassinations of Trotsky and Lenin.[50] This proposal would very nearly cost him his life when he did eventually visit Russia in 1920, as it appears a document drawn up by Londres and Helsey, and submitted to the Ministry, outlining their plans for counter-revolution, had somehow found its way into Russian hands.[51] Apparently Londres had returned from Russia just in time to save himself.

The Press Mission

In September 1917, Albert Londres returned to France. Changes were taking place. In the wake of the French mutinies at Craonne in the early summer, the French War Ministry had established a Press Mission – conceived by General Nivelle and overseen by Pétain – in Chateau D'Offremont, near Compiègne. Its aim was to allow the French journalist the same liberty to report the war that other foreign correspondents enjoyed.[52] Together with a select band of journalists, Londres went there to cover the war. The real aim of the Mission, however, was to exploit the presence of the reporters for propaganda purposes;[53] what could actually be reported remained strictly controlled. Along with the other reporters, Londres signed a contract with the army, placing himself under martial law, requiring the submission of his articles and all of his correspondence, private as well as public, to the Mission Chief, undertaking not to write anything prejudicial to the interests of the army or damaging to the morale of the troops, proscribing any criticism of army actions and forbidding him to name regiments, describe terrain, tactics or infrastructure.[54] On forays from the Chateau, the journalists, travelling in groups, were accompanied everywhere by army officers.[55] Reporting from the front, Londres' only recourse was to paint edifying portraits of the common soldier, ironically in the vein of reporting he himself had helped initiate. As time went by, however, he became increasingly dissatisfied with the restrictions placed upon him, which allowed only anodyne, indifferent war reports. He denounced repeatedly the role of the censor and quickly established a reputation as a troublemaker. A breach with the authorities was inevitable. A confrontation with one of the officers, in which Londres accused the officer of 'lying all the time – and you will understand, Captain, that is not very nice for us to be directed by a liar' constituted the final straw.[56] Londres found himself attached, in disgrace, to a regiment of cavalry.[57] Later, he joined the Italian and British fronts. It is probable in the end that Londres' attitude cost him the 'War Cross' bestowed on six other French reporters at the end of the war. Notably, however, he was made an Honorary Officer of the Order of the British Empire by George V in 1920.[58]

As the war ended, Londres continued to report on it, following the Allied advance as finally the stasis broke. His reports offer a constantly recurring, breathlessly appalled, nightmarish vision of the devastation of war, as city in ruins follows city in ruins. In this world of perpetual recurrence, his articles feature a litany of ruined cathedrals: Saint-Quentin, 'we saw her corpse [...] She was scalped';[59] Soissons, a 'tragic ruin [...] her towers wounded';[60] Reims, 'I will say nothing of her, I do not like to speak while sobbing fills my throat';[61] Amiens, 'defenceless, and still they wounded her';[62] Cambrai, 'with all her sides broken'.[63] In the spring of 1918, he revisited Reims and then Amiens. His writing had by then developed an acerbic, derisive edge, a sort of sharp, black humour that often typifies it, both during and after the war. Londres' writing style was undoubtedly sharply honed by his experience of war.

> There are blood stains on the ground. It's dogs' blood. Posters on the walls proclaim, 'any dogs found wandering the streets will be put down'. But the posters were too high and the dogs couldn't read them. They continued to wander. And so they were killed.[64]

Cambrai was the town that most left its mark. 'They're barbarians', Londres railed against the Germans. 'There is no other word for their nastiness. They burned Cambrai for nothing, simply from tradition'. But there was something more to Londres' experience of Cambrai. Wandering the streets of the town in the company of an English officer, a piano miraculously came into sight in the middle of the devastation. A Beethoven sonata rested, waiting to be played, on the music stand. Londres sat and played inexpertly with one finger before giving up. The English officer sat in his turn at the keyboard. 'Play all of it', Londres encouraged the officer as he moved away, 'there's at least twenty pages'. Soon after, the music was swallowed up in a sudden explosion rising from beneath it, instrument and pianist blown to pieces.[65] Understandably, Londres found this experience difficult to forget as he followed the advancing Allies into liberated Belgium and, finally, to Germany. At this time it was his custom to end each article with a single word: 'Vengeance!'.

After the war is over

The war over, Londres returned home for a brief stay. His parents noticed how much he had changed, aged. The war was at the heart of everything he spoke about. And he was so restless. Announcing to his daughter, Florise, that he was leaving again, she asked him 'Why?'. 'I am going to look around, and I am going to write all that I see [...]', he answered. 'My business is to plunge the iron into the wound. There is too much unhappiness in this great big world for me to remain sitting at home.'[66] The war had undoubtedly changed him; how could it have done otherwise? Was the 'wound' in him as much as it was in the world of which he was the constant observer?

> [Londres] was no longer the same man. He had been mixed up with too many horrors [...] In their thousands, in the tens of thousands, he had seen soldiers [...], civilians, old people, women and children, wounded or killed.[67]

Londres said reporting allowed him to indulge his real vice – travel – but certainly there is more to his incessant post-war movement than this. While much of his writing has the exoticism of travel literature, and there is a clear fascination with the distant and the strange, foreign fields provide mainly a rich backdrop to the real recurring concerns of his journalism. Londres' subjects have a clear preoccupation, as Redfern suggests, with the alien and the alienated. His business was to 'dip the pen into the wound', he wrote in the preface to his *Terre d'Ébène*, his denunciation of the slave traffic in France's African colonies.[68] He was driven to enter spaces of estrangement and turmoil. He explored in particular modes of confinement or entrapment, writing about the imprisoned and the enslaved, the exploited and the marginalized. There is, too, a concern with the hidden, the occulted, and with the many modes of violence and injustice, which may be considered modes of alienation. At the core of most of his work there is a key figure: the 'victim', whether it be the mental patient, the prisoner, the slave, the prostitute or the Jew. And then there is the other, obverse, presiding 'face' of the experience of victimization: the revolutionary, the terrorist, the oppressor, the executioner. All in all, his writing offers an

eclectic mix of travel, exoticism, news and animated polemic – constitut-
ing indeed a very post-WWI mix – contaminated too perhaps with 'the
germ of literature'.

Peace was perhaps for Londres the continuation of war by other means.
In the 1920s, he became the very model of the modern journalist–adventurer, forever on the move, plunging into worlds of entrapment, estrangement and turmoil. Everywhere that the fabric of the world was torn or
threatened by movements of violence, Londres was pulling the threads
in an effort to unravel and record them. In 1919, he joined the Italian
soldier–poet, Gabriele D'Annunzio, in Fiume, which the proto-fascist
D'Annunzio had just seized for Italy. Londres continued to provoke the
wrath of officialdom as if he delighted in it, as if finally he was avenging
himself on the censor's attacks on his wartime reports. His reporting of
Italian dissatisfaction with the terms of the Peace that had concluded the
war, excited the disapprobation of the French government to such an extent,
that Londres was removed from his post at *Le Petit Journal*, from where he
moved on to join the staff at *Excelsior*.[69] In late 1919, Londres journeyed to
Syria, Egypt and Palestine, covering the rising fervour of Arab nationalism.
In 1920, he plunged into the tumult of post-revolutionary Russia, visiting
Saint Petersburg and Moscow, catching glimpses of Lenin and Trotsky,
men he had plotted to kill. There were travels too to Greece, Bulgaria and
Germany, followed by Japan, China and Indochina.

Dipping the pen

In 1923, Londres penetrated one of France's most notorious spheres of
confinement and exile where he had a career-defining encounter with the
prisoners held on the island penitentiary system of French Guyana. He
travelled to the system's islands – among them the hellish Devil's Island – to
investigate the conditions of detention. He travelled from island to island
meeting the most notorious prisoners, among them one Eugène Dieudonné,

a furniture maker exiled and imprisoned for suspected involvement with the infamous Bonnot anarchist gang but whom Londres believed innocent. Londres was deeply moved by his meeting with Dieudonné and did not forget him. He concluded his series on the islands and their captors with an open letter to the Minister for the Colonies seeing reform for the system that governed them.[70] The series constituted a news sensation, enthusiastically followed by the public. The following year Londres published a book based on the series, a pattern that from then on constituted his *modus operandi*, book following on series, as he continued his investigations. In succeeding years, he continued his campaign on behalf of Dieudonné, until finally the affair came to an extraordinary conclusion.

In 1927, Londres learned that Dieudonné had escaped and was hiding in Rio de Janiero. Londres journeyed there to meet him and returned with him to France, where they were met in Marseille by cheering crowds. Dieudonné remarried his wife and settled back to his former career. Later he wrote and published his memoirs, prefaced by Londres, and later still played a part in a play based on Londres' account of the prison system that had held Dieudonné. After Londres' death in the summer of 1932, Dieudonné would close each performance with a homage.[71]

By this time Londres' star could not have been higher with his public and his career now had a new definition. One by one he began to investigate a whole series of quite literally imprisoning spaces. His next major investigation was of France's military prisons in North Africa. Later he revealed the horrific conditions in which the mentally ill were maintained in France's asylums. In 1927, he wrote a sensational series on the white-slave trade involving French prostitutes in Argentina; in 1928, he exposed the black-slave trade in France's African colonies. Londres had become a crusading journalist, revealing the injustice and abuse underlying degraded and degrading systems of condemnation, entrapment and exploitation. 'Until the end of his days', wrote Paul Mousset, 'Londres would carry inside him an abomination of injustice'.[72] Londres now had a supreme mission: not just to dip his pen into 'the wound' but to *heal* 'the wound'. His report on the island prisons of French Guyana started the process of reform that would eventually lead to their closure in 1953.[73]

The death of a journalist

As Londres reached his late forties he developed a deeply melancholic
streak. He seemed full of fatigue, dejection and morbid foreboding. Perhaps
it had something to do with the recent death of his father, with an increasing sense of age and decline, or simply having looked too long into 'the
wound', the growing 'wound' of the world. 'I am going to die, I feel it', he
told his daughter. 'My heart has nothing left, I tell you I am going to die
[...] I'm unwell [...] There are bad years ahead [...]'.[74] His days were indeed
numbered. Like much of his life and career his death, in May 1932, would
also have something of the extraordinary and even mysterious about it.
Cruelly, it provided Londres' life with a final burning image of entrapment,
which tragically, however, he could neither escape nor survive.

Londres had gone back to war. In 1931, he travelled to the Balkans
– Sofia first, followed by an expedition to Macedonia – to report on the
intensely murderous internecine conflict within the Bulgarian-sponsored
Komitadji, a violent nationalist group dedicated to achieving the independence of Macedonia from Serbian domination. About this time he became
obsessed with China. Returning to France, Londres approached his editor,
the same Élie-Joseph Bois who had given him his start in journalism, and
proposed a series on China but, when pressed, Londres would not reveal
the essential purpose of his journey. Bois refused to back Londres, only
to be handed his resignation. A rival newspaper, *Le Journal*, was only too
glad to commission Londres and so, in early 1932, he left France for China.
He arrived in Shanghai as the Battle of Shanghai was breaking out and
soon he was living under siege and under bombardment. From January to
March, Londres despatched report after report home on the city at war,
until finally, inevitably it fell. Now free to do so, Londres left Shanghai for
Mukden, in Manchuria, and there mystery falls upon him.

No-one knows where Londres went during the following month or
what he did. It is likely that he made his way into that part of China under
the control of Mao and the Chinese Communists but, even if that is so,
no-one knows what happened or what discoveries he made there. A month

later, however, he returned to Shanghai and immediately booked his passage home by sea on the *Georges-Philippar*.

The last chapter in Londres' life belongs perhaps more to a spy novel than a biography. On the journey home, he worked tirelessly on the documents he was carrying with him, tearing himself away only to spend time with a couple he had become acquainted with in Argentina, the Lang-Willars. It is clear Londres was tremendously excited by the knowledge he was carrying home with him. It is 'dynamite', he told the Lang-Willars over dinner. This new series on China would 'crown' his career.[75]

In the early morning of 16 May, after Londres returned to his cabin from dinner with the Lang-Willars, a fire broke out on the *Georges-Philippar* and quickly spread. Over forty passengers perished without trace, burned or drowned, Londres among them. For some reason – perhaps taking time to gather his precious documents together – he delayed leaving his cabin and then found he was encircled by fire. He also, inexplicably, refused to jump into the water. The last sight of him was as he struggled to emerge from his cabin window. One of the crew threw a hose to him and Londres seemed to catch it but he either fell back into the flames or fell down into the water. Londres could not swim.

Londres was dead but the plot was still to thicken. The Lang-Willars survived and they announced to the press that they were aware of the findings of Londres' investigations in China but they would reveal them only to the French government. Flying from Djibouti in French Somalia, their plane crashed in Italy, killing all of its four passengers. Londres' demise had acquired all the necessary ingredients of a conspiracy theory. Was his death an accident or an assassination? Even the Lang-Willars were under suspicion. In France, a commission of enquiry was set up. It found the shipping company guilty of negligence; an electrical fault was the cause of the fire. Later, a group of French Communists claimed that Chinese Communists had been responsible for the burning of the ship, which they said was being used to traffic arms for the benefit of Japan. And all the while speculation continued as to the nature of Londres' findings. What had he found? Had it to do with drugs? Arms? The involvement of Bolsheviks in Chinese Communism? The great reporter's last mission remains to this day secret and unknown.

When all is said and done

Albert Londres was the archetypal accidental journalist. Emerged in almost
haphazard fashion from the transforming flames of the Great War 1914–18,
he would define and embody a new style of reporter for a new age, an age
of war, turmoil and myriad alienations. Engaged and committed, his being
and his voice as a journalist had come out of war, rising out of its flaming
wound, and he would be the plaintive voice of that wound and others.
Londres inhabited the wound and he was never indifferent to it. His pen
gave expression to the wounded fabric and soul of the world, and at the
same time sought to bring solace to it. 'Dipping his pen into the wound',
Londres sought both to *write* and to *right* it. His writing had a profoundly
moral dimension and an over-riding clear preoccupation with injustice.
Drawn to the flame, in a world in flames, perhaps it was inevitable in the
end that the flame would have the better of him, and that he would finish
in the embrace of the tragic and the unknown. The prize that bears his
name remains his best memorial and still holds a value which he earned
for it, face to war, entrapment, alienation and injustice – uncompromising,
persevering and dedicated: Albert Londres, the writer, and the wound.

Notes

1   W. Redfern, *Writing on the Move: Albert Londres and Investigative Journalism*
     (Bern: Peter Lang, 2004), 32–33.
2   P. Mousset, *Albert Londres* (Paris: Grasset, 1972): 85–86. The translation from
     the original French here and all translations that follow in this chapter are my
     own.
3   P. Assouline, *Albert Londres: Vie et mord d'un grand reporter 1884–1932* (Paris:
     Editions Balland, 1989), 123. [Cited in French.] This chapter makes extensive
     use of Assouline's biography for factual information about the life and career of
     Albert Londres.

4   P. Assouline, 26.

5   Marcelle Laforest died in November 1905.

6   Cited in P. Assouline, 36.

7   *Suivant les heures* (1904), *L'âme qui vibre* (1908), *Le poème effréné I, Lointaine* (1909) and *Le poème effréné II, La marche à l'étoile* (1910) are the titles of Londres' four volumes of poems.

8   'La vie fait bien les choses' is the French expression.

9   P. Assouline, 59–60.

10   The full text of Londres' article is reproduced in P. Assouline, 12–16.

11   W. Redfern, 36.

12   See P. Assouline, 87. 'If the Germans had had the good taste to spare monuments, it is hard to say if Londres' antiboche sentiment would have remained as strong.'

13   W. Redfern, 32–33.

14   Reims had been the site of coronation of many of the French kings, including Charles VII, whose coronation was attended by Joan of Arc.

15   P. Assouline, 77.

16   P. Assouline, 78.

17   W. Redfern, 35.

18   See T. Ferenczi, 'Les transformations du journalisme', in S. Caucanas & R. Cazals (Eds), *Traces de 14–18, Actes du colloque de Carcassonne* (Carcassonne: Les Audois, 1997), 59–66. The second and third key moments in Ferenczi's transformation of journalism in France are Maurice Maréchal's founding of the satirical trench newspaper *Le Canard enchaîné* in 1915, and the founding of the Union of Journalists in 1918.

19   P. Assouline, 89.

20   Cited in P. Assouline, 82.

21   P. Assouline, 84.

22   W. Redfern, 33. The French soldier was familiarly described as a '*poilu*', perhaps meaning unshaven, but often though to indicate 'plucky'.

23   P. Assouline, 88.

24   C. Delporte, *Les Journalistes en France (1880–1950)* (Paris: Éditions du Seuil, 1999), 180.

25   F. d'Almeida & C. Delporte, *Histoire de medias en France de la Grande Guerre à nos jours* (Paris: Flammarion, 2003), 29.

26   Cited in F. Terrou, C. Berranger, J. Godechot & P. Guiral (Eds), *Histoire générale de la presse française* [*De 1871 à 1940*] III (Paris: Presses universitaires de France, 1969–1976 [1972]), 417. [In five volumes.]

27   F. Terrou, C. Berranger, J. Godechot & P. Guiral, 418.

28   F. Terrou, C. Berranger, J. Godechot & P. Guiral, 416.

29   C. Delporte, 187.

30   For background on the Section d'Information, Trench Journals and journalists
      forbidden to visit the Front, see F. Terrou, C. Berranger, J. Godechot & P. Guiral,
      420–421. As said, Thomas Ferenczi lists the founding of Maurice Maréchal's
      Trench newspaper *La Canard enchainé* as the second of three key-turning points
      in history of French journalism during World War I. Another trench newspaper
      of note was *Le Crapouillet*, founded by Jean Galtier-Boissière.

31   M. Bloch, *Réflexions d'un historien sur les fausses nouvelles de la guerre* (Paris:
      Éditions Allia, 1999), 50–51.

32   T. Ferenczi, 59–66.

33   Édouard Helsey cited in C. Delporte, 184.

34   F. Terrou, C. Berranger, J. Godechot & P. Guiral, 426–427.

35   C. Delporte, 185.

36   F. Terrou, C. Berranger, J. Godechot & P. Guiral, 419.

37   F. Terrou, C. Berranger, J. Godechot & P. Guiral, 416.

38   Cited in F. Terrou, C. Berranger, J. Godechot & P. Guiral, 423.

39   Cited in French at http://www.1914-1918.be/civil_horta.php (accessed 1
      November 2007). This quote from Baroness Horta refers to her visit to Verdun
      in 1916, a battle which took place in near total secrecy.

40   J.-P. Guéno & Y. Laplume (Eds), *Paroles de Poilus: Lettres et carnet du front
      1914–1918* (Paris: Librio, 1998), 8.

41   See Antoine Prost on the Louis Marin reports on war casualties in A. Prost, *Les
      Anciens Combattants et la société française 1914–1918* [*Sociologie*] II (Paris: Presses
      de la Foundation Nationale de Sciences Politiques, 1977), 2 and following pages.
      [In three volumes.] Prost suggests that Marin's figures were undermined by the
      unwillingness of the French War Ministry to reveal the true extent of the nation's
      manpower losses. Officially France suffered more than 1,300,000 dead in the
      Great War, one of the highest rates of casualties among combatant countries.

42   Jean Guéhenno cited in F. Terrou, C. Berranger, J. Godechot & P. Guiral, 425.

43   P. Assouline, 90.

44   C. Delporte, 187.

45   P. Assouline, 122. Assouline writes that the circulation of *L'Écho de France* rose
      to 20,000 copies.

46   P. Assouline, 123.

47   P. Assouline, 126–127.

48   P. Assouline, 127–129.

49   P. Assouline, 130–132.

50   P. Assouline, 145–151.

51   P. Assouline, 219–220.

52 F. Terrou, C. Berranger, J. Godechot & P. Guiral, 422.

53 C. Delporte, 188. F. d'Almeida & C. Delporte, 30.

54 P. Assouline, 138.

55 C. Delporte, 189.

56 Cited in P. Assouline, 144.

57 P. Mousset, 89–90.

58 P. Assouline, 219.

59 A. Londres, *Contre le bourrage de crâne* (Paris: Arléa, 1998a), 27–28.

60 A. Londres (1998a), 67, 76.

61 A. Londres (1998a), 119, 146–149.

62 A. Londres (1998a), 164.

63 A. Londres (1998a), 235.

64 A. Londres (1998a), 163.

65 P. Assouline, 154–155.

66 P. Assouline, 157. Londres' war reports have been published by the Paris-based publishing house Arléa in a collected edition, *Câbles et reportages* (1993), which contains a section devoted to his Great War journalism, and also his *Contre le bourrage de crane* (Against Brain-Washing). This latter, which brings together texts following his return to the Western Front in 1917 has also been re-published separately in a new edition by Arléa (2008).

67 P. Mousset, 85.

68 A. Londres, *Terre d'Ébène* (Paris: Arléa, 1998b), 111.

69 P. Assouline, 163–164.

70 P. Assouline, 335.

71 P. Assouline, 469–476, 592.

72 P Mousset, 85–86.

73 F. d'Almeida & C. Delporte, 382.

74 Cited in P. Assouline, 562. All of this last section is indebted again to Assouline's biography.

75 P. Assouline, 578.

YVONNE MCEWEN

Behind and Between the Lines: The War Diary of Evelyn Kate Luard, Nursing Sister on the Western Front and Unofficial Correspondent

On 5 August 1914, *The Times* carried the headline, 'War Declared'.[1]

After weeks of political brinkmanship while trying to avert war in Europe, on 4 August, Sir Edward Grey, the British Foreign Secretary, delivered an ultimatum to Germany demanding the termination of military action against neutral Belgium or face war with Britain.

On the same day, newspapers were already predicting the outcome of the faltering negotiations. The *Daily Mail* Editorial stated that 'The shadow of an immense catastrophe broods over Europe today. All hope of peace has disappeared with a crash [...] Our duty is to go forward into the valley of the shadow of death with courage and faith – with courage to suffer, with faith in our God and country'.[2] According to *The Times*, the position in Europe was 'one of breathless anticipation of the beginning of hostilities on a large scale. France and Russia await with evident anxiety the decision of Great Britain as to her attitude towards the crisis'.[3] The *Daily News*, which had been so adamant that Britain should not be embroiled in a European war, had to concede, 'Let us fight, if we must, without bitterness and without malice, so that when the tragedy is over we may make an honourable peace'.[4] In Scotland, the national newspaper, *The Scotsman*, predicted that stoicism would prevail. 'At any moment Great Britain may be at war with the German Powers. Her people will accept this destiny with quiet and enduring courage.'[5]

After days of newspaper speculation, and the declaration of hostilities finally announced, the nursing press responded. The *Nursing Times* Editorial prophetically lamented, 'What was nominally a quarrel between Austria and Serbia has led to a European Armageddon' and predicted that,

'The conflict will be terrible, and every soldier will be required for fighting and every nurse for the care of the wounded'. In a spirit of patriotism, if not professional determination, it concluded, 'The call has come and the nurses are ready'.[6] Its rival, *The British Journal of Nursing*, arguably the most politically astute within the nursing press, declared, 'The call to arms which has reverberated through this country with such sudden urgency since our last issue has its echo in the equally urgent call to trained nurses to be prepared to respond to any summons to place their services at the disposal of the sick and wounded [...] There is probably not a woman in the country who does not desire to place her services at its disposal, and time will show the many ways in which women's work can be utilised, but, in the supreme care of the moment, the provision for the sick and wounded, it is to trained nurses the call is made'.[7] The emphasis of the Editorial was on 'trained nurses' caring for the casualties of the war, not volunteers. Within the first few days of war being declared it was estimated that, in London alone, 50,000 women from a variety of backgrounds, with little or no nursing experience, were volunteering to nurse the anticipated casualties in the British Expeditionary Force (BEF).

Nursing in peacetime was neither exciting nor glamorous, and the day-to-day ministrations of caring for the sick and injured brought little financial reward or public recognition. In the eyes of professional nurses, nursing was a vocation and they believed that volunteer nurses, with limited or no training, would devalue the worth of the profession, compromise professional development and have a negative influence on the success of the Nurse Registration Bill being passed in Parliament. It was, therefore, not surprising that trained nurses expressed their concerns about volunteers whose motives for nursing were founded in wartime altruism. Furthermore, trained nurses were fearful that when the war ended, the unskilled volunteers would swamp the labour market and affect the employment prospects of trained nurses.[8]

Notwithstanding the professional concerns, *The Nursing Mirror and Midwives' Journal* took a more balanced view of the situation and advised trained nurses, and potential volunteers, not to get carried away with the excitement of war fever that was gripping the country. Furthermore, urging caution against gossip and the reliability of the press, the article stated that nurses should not become 'bewildered by the strife of tongues, the unreliability of news or demoralised by the contradictory reports of victories or defeats'.[9] There were, however, particular groups of professional nurses called upon by the War Office to mobilize for war service: The Queen Alexandra's Imperial Military Nursing Service (QAIMNS), the Queen Alexandra's Imperial Military Nursing Service Reserve (QAIMNSR), the Queen Alexandra's Royal Naval Nursing Service (QARNNS) and the Territorial Forces Nursing Service (TFNS).

Called up in the mobilization order was forty-seven-year-old Evelyn Kate Luard, a QAIMNSR and a veteran of the war in South Africa. On 11 August, she left her job as Matron of the Berks and Bucks County Sanatorium in England and travelled to Ireland where she joined her army unit, Number 1 General Hospital, temporarily stationed at the Hotel Metropole, Dublin. In her first letter to her family while on active service she writes, 'no one knows where or when we are going – probably only a day's notice [...] All the foreign waiters here were arrested last night so they are rather up a tree with a few Irish got in, in a hurry. Miss Hodgens [Matron] wants us to do for ourselves as far as possible. I miss *The Times*, the *Daily Mail*, the *Daily Mirror* terribly, not to mention my immediate family'.[10] This was the first of hundreds of items of correspondence exchanged between Kate Luard and her family, and it was the beginning of her war diary.

On 20 August, Kate Luard landed at Le Havre, France. However, her expectations of Number 1 General Hospital being immediately established for casualty admission were not realized. Two weeks after the arrival of her unit she recorded in her diary the frustration of having no work except 'fatigue duty'. The lack of activity led her to wonder where the casualties were that she was sent out to care for and when her unit would receive them. There was little information available about the activities of the BEF, even for those waiting to care for them. Kate Luard was an avid reader of the press and she relied on letters from home and the British press to keep her informed about the progress of the war. A press blackout on the movement and activities of the BEF was enforced as soon as the mobilization order was given. Those who criticized the lack of news from the fighting front were assured by the Prime Minister, H. H. Asquith, that military considerations necessitated that all steps should be taken to minimize any advantage the enemy might gain from British press reports.

At the beginning of the war, in order to gain wider powers over national security, the government introduced The Defence of the Realm Act, 1914 (DORA). Under the new legislation, the government, if need be, had the power to censor the press. On 5 August, Lord Kitchener was appointed Secretary of State for War. During his earlier campaigns in the Sudan and the war in South Africa, Kitchener had a troubled relationship with the press and he was determined they would not cover the conflict in France. At his behest, correspondents were banned from the front. Under the new legislation and military authority, the coverage of the war in its early stages was speculative; there were many generalizations and few, if any, facts.

Official information and confirmation regarding the care and number of casualties was nonexistent. This was not surprising as the medical and nursing arrangements in the early weeks of the war were confused, if not in disarray. On the Lines of Communication, experienced medical and nursing staff were not being utilized to full advantage; whole medical units had been stood down since their arrival in France. At the fighting front there was a desperate shortage of appropriate transportation for the removal of the sick and wounded. The problems were rightly attributed to the lack of cooperation and information sharing between the War Office in London and the administrative medical officers on the fighting front. As a consequence, there was a disturbingly poor management of services and long delays in the supply of much-needed equipment.[11]

In the month of August, from the Battle of Mons and the tragedy of the retreat to the British stand at Le Cateau, followed by the advance on the Marne in September, the reality of the military situation and deficiencies in the medical arrangements were not reflected in the national press reports. However, the nursing press ran anonymous stories and eye-witness accounts of what was happening with the casualty care arrangements at the front. Many of the reports were critical of the War Office and its ability to manage the collection, care and distribution of the sick and injured.

Following the BEF's first military engagement at Mons, then its disastrous retreat, a political storm broke out between the Northcliffe Press and the government. On 30 August, *The Times*, in a special Sunday edition, published the first accounts of the army's retreat, reporting that, 'The German advance has been one of almost incredible rapidity [...] The pursuit was immediate, relentless, unresting [...] regiments were grievously injured and the broken army fought its way desperately with many stands [...] Our losses are very great. I have seen the broken bits of many regiments'.[12] The dispatch, filed by Arthur Moore, was widely attacked and was viewed by the government as unpatriotic, and liable to affect public morale and support for the war. Yet, seven days later, *The Times* reported that 'Sir John French's reports dwell on the marked superiority of the British troops of every arm over the Germans. The shooting of the German infantry is poor and it is officially stated that the vast majority of the British wounded now in hospital will return to their regiments. Very few of them were suffering from rifle bullet wounds'.[13]

The conflict had entered a new phase – the propaganda war had begun.

In September, nearly a month after her arrival in France, Kate Luard was posted to Le Mans where she dealt with the casualties from the Battle of the Marne. She worked in a variety of treatment facilities and carried out temporary duty in casualty evacuation trains on the Lines of Communication. On 25 September, she wrote to her family from the hospital ship *Carisbrook Castle*, 'At last a chance to write uncensored [...] I brought down 450 wounded and sick yesterday from Le Mans [on train]. Arrived 8:30 pm and slept in railway carriage in the station when they were all lifted off. Came on here this morning to get my last up-to-date instalment of diary posted [...] There are a lot of wounded officers on board, limping haggard wrecks. I read French's dispatch about the Great Retreat, the most heroic and brilliant thing in history. Surely no one grudges their best of sons and brothers and husbands who gave their life in that. And this battle of the Marne is doing the same [...] When you stand off for a few hours from the gruesome details and pathetic streams of broken, dirty, ragged bandaged cripples that one is occupied with all day it gets more and more unfathomable and heartbreaking'.[14]

From the diary entry, it would appear she was experiencing ambivalent feelings – patriotism, yet reluctantly accepting that sacrifices had to be made. On Sunday, 20 September, Kate Luard had faced her baptism of fire. At Le Mans, three trains full of wounded numbering 1,175 cases, arrived at the station; she was detailed to care for 510 of the casualties. In her diary she describes the horror of the situation.

> You board a cattle-truck, armed with a tray of dressings and a pail; the men were lying on straw; had been in train for several days; most had been only dressed once [field dressings] and many were gangrenous. If you found one urgently needed amputation or operation, or was likely to die, you called the MO [Medical Officer] to have him taken off the train for Hospital. No one grumbled or made a fuss. Then you joined the throng in the dressing station, and for hours, doctors of all ranks, Sisters and orderlies, grappled with the stream of stretchers, and limping, staggering, bearded, dirty, men [...] The Black Watch and Camerons were almost unrecognisable in their rags [...] They were nearly all shrapnel shell wounds, more ghastly than anything I have ever seen or smelt.[15]

In a letter to her sister she explained that when she attended the cathedral at Le Mans the morning after 'that awful Sunday of carnage at the station', it was 'suddenly horribly upsetting'.[16] Despite her rationalization of the consequences of the military engagements, the reality of what she witnessed disturbed her; doubts were beginning to formulate.

On 27 September Kate Luard informed her family that she was about to take up permanent duty on an ambulance train. The following day in a more detailed letter to her father, she wrote, 'trying some letters through the French post, let me know if they get through uncensored and in how many days'. The letter described the difficulties the Royal Army Medical Corps (RAMC) was having at the front, the work and movements of the ambulance train, and she wrote that, after nearly two months, the original unit with which she arrived in France was still not operational.[17]

The content of the letters breached DORA and the implications for her or anyone violating the Act were extremely serious – imprisonment or the death penalty. The letter sent to her father through the French postal service was intercepted by the military censor but, surprisingly, it was passed with the warning, 'This letter is only passed as a concession. Attempts to evade Censorship only defeat their own ends, kindly inform writer of this. Letters posted by members of the Expeditionary Force in French post offices are liable to be destroyed'.[18]

The censor's message was understood but only temporarily adhered to. The frustration of censorship was evident in a letter to her sister. 'You say you are aching to hear from me but you've no idea what it is like to bottle it all up and not be able to tell you all about it [...] That is why my diary oozes out of me, as a vent [...] Do let me know if the 3 instalments have reached you.'[19] For a short period, her letters home were mostly about family, friends and her struggle to keep infection free from the body lice being transmitted from the sick and wounded on the ambulance train. 'Found one doing a brisk route march on my back and two more strongly entrenched in my combinations. I wonder if Aunt Lucy would send me a nice fat sultana cake to make up for it?'[20]

By late October, she was caring for the casualties of the fierce fighting that was taking place in and around Ypres. Furthermore, she was back to breaking the censor's rules. In a diary entry for 25 October she records the frantic fight it had been to care for the wounded on the ambulance train. 'They were bleeding faster than we could cope with it and the agony of getting them off stretchers and on to the top bunks is a thing to forget. All night, and without a break till we got back to Boulogne at 4 pm next day, we grappled with them [...] The head cases were delirious and trying to get out of the window, and we were giving strychnine and morphia all round.'[21]

In a letter to her father she described some of the recent activity. 'We have been up to the Front and remained there 3 days, taking up the wounded and sick including 4 French women severely wounded [...] They shelled the church of the village we were at, shells came whizzing into the wood and burst close to the train, two came right over the train, it was an exciting afternoon.'[22] In further correspondence with her family she explains that 'No 7 train was in the station at Ypres when they were shelling it like mad: the train windows were broken and the engine ran away!'[23]

Kate Luard was morally challenged by the imposed censorship, a rule she clearly had difficulty adhering to. She was disturbed by what she witnessed and the testaments of the men she nursed. In a diary entry on 11 November she records the value of listening to what the men had to say about their experiences. 'Their conversation to each other from the time they are landed on the train until they are taken off is never about their own wounds and feelings, but exclusively about the fighting they have just left. If one only had time to listen or take down it would be something worth reading, because it is not letters home or newspapers stuff, but told to each other, with their own curious comments and phraseology, and no hint of a gallery or a Press.'[24]

For weeks she had tried to follow the developments of the war in the press. In her diary entries between 23 August and 17 December, she makes numerous references to her desire to obtain newspapers, particularly *The Times* and *Daily Mail*. Yet, on 27 October she had recorded '*The Times* of yesterday which you can get here and to-day's *Daily Mail* say the fighting beyond Ypres is "severe", but that gives the British public no glimmering of what it really is'.[25] A very brief diary entry on 12 November states, 'News from the front handed down the line coincides with the *Daily Mail*'.[26] Kate Luard was clearly trying to establish whether the press coverage, particularly in the popular and quality press, actually reflected the realities of what was taking place.

As her unofficial dispatches could, and would later, attest, her experiences of the war being fought on the Western Front were very different from the propaganda war being waged by the government and press. In the first four months of the war, the British casualty rate, battle and non-battle, amounted to 190,000.[27]

Kate Luard's initial plan was to record her thoughts and experiences of the war purely for personal use. She described the closest members of her family as the 'inner circle' but, by November 1914, they were urging her to publish the war diary. It is clear from the letters she sent home between autumn 1914 and spring 1915, that, despite the experiences she had been through and continuous bouts of bad health, she was utterly devoted to caring for the casualties of the conflict. In a letter in January 1915 and addressed to the 'inner circle' she wrote, 'Sometimes it flashes across me what a devilish lucky beggar I am to be in France at all, in the King's uniform, and paid by HM Government for personal services with the British Army in the Field'.[28] She had been on active service throughout the battles of the Aisne and the first battle of Ypres, witnessing first hand, the enormity of the carnage. While obviously committed to the men she nursed, she was equally committed to recording their suffering. Furthermore, believing the public had a right to know the human cost of the conflict, with the encouragement of her father, brothers and sisters, she decided to submit her diary for publication.

By April 1915, Kate Luard was no longer working on the ambulance train and was detailed for duty at a field hospital. While travelling to Beuvry, she records that she passed 'an unending stream of khaki, the men marching back from their four days in the trenches, infantry officers and all, steadily trudging on with the same coating of mud from head to foot, packs and rifles carried anyhow, and the Trench Look, which can never be described, and is grim to the last degree'.[29] A few days later she wrote a lengthy letter to her sister Daisy who was working as a Voluntary Aid Detachment (VAD) nurse on the home front. 'I am writing in the ward while the orderly has his meal downstairs – opposite me is a boy of 22 with his shoulder arm and left leg all shell holes. He has curly hair, blue eyes and a serene face [...] he has to have enemas and rectal salines – all sorts of unknown horrors, morphia and castor oil and brandy. He never questions or rebels against any of it. His dressings this morning was half an hour of agony – when he moaned you felt sick.'[30]

After nearly eight months of serving at the front her letters home became more expressive; for example, the word 'damned' was now used liberally. In the letter to her sister she remarked on her language, and that of other nurses. Instead of referring to 'the war' it became the 'damned war'. However, she mused that her language was not as bad as some of her nursing colleagues. 'I thought I was pretty hot but my language is nursery tea compared to theirs.' Furthermore, she was even inclined to pass cynical comments on the high command. Referring to Sir John French, she wrote, 'Yes, Johnny French has mentioned the nurses for the first time for nearly a year of war [...] So I suppose that someone has got it into his head that we do a little work sometimes'.[31]

In May 1915, weeks before the final submission of her diary, she was dealing with the casualties from the Battle of Festubert. The British offensive started on 15 May and concluded on 25 May. Ten days of fighting saw 12,419 casualties in the ranks of the BEF.[32]

In a diary entry for 10 May, Kate Luard highlights the demands that were made on the medical services. 'We have had a night of it. Every Field Ambulance, barge Clearing Hospital and train are blocked with them

[casualties]. The MOs can neither eat nor sleep [...] I went down to the
barge to see if they wanted any extra help and had a grim afternoon and
evening there [...] It was packed with all the worst cases – dying and bleeding and groaning.'[33]

She concludes the first diary with an entry on 26 May. 'No time to
write yesterday; had a typical Clearing Hospital Field Day. The left-out-
in-the-field wounded, mostly Canadians, had at last been picked up and
came pouring in. I had my Tent Section of eighty beds nearly full, and we
coped in a broiling sun till we sweltered into little spots of grease. In the
middle of it all at 5 pm orders came for me to join Number [...] [censored]
Ambulance Train for duty [...] these orders were afterwards cancelled, and
I am for duty at a Base Hospital.'[34]

The war diary of Kate Luard was published in the autumn of 1915 by
William Blackwood and Sons under the title *Diary of a Nursing Sister on
the Western Front*, the author, anonymous. The book was an immediate
success. The review in *The Daily Telegraph* stated, 'No one should miss this
"*Diary*". It will make them realise what war means, and what the British
Army endured, and is enduring, as they have never realised it before'.

The *Daily News* was more than praiseworthy, it was a little envious.
'This diary will tell you more about war than leader writers on impartial
prints ever get the chance, worse luck, to learn. From her side of it the
nursing sister is a realist.'

The *Manchester Guardian* claimed the book was 'A book of heroes.
Few books about the war bring it so closely to us, and this enormous mass of
memoranda is thoroughly alive [...] We are drawn to sympathy and admiration for the woman whose great adventure is in such terrible and daunting
circumstances. It is terrible, but there are times when it is strangely exalting'.
There was a strange irony with *The Guardian*'s review as the paper's middle-
aged leader writer and deputy editor, C. E. Montague, had left his job to
enlist as a private then, ironically, was transferred to the Intelligence Corps,
where he worked as a press censor. The *Yorkshire Post* recommended there
should be 'a cheap reprint for the widest possible circulation [...] It is the
most vivid and the most painful description of life and death at the Front
that has been printed, and at the same time the most buoyantly cheerful'.
The society journal, *The Lady*, which throughout the war continued as if

it were business as usual, commenting on the social scene, fashion, and the virtues of being a good hostess and wife, carried out a review of the book. In a slightly patronising tone it was described as 'A wonderful inspiring and intensely moving little book'.[35]

On Christmas Day 1915, the book was featured in *The Scotsman*'s book reviews, with the reviewer claiming 'It is well, therefore, that among those who minister to the wounded there should be some whose experiences and impressions may be made available for a wider circle than that of relatives and friends. In this volume what the anonymous writer has to say about the wounded soldiers forms part of a more comprehensive diary which furnishes a vivid and well-filled picture of the life of a nursing sister in France and Flanders [...] One of the general conclusions which she draws from her varied experiences is that "it is only when things are prosperous and comfortable that Tommy grumbles and has grievances" and that the fortitude of the wounded is "a revelation of what the British soldier will stick without grumbling"'.[36] At the outbreak of the war, the paper had predicted that stoicism would prevail and it did. By the time the book was reviewed, 84,085 families had lost loved ones serving in the first year of the conflict.[37]

With the publishing of *Diary of a Nursing Sister on the Western Front*, Kate Luard's narrative of the human cost of the war said what the newspapers were unwilling or unable to print. Press censorship had been imposed two days before the declaration of war and there was little opposition from the press against this measure. Moreover, when the fighting began, some newspapers called for even greater restrictions. The language of the press became emotive; advocating stronger censorship, the *Daily Sketch* claimed it was voicing the wishes of 'the mothers of soldiers'. Fearing that national moral could be damaged, *The Daily Telegraph* came out against 'alarmist stories'. The voice of the Northcliffe Press dissented but only for a while. The *Daily Mail* had initially challenged the government to explain to the people of Britain why there needed to be a total news blackout on the activities of the BEF. In an appeal to the government, the paper claimed it did not wish to print anything that might be 'injurious to the military interests of the nation'. However, it then went on to say, 'while we all agree that careful censorship is necessary for success, it might seem that the reticence

in Great Britain has been carried to an unnecessary extreme'.[38] Following
the Allied success on the Ainse, Lord Northcliffe, despite his previously
hostile stance to Britain's entry into the war, put money and his influential
newspapers, *The Times* and *Daily Mail*, at the disposal of the war effort.
The last dissenting voice had joined the propaganda war.

By early 1915, the government had relaxed the ban on correspondents
from the front by allowing *selected* journalists to report on the war. The shift
in mindset was primarily the result of international and domestic pressure
being brought to bear on the government for a more relaxed censorship of
the press. To this end, five men were chosen as 'war correspondents': Philip
Gibbs, Percival Philips, William Beach Thomas, Henry Perry Robinson and
Herbert Russell. However, the political and military authorities were not
as accommodating as the correspondents believed they would be. Indeed,
before their dispatches could be sent back to Britain for publication, they
had to be submitted to the military censor. Apparently, the correspondents had a clear conscience about this compromise as they lived relatively
charmed lives at the front. They wore officers' uniforms, minus insignia,
held the honorary rank of captain, and had orderlies, drivers and cars at
their disposal. Additionally, the Army supplied their accommodation.[39]
The arrangement was hardly conducive to impartial dispatches, a point
made by Philip Gibbs four years after the end of the war. 'We identified
ourselves absolutely with the Armies in the field [...] there was no need of
censorship of our despatches. We were our own censors.'[40] There was a general consensus amongst the gentlemen of the press (there were no women
of influence working in newspapers) that, in order to win the war, some
freedoms had to be sacrificed. As in previous wars, the truth in print and
honour amongst correspondents became the first casualties.

Kate Luard's published account of the first eight months of the war on
the Western Front challenged what little authorized reportage there was
and, in doing so, it also breached DORA. The book was not an attempt
to sabotage anything of national security; it contained little if anything
that could identify locations, units or people. She did not engage in anti-
war rhetoric, name-and-shame individuals, apportion blame, criticize the
government or the military high command. She wisely let the diary entries
speak for themselves; the message was between the lines. Kate Luard was

not unpatriotic; she just wanted the public to realize that patriotism came with a high price. The diary was not the product of vainglory, rather it was a bold attempt to inform the public and press of the human cost of the victory they were looking for and, indeed, expected.

The political consequences of her decision to publish the war diary should not be underestimated. The diary was significant, as this first-hand account of the physical and psychological effects of warfare on the fighting forces directly contradicted official press reports and government propaganda. Moreover, it was the earliest account in book form of life at the front in the early months of the war, written by a member of the BEF and published without War Office clearance. She published the diary with the full support of her family and in the knowledge that it could have serious political, professional and personal repercussions. By publishing, Kate Luard made herself vulnerable to charges of being unpatriotic and an enemy propagandist. Additionally, the disturbing content of the book could have been viewed as alarmist thus having the undesirable effect of lowering troop and civilian morale. Ultimately, it could have inflicted damage on recruitment, and strengthened the arguments of pacifists and conscientious objectors.

The risks of personal consequences were no less serious. Kate Luard was the granddaughter of Admiral Sir William Garnham Luard, her father was a Church of England clergyman as was her brother, Percy. She had three brothers serving in the forces; one in the Royal Navy and two in the British Army, all holding commissions. Another brother was a doctor with a well-established medical practice. In addition, an uncle was a Naval Commander and three nephews were serving officers in the British Army. Obviously, her actions could have brought shame on the family name and caused great embarrassment to the serving members of her family.

Equally, her actions could have damaged the standing of professional nurses and compromised hard-won political support for the Nurse Registration Bill. It had not been long since some doctors voiced their concerns about nurses being given too much autonomy. One doctor went as far as to suggest that nurses possessed 'just enough knowledge to make them dangerous'.[41] It had been a long, hard battle to achieve professional recognition and on the eve of war being declared the Nurse Registration

Bill was near implementation. However, the reading of the Bill was suspended for the duration of the hostilities. The nursing profession had much to lose and Kate Luard's actions could have further fuelled long-held beliefs amongst those in medicine and the military who were unwilling to recognize nursing as a profession or to accept the suitability of nurses to be with the army and at the front. Much of this prejudice was based on the notion of hysteria, an alleged female condition. It was not uncommon then for women to be accused of hysterical utterings or behaviour when they spoke out for their rights or the rights of others. Likewise, if they tried to assert their position within the home, marriage, profession or community, they were often labelled as neurasthenic (being physically and psychologically weak). In the same way, Kate Luard's actions and book could have been attributed to the behaviour of a hysteric and any suggestion of emotional instability would have had devastating consequences for her career as a nurse.[42]

From the available evidence, however, any concerns voiced within the military and political establishments were not acted upon, with a number of factors undoubtedly influencing the decision not to react, for instance the potential effect on nurse recruitment. Despite the thousands of women who had volunteered at the outbreak of war to nurse in the BEF, in reality there was a serious shortage of nurses. The early enthusiasm had given way to the realization that there was little financial reward or glamour in nursing the sick and wounded. The shortage of skilled professional and volunteer nurses was a real problem for the War Office and the war effort. Consequently, the government could not afford to engage in any form of negative rhetoric or in actions that would compromise or affect nurse recruitment and retention. To make an example of Kate Luard would probably have done both.

The politics of universal suffrage had been pre-eminent prior to the outbreak of war. The National Union of Women's Suffrage Societies (NUWSS) and the militant wing, the Women's Social and Political Union (WSPU), had mounted campaigns and lobbied for political and social inclusion. However, with the declaration of war, the fate of husbands, brothers and sons, and a sense of patriotic duty, overshadowed the franchise demands. It was agreed amongst the women's suffrage societies that political agitation on equality rights would be suspended for the duration of the war. There were women, however, who objected to the suspension of activity. There was an uneasy truce between the government and the franchise lobbyists and, despite the politics of compromise, a strong ethos of sisterhood still prevailed. Many professional nurses were members of suffrage societies and *The British Journal of Nursing* was highly political in its support of women's rights and the franchise. If Kate Luard was made an example of there could have been repercussions, particularly within the militant wing of the suffrage movement. The government needed the support of women and fighting political wars on the home front could not be allowed to distract it from trying to achieve victory on the fighting fronts.

There was, of course, the Cavell factor. By the time *Diary of a Nursing Sister on the Western Front* was published, Edith Cavell, a professional nurse who had been working as a Matron in Dr Depage's School of Certified Nurses in Brussels' Barkendalle Medical Institute, had been executed by the Germans. During the war the Institute was transformed into a Red Cross Hospital at which Allied and German wounded were treated. The Germans, however, accused Edith Cavell and others of helping Allied soldiers to escape across the frontier. Despite diplomatic representation and pleas for clemency, Edith Cavell was executed by firing squad on 12 October 1915. The press reported widely on the manner of her death, which was met with public and political outrage. Her last few words, also reported, led many to believe she died a martyr. The night before her execution she told the Reverend Stirling Gahan: 'Standing as I do in view of God and Eternity, I realise that patriotism is not enough. I must have no hatred or bitterness towards anyone'. In a last letter to a friend she claimed, 'I am neither afraid, nor unhappy, but quite ready to give my life for England'.[43]

The image of the dedicated, self-sacrificing nurse was a potent force in shaping public opinion and their perceptions about the difficulties of nursing on the fighting fronts. In the weeks following Edith Cavell's death, public revulsion about the killing did not abate and she became a symbol of martyrdom. The War Propaganda Bureau, seizing the opportunity, prepared recruitment posters urging men to join up and avenge her death. The message was constant: Edith Cavell had been 'murdered' by the enemy. Therefore, given the strength of feeling, it would probably have been incomprehensible to the public for Kate Luard to have been prosecuted for telling the truth about the obscenity of war. Consequently, any government censure of her could be seen as yet another nurse paying for her actions and beliefs. Given all the variables, on balance the government may have decided it was unwise to express disapproval or condemnation.

Although the diary primarily dealt with the day-to-day activities of a nursing sister working under difficult conditions, and dealing with sickness and wounding on a gargantuan scale, it did not speak only of tragedy and trauma. The diary entries were balanced with humour and examples of individual acts of kindness and bravery – a point the government war propagandist could have exploited, by highlighting the 'pluck' of the BEF. The book and its author were best summed up in a review in *The British Journal of Nursing*: 'It is a first-hand, simple record of the daily experiences of what we judge to be one of the pick of the nursing profession in charge of an ever changing convoy of wounded men on a hospital train [...] The book is full of priceless, deathless records of otherwise unrecorded valour. The Sister jots them down along with her own experiences, without any appeal to the gallery, without any strained sentiment'.[44]

Kate Luard was a woman of big deeds and eloquent words. She was also a paradox. As references and testimonials from medical officers, nurses and orderlies would attest, she was the ultimate dedicated, disciplined, professional nurse. The discipline, however, was selective. Not only was she prepared to break the censorship rules but on more than one occasion she also breached military orders and protocols. Her diary entries highlight just how much she and her medical and nursing colleagues were prepared to break the rules, particularly the absurd ban on nurses and medical officers having any kind of social interaction, which, living and working in the confines of an ambulance train, could not be avoided. Fraternizing with the other ranks and drinking alcohol was strictly forbidden but she did both. Her diary entry for Christmas 1914 highlights the camaraderie that existed between the sexes and ranks.

Describing Christmas dinner on the Ambulance Train she writes, 'We had a very festive Xmas dinner [...] soup, turkey, peas, mince pie, plum pudding, chocolate, champagne, absinthe, and coffee. Absinthe is delicious, like squills. We had many toasts in French and English. The

King, the President, Absent Friends, Soldiers, Sailors, and I had the *Blesses* and *Malades* [...] Our great anxiety is to get as many orderlies and NCOs [non-commissioned officers] as possible through the day without being run in for drunk, but it is an uphill job'.[45] On Boxing Day the Sisters were invited to the Orderlies' Mess Truck and she records that, 'The OC [Officer Commanding] made a speech, and the QMS [Quarter Master Sergeant] dished out drinks for us to toast with [...] it ended in a healthy splodge all round'.[46]

According to her diary and letters home, she played bridge with medical officers and attended the cinema with them. At times, when they were 'stood down', she would commandeer a car or truck and drive colleagues into the French countryside. She understood the physical and emotional demands made on the medical and nursing staff, and tried to bring a degree of normality and pleasure into their lives. She was a pragmatist, even in her dress code. Abandoning the army nursing apron, she had special aprons made that were more suited to the type of nursing in which she was engaged. She designed and made a satchel that was practical for carrying dressings, scissors, probes and her diary. In cold or wet weather, she wore artillery boots. To protect her feet and ankles from the effects of standing too long, she wore puttees over her regulation shoes. During the war she was only one of eight women to visit Toc H, a club in Poperinghe, Belgium, opened by army chaplain, the Reverend Philip 'Tubby' Clayton. This social club was an oasis of peace in a violent war. It was rare in as much as it was a soldiers' club for all ranks. Over the front door was a notice, 'All rank abandon, ye who enter here'. It was a home-from-home, furnished with soft chairs, curtains, books and a piano. Kate Luard became a frequent visitor and after the war served on the first committee of League of Women Helpers for Toc H.

Despite her actions and unorthodoxy Kate Luard remained in continuous service with the BEF until 1918. Her work was rewarded with the Royal Red Cross (First Class) and Bar and she was twice Mentioned in Dispatches.[47] After the publication of *Diary of a Nursing Sister*, she continued to keep a war diary and, thirty years later, she published the remainder in *Unknown Warriors* under her own name. The preface of the book was written by Field Marshal Viscount Allenby.[48] The book was published to critical acclaim and was an immediate success. She received letters of praise and cards of thanks from nurses, orderlies, doctors and soldiers she had nursed or known during the war.[49]

In the post-war years Kate Luard worked as Matron at the South London Hospital for Women and Children. She toured the battlefields on the Western and Eastern Fronts with her brother, Percy, searching for the graves of family members and laid little remembrances at the graves of unknown warriors. Kate Luard had to deal with grief professionally in warfare but the war also took a heavy toll on the Luard family. Between 1914 and 1918 eight members of her family had died, five of them on active service.

In her sixties, she embarked on a new nursing career; she and her sisters opened a nursing home for disabled and elderly war veterans. By the time the Second World War broke out Kate Luard was in her seventies but she was still active in the community, carrying out gas-mask and first-aid training. In 1962, at the age of ninety, Evelyn Kate Luard, nurse and author, who was quite irrepressible in work and indomitable in spirit, gave up the fight. The humble headstone with her name followed by RRC and Bar, date of birth and death, gives no indication of a life well loved and lived. It is very much in the fashion of Kate Luard.

Since its publication in 1915, *Diary of a Nursing Sister on the Western Front* has consistently been reviewed as a masterpiece of war testament. Furthermore, it was the earliest first-hand account of life at the front to challenge the reporting of the war and it became a classic in the historiography of World War One. However, in the past few years, some feminist writers and nurse historians have described the book as nothing more than propaganda, claiming Kate Luard was an apologist for war and that her diary glorified it. This rather naïve, if not ridiculous assertion, is at odds with some of the less-tempered entries in her diary, such as the one written on 22 February 1915: 'It is such a vast upheaval when you are in the middle of it, that you sometimes actually wonder if everyone has gone mad, or who has gone mad, that all should be grimly working, toiling, slaving from the firing line to the base, for more destruction, and for more highly-finished and uninterrupted destruction, in order to get peace. And the men who pay the cost in intimate personal and individual suffering and in death are not the men who made the war'.[50] Had she lived to hear the accusations, it is doubtful if Kate Luard would have cared much about them. What mattered most to her was truth and gaining approval for her actions from the people she spoke out for.

In the post-war years, when some war correspondents were beating their breasts for being less than truthful, William Beach Thomas declared: 'I was thoroughly ashamed of what I had written, for the good reason that it was untrue. The vulgarity of enormous headlines and the enormity of one's own name did not lessen the shame'.[51] Kate Luard had no such haunting – truth was at the heart of her testament.

In 1924, she was asked to write an article on the importance of character in nursing the sick. Amongst the many qualities she listed were gentleness, cheerfulness, courage and tolerance. And Kate Luard believed truthfulness to be the greatest of these, stating, 'Without it a nurse will come to grief and probably her patients too [...] Whatever else you are afraid of, don't be afraid of telling the exact truth and face the consequences'.[52]

Thankfully, for the recording of war, journalism and history, *she* stayed true to her beliefs.

Notes

1　*The Times*, 5 August 1914.
2　*Daily Mail*, 4 August 1914.
3　*The Times*, 4 August 1914.
4　*Daily News*, 4 August 1914.
5　*The Scotsman*, 4 August 1914.
6　*Nursing Times*, 8 August 1914.
7　*The British Journal of Nursing*, 8 August 1914.
8　Y. T. McEwen, *It's a Long Way to Tipperary: British and Irish Nurses in the Great War* (Dunfermline: Cualann Press, 2006), 42.
9　*The Nursing Mirror and Midwives Journal*, 15 August 1914.
10　Essex Record Office, Chelmsford, UK: Papers of Bramston and Luard Families: D/DLu/55/13/4.

11   T. J. Mitchell & G. M. Smith, *History of the Great War based on Official Documents. Medical Services: Casualties and Medical Statistics* (London: HM Stationary Office, 1931).

12   *The Times*, 30 August 1914.

13   *The Times*, 7 September 1914.

14   Essex Record Office: K. Luard letter to brother and sisters, 25 September 1914: D/DLu/55/13/4.

15   Anon., *Diary of a Nursing Sister on the Western Front, 1914–1915* (Edinburgh & London: William Blackwood and Sons, 1915), 40, 41.

16   Essex Record Office: Undated letter: D/DLu55/13/4.

17   Essex Record Office: K. Luard to Rev. B. G. Luard, 28 September 1914: D/DLu/55/13/4.

18   Essex Record Office: Undated note: Captain, Chief Censor: D/DLu/55/13/4.

19   Essex Record Office: K. Luard letter to family, undated, 1914: D/DLu/55/13/4.

20   Essex Record Office: K. Luard note to family, undated, 1914: D/DLu/55/13/4.

21   Anon. (1915), 89.

22   Essex Record Office: K. Luard to Rev. B. G. Luard, 28 October 1914: D/DLu/55/13/4.

23   Essex Record Office: K. Luard letter to family, undated, 1914: D/DLu/55/13/4.

24   Anon. (1915), 104.

25   Anon. (1915), 96.

26   Anon. (1915), 105.

27   T. J. Mitchell & G. M. Smith, 121.

28   Essex Record Office: K. Luard to family, 28 January 1915: D/DLu/55/13/4.

29   Anon. (1915), 251.

30   Essex Record Office: K. Luard to D. Luard, 2 May 1915: D/DLu/55/13/5.

31   Essex Record Office: K. Luard to family, 2 May 1915: D/DLu/55/13/5.

32   T. J. Mitchell & G. M. Smith, 135.

33   Anon. (1915), 281.

34   Anon. (1915), 299.

35   Essex Record Office: Blackwood's Advertiser, undated review: D/DLu/62/1.

36   *The Scotsman*, 25 December 1915.

37   T. J. Mitchell & G. M. Smith, 122, 136.

38   *Daily Mail*, 27 August 1914.

39   P. Knightley, *The First Casualty. From the Crimea to Vietnam: The War Correspondent as Hero, Propagandist, and Myth Maker* (New York, NY: Harcourt Brace Jovanovich, 1975).

40   P. Gibbs, *Adventures in Journalism* (London: Heinemann, 1923), 231.

41   Anon., 'Editorial', *Lancet*, 109 (1877), 62.

42   E. Showalter, *The Female Malady. Women, Madness and English Culture 1830–1980* (London: Virago Press, 1987), 18.

43   J. Evans, *Edith Cavell* (London: Royal London Hospital Archives and Museum, 2008), 46–47.

44   *The British Journal of Nursing*, 12 August 1916, 141–142.

45   Anon. (1915), 155.

46   Anon. (1915), 157.

47   Essex Record Office: K. Luard papers: D/DLu/62/2.

48   E. K. Luard, *Unknown Warriors* (London: Chatto and Windus, 1930).

49   Essex Record Office: K. Luard papers, Correspondence File: D/DLu/62/2.

50   Anon. (1915), 126.

51   W. B. Thomas, *A Traveller in News* (London: Chapman and Hall, 1925), 109.

52   Essex Record Office: K. Luard papers: D/DLu/65.

PATRICK S. WASHBURN

George Padmore of the *Pittsburgh Courier* and the *Chicago Defender*: A Decidedly Different World War II Correspondent

On 31 July 1943, the *Pittsburgh Courier* ran an eight-column feature story about George Padmore, the paper's World War II London correspondent since 1941. Noting that readers were constantly asking about his background, it said he had been 'a colonial expert' for the Communists in Moscow, where he knew Russian Premier Joseph Stalin; he had a worldwide reputation as 'a racial zealot' who vigorously fought imperialism; and he was in the 'forefront' of black journalists. 'In his reporting for *Courier* readers of world events affecting colored peoples, he has achieved almost complete objectivity', the paper continued. 'He has perfected the knack of embracing in paragraphs of interpretative background data, the significant currents in the advancing social, political and economic trends of colored peoples. He is reporter, writer, analyst and interpreter all heaped into one.' It concluded by labelling him 'one of the best informed writers of developments in the present war as they affect colored races'.[1]

Such effusive praise by the *Courier* was not surprising. Like all of the black newspapers in the United States, it ignored the white press' reportorial goal of objectivity and instead practiced a powerful form of advocacy journalism, continually mixing straight, factual writing with editorialized comments in news stories. In doing so, it pushed hard for more equality for blacks and more recognition of what they were doing to help win the war, both of which were constant themes in Padmore's articles. But that made him no different from the other twenty-six black newspaper war correspondents from the U.S., including seven on the *Courier*.[2] They all played up black accomplishments and inequalities. However, none of them, including Padmore, who was only one of two black press correspondents to serve in that capacity for the entire time that the U.S. was in World War II (1941–45), achieved widespread national fame for their reporting and their work has been largely forgotten.[3]

Upon close inspection, Padmore stands out because of one area that he wrote about far more than any other U.S. black-press war correspondent. He may have been the only one never to go on a bombing run, never sail on a naval raid, never go on a patrol or never be on the front lines. Instead, he covered the entire war from the relative safety of London – his home was destroyed by German bombers in 1941 but he was never injured – except for occasional visits to American army camps in England.[4] While he wrote about black U.S. troops, which was not unexpected because of the large number of them sent to Great Britain after America entered the war, he far more frequently focused on non-U.S. people of colour. What were they doing to help win the war, what inequalities did they endure because of the colour of their skin and, particularly, what were their chances of being freed from their imperialistic masters when the war ended? His well-known, anti-imperialism agenda, which he had been aggressively honing for more than ten years before the U.S. entered the war in 1941, was clearly welcomed by the *Pittsburgh Courier* and the *Chicago Defender*, the country's two largest and most-influential black newspapers, both of which ran his stories regularly in World War II.

Numerous scholars have written about Padmore's work from the 1930s through the 1950s in the Pan Africa movement, with some labelling him the 'Father of Pan–Africanism' and the 'Father of African Emancipation' because he was an originator of the movement for political independence for Africans.[5] However, they have virtually ignored his extensive war correspondence in black newspapers. For example, James R. Hooker, who authored the lone book-length biography of Padmore in 1967, *Black Revolutionary: George Padmore's Path from Communism to Pan–Africanism*, noted briefly that he worked for black newspapers both before and during the war, but he did not examine what or how much he wrote.[6] John Stevens' 1973 monograph about black press correspondents in World War II also did not discuss Padmore's articles and the only other mention of him by a mass-communication historian, Lee Finkle, in his 1975 book about the black press during the war, confined him to one paragraph.[7] Thus, this chapter fills a gap in Padmore's history because it shows that, during World War II, his stories in the *Pittsburgh Courier* and the *Chicago Defender*, often on their front pages, actively and continually promoted what he already was becoming famous for internationally: anti-imperialism.

Knowing more about Padmore's journalistic career is not nearly as significant historically as what the appearance of his articles in World War II revealed about black U.S. newspapers. Historians have noted how the black press continually played up the inequalities of American blacks as well as their wartime gains, both in civilian life and in the armed forces, as it walked a thin line between supporting the U.S. war effort while threatening to hurt black morale with continuous complaints about injustices, such as lynchings. The leader of the black press, particularly with its famous Double V campaign (victory over totalitarian forces overseas and victory over the same types of forces in the U.S.), was the largest of the papers, the weekly *Pittsburgh Courier*, which rose during the war from 190,000 circulation to 350,000.[8]

As this chapter shows, historians have been so fixated on studying what the black newspapers were writing about American blacks during the war that they have failed to notice that the *Courier* and the *Chicago Defender* also ran a large number of articles about non-U.S. blacks. This was not the first time that the black press had written extensively about blacks outside America. As recently as 1935–36, for example, the *Courier* had sent a war correspondent to cover the Italian invasion of Ethiopia. J. A. Rogers' stories were sometimes overly dramatic and grandiose, such as one that called Emperor Haile Selassie 'Ethiopia's triumphant God, hurling his thunderbolts [at the Italians] from sky-tipped mountain peaks'. But readers expected this type of colourful writing and embraced it, which was shown by the paper's circulation increasing quickly by about 25,000 during the invasion of Ethiopia.[9]

While Padmore's bylined articles about foreign blacks in the *Courier* and the *Defender* cannot be tied to their circulation gains during World War II, it is possible that they may have played a part. What is clear, given the large number of his articles that ran, is that the papers unquestionably felt his dispatches were important. These stories sent a strong message – a victory for equality by blacks anywhere in the world, not just in the U.S., was significant – and the papers wanted their readers to recognize that.

Over all of the world's blacks

Padmore's journalistic message, particularly about anti-imperialism, was not surprising because of his experiences before World War II. Born in the British colony of Trinidad in 1902 or 1903, his given name was Malcolm Ivan Meredith Nurse and he would not begin calling himself George Padmore until the latter part of the 1920s. His abhorrence of imperialism began after graduating from high school and becoming a reporter of shipping news for six years on a Trinidadian newspaper. The work not only bored him but also he detested his white British editor, Edward J. Partridge, who treated blacks on the staff subserviently. '[He was] one of the most arrogant agents of British Imperialism I have ever encountered', Nurse recalled, 'I held him in utter contempt, and had hoped to use my pen in exposing his role before the colonial workers and peasants whom he oppressed through his dirty sheet the *Guardian*'. When Partridge criticized his reporting in 1924, they had a heated argument and Nurse was fired.[10]

Deciding that he wanted to study medicine, although later he switched to law, Nurse sailed to the United States late in 1924 and for the next four-and-a-half years took classes at Columbia University, Fisk University and Howard University, but he never earned a degree from any of them. He also enrolled at New York University, never attended and was dropped. While going to college, he quickly became aware of what he called a 'fundamental distinction in modern society based on color' with blacks occupying 'an inferior social status'. This led to him forsaking individualism because he came to believe that '[a]ll colored peoples remained down or all went up [as a group]' and, as a result, he joined the Communist Party in New York City in 1927, feeling that it could help blacks move upwards. Shortly afterwards, he began referring to himself as George Padmore when doing party business and used that name for the rest of his life. 'You see, all revolutionaries are compelled to adopt false names to hide their identity from the Government', he naïvely wrote a friend'.[11] While in New York, he edited a Communist paper in Harlem, the *Negro Champion*, but, needing more money, he also worked on a boat and as a janitor, adding to his small wardrobe by sometimes keeping cast-off clothes that he found in wastebaskets. Hooker noted that he 'provided an excellent example of the astonishing vigour and singleness of purpose one associates with the determined party activist'.[12]

In late 1929, a Communist Party official took Padmore to Russia, where he quickly began moving in high government circles, first as an authority on the United States and then as head of the Red International of Labour Union's Negro Bureau. In this position, he wrote articles about American blacks and Africans for the *Moscow Daily News*, an English-language newspaper; supervised party activities involving blacks all over the world and organized the first International Conference of Negro Workers; denounced American racism; and occasionally took money to party functionaries in other countries. In 1930, the party moved him to Vienna, Austria, and he began travelling widely, coordinating the activities of blacks fighting imperialism, particularly in British colonies.[13] During a trip to London, he jokingly told an Englishman that he was over all of the world's blacks and then, becoming more serious, he said he was pushing for two revolutions: one was encouraging black leaders in various countries to overthrow their white imperialist masters and to put their own people in power, and the second was class based.[14]

His life changed radically in 1933. When Adolf Hitler came to power, the Nazis cracked down on Germany's Communist Party and Padmore was one of many who were arrested. After several months in jail, he was deported to England, which was not pleased to see him because of his Communist background but had no way of keeping him out because the party was not illegal in the country and he had a British passport. At this time, Russia reduced its anti-imperialistic activities in order to curry favour with western countries and ordered him to cease attacking British, American and French imperialism, leaving only the Japanese as a target. This frustrated and angered him because, as his nephew told Hooker years later, Padmore felt that the Japanese were not the imperialists with 'their boots across the black man's neck'. Feeling strongly that backing away from anti-imperialism was 'a betrayal of the fundamental interests of my people', he resigned from the Communist Party in 1933 and a year later the party made it official by expelling him, saying he had a 'petty-bourgeois nationalist deviation'.[15]

Left with no livelihood and no income, Padmore moved in with a group of destitute West Indians in London and struggled to make a living by conducting political-science classes for colonial students, who paid small amounts for his lectures. He also started writing and his 1936 book, *How Britain Rules Africa*, which indicted British imperialism, received generally good reviews. The foreword to the book was blunt: 'The one safety for the common man of [Great Britain] or any other country is to destroy imperialism'. Then, a year later, he established the International African Service Bureau. Its goal was to 'fight for the demands of Africans and other colonial peoples for democratic rights, civil liberties and self determination', and one of the main ways it tried to accomplish this was by making the press more aware of the grievances of people of colour in British colonies. The Bureau's motto was blunt: 'Educate, co-operate, emancipate. Neutral in nothing affecting the African people'.[16]

As time passed, Padmore became more outspoken. For example, less than three months before the start of World War II in 1939, he wrote in the Independent Labour Party's weekly journal, the *New Leader*, that he was opposed to conscripting British citizens into the military because a future war would be imperialistic and support capitalism. He added ominously, in words that could not have pleased the English authorities, 'The enemy is at home!'. Then, only days before the war began on 1 September, his Service Bureau put out a 'Warning to the Coloured Peoples', which labelled Nazis, fascists and democrats, as imperialistic bandits. After the war began, despite feeling that blacks in the military were doing white man's work, he and others who shared his viewpoints argued successfully for the induction of blacks into the armed services, both in Great Britain and in the English colonies. However, he wrote to the Minister of Labour that he would go to prison rather than accept a position that he was offered in the Ministry of Information because he would not 'help in any way the war effort of British Imperialism or any other Imperialism'. A friend speculated that the government chose to ignore his refusal to work for it and to take no action against him because it did not want to make him a martyr.[17]

As Padmore's prominence as an anti-imperialist had risen in the mid-1930s, he had added to his income by starting to write regularly for a number of black publications. These included two newspapers, *Public Opinion* in Jamaica and the *Ashanti Pioneer* in the Gold Coast, as well as *The Crisis*, a magazine published by the National Association for the Advancement of Colored People in the U.S. His articles noted what was happening to blacks around the world, particularly in colonized countries, such as in South, West and East Africa. Then, in 1938, he wrote an article for the *Chicago Defender* about a British Royal Commission that was preparing to investigate conditions in the West Indies and Metz Lochard, one of his former Howard professors who worked at the paper, liked the story so much that he hired him as a European correspondent.[18] By 1940, Padmore was also writing for the *Pittsburgh Courier*.[19]

Thus, the two largest and most influential black newspapers in the United States, which were fierce competitors, found themselves in the unusual position of having the same war correspondent in London following the Japanese bombing of Pearl Harbor in Hawaii on 7 December 1941, which brought the U.S. into the war. He would write for both of them throughout World War II, gathering his information by reading a large number of newspapers and magazines as well as interviewing government leaders and making daily visits to the Ministry of Information in London.[20] By the time the war ended in Europe with the German surrender in May 1945, the two weekly papers had published 575 of Padmore's bylined stories (an average of 3.2 per week) and he may have written even more. There also were numerous non-bylined articles that had a London dateline but it is impossible to know who wrote them because both papers had other war correspondents in England at various times.

Writing about the 'Dixie boys'

Padmore's World War II newspaper stories, which dealt totally with blacks and people of colour, fell into two broad categories: those about Americans and the U.S., and those about non-Americans and countries other than the United States. Most of the stories in the former category were about U.S. troops, particularly those in Great Britain. As historian David Reynolds noted in *Rich Relations: The American Occupation of Britain, 1942–1945*, the arrival of the blacks after the U.S. entered the war was like a sudden flood. There were only about 8,000 blacks in Great Britain in 1939 and the British government was not keen on having black GIs. This caused the U.S. army commander in Great Britain to cable Washington on 17 April 1942: 'Colored units should not, repeat not, be sent to British Isles'. The War Department, however, rejected that suggestion, saying that blacks sent to Great Britain would be 'in reasonable proportion for any type of Service Units'. By 12 May, 811 black troops were in the country and their numbers grew rapidly after that, reaching 7,315 by the end of 1942, 65,000 twelve months later and 130,000 by D-Day (6 June 1944).[21]

Although black American troops began arriving in Great Britain in the spring of 1942, Padmore inexplicably did not write his first article about them until 1 August. In an upbeat story in the *Chicago Defender*, he said the blacks had made 'a good impression' on the British, who welcomed them warmly, and he called them 'a fine body of well disciplined men'. He concluded with a prediction: 'Coloured American soldiers will therefore experience little of the type of racial chauvinism and arrogance which is so blatantly manifested by white Americans at home. From observation on the street and other public places, it is remarkable to see the number of white and coloured American soldiers together. Coloured Americans are also beginning to make pals among the Britishers, men as well as girls, with whom they move about quite freely'.[22]

Two weeks later in a front-page story in the *Defender*, Padmore again played up how much the British liked the black soldiers. He noted, however, that there had been several 'racial incidents', including a dance-hall owner who had refused to admit black GIs because of complaints from white American army officers as well as regular patrons of the club.[23] Nevertheless, he continued his upbeat coverage a week later in another story on the front page, saying 'Southern cracker arrogance in the Dixie tradition is getting a sound trouncing' in Great Britain. As an example, he noted that some American sailors in London 'had a rollicking time escorting good-looking British blondes and brunettes [...] [T]axis were packed with groups of visitors and their girl friends busy sight-seeing'.[24] This was followed by another story praising black troops at a military ball in Liverpool.

> It was an exciting picture as Dixie boys of all colors – some ebony chocolate, some near white – stepped out to the popular strains of 'Dark Town Strutters Ball' and other numbers a little out of date, we think, in Harlem.
> The Afro–Americans strutted their stuff with vigor, their teeth flashing, eyes shining, while they threw light weight partners about in latest jitterbug antics.
> Britishers had never witnessed such jollity.[25]

Padmore wrote the same types of articles in 1942 for the *Pittsburgh Courier* even as he noted that there was evidence of racial tension, such as blacks being denied hotel accommodation, refused service in restaurants and being harassed for dancing publicly with white women. Just as in the *Defender*, he played down the problems, claiming the majority of the British felt 'if the colored are good enough to come over here and help the British defend their country against the so-called pure blooded Hitler Nordics, they are good enough to enjoy the democratic rights of selecting their friends, regardless to race, creed or color'.[26] Meanwhile, amid such concerns, Padmore praised the black U.S. troops, such as stevedores on the docks, frequently in almost breathless prose.

> This sunless land is a far cry from the tobacco and cotton fields of Dixieland, but the colored boys still sing and laugh while they work, bringing with them their Southern gaiety and good will.
> Theirs is a long and busy day. They are up at five, down to the docks by six-thirty, where they tote crates and boxes laden with supplies for the different United States camps and fighting units, 'til seven at night. In fact, fourteen-hour shifts are not uncommon and work goes on, night and day.

Negroes from small towns where the sun beats down summer and winter are now in a land which is always wet and cold [...] where sirens break up the night peace [...] where planes drone overhead all the time and big guns roar incessantly. These big, strong men from down South, husky, slow of speech, sing lustily as they ceaselessly unload enormous boxes from the ships into the U.S. Army trucks.

Standing on a quayside, a British dock superintendent declared:

'These colored boys have broken several records since they have started unloading here. They shift stuff faster than I've ever seen in 40 years on this quay.'[27]

However, as the autumn of 1942 rolled on, Padmore's writing subtly changed. He no longer gushed excitedly about the 'Dixie boys' – perhaps he had succumbed to the grimness of the war as it dragged on for month after month and maybe he realized that the black soldiers came from all over the U.S., not just the South – but he did keep praising their accomplishments. Examples of what he lauded over the final two-and-a-half years of the European war included: black soldiers in Great Britain who collected $111,516 for British war orphans; a black army truck driver who saved numerous lives when he ran frantically through an English village, warning people to take cover because a number of bombs on timer devices were about to explode; two black soldiers who ignored their own safety and leaped into the water to save a man who had fallen off a dock and was almost crushed by a ship; and a black soldier who saved a girl from a burning house and another who rushed into the ocean to keep a woman from drowning.[28]

Occasionally, he also wrote about U.S. blacks involved in the fighting. One story was about troops manning anti-aircraft batteries on the English coast, trying to shoot down German bombers; another noted that black soldiers had landed at Tripoli in the invasion of North Africa; and a third praised two black sailors who had successfully steered their munitions ship through a fierce German bomber attack in the North Atlantic.[29] These types of stories frequently gave Padmore an opportunity to mention past black injustices and he rarely passed up the chance to do so. For instance, his article about the landings in North Africa was a typical example of black press advocacy journalism: 'American descendants of Africans have returned to their ancestral homes whence three centuries ago they were taken away as bondmen, and with their tears, toil and sweat helped lay the foundation of the now mighty United States'.[30] In other stories, he noted that blacks were impressing whites with their heroism. He wrote that many of the white sailors on the ship in the Atlantic were from the South and the Midwest and had never been around blacks much and, thus, did not like to eat with them. But when the two black men showed 'staunch courage' in guiding their ship unscathed through the bomber attack, he said all prejudice disappeared and the crew came together in 'a common bond of understanding'.[31]

However, as the war roared onward, Padmore noted increasingly in his stories that not everything was so cheery for the U.S. black troops in Great Britain. Despite his early optimism that racial problems and prejudice would remain minimal, colour barriers sprang up at numerous places, such as weekly dances 'for whites only' in East Anglia in 1944. A dance organizer explained blacks had attended the dances for several weeks without any problems but then white Americans warned 'a clash' would occur if the blacks were not barred because they were dancing with white women. So, the organizing committee decided to exclude blacks from the dances because this was 'in everybody's interest'.[32]

Equally problematic were U.S. black soldiers who had legal problems. For example, forty-one blacks were found guilty of rape in Great Britain at Army court martials during the war.[33] One case that particularly drew wide attention, and resulted in front-page articles by Padmore in both the *Courier* and the *Defender*, occurred in Bath in May 1944. A woman sleeping with her husband was awakened before midnight by knocking at her parlour door. Looking out her bedroom window, she saw a black GI who wanted to know how to get to the train station and, although dressed only in a nightgown, she offered to walk with him. She told police that he raped her several minutes later in a field and he was arrested shortly afterwards, signed a confession, was found guilty and sentenced to be hanged. Following 50,000 British signing a petition on behalf of the soldier, asking for clemency and reconsideration of the verdict, General Dwight Eisenhower reversed the court-martial decision. He did so after being advised it was clear the confession was not voluntary and it came from a soldier who the army found was 'ignorant' (he only had seven years of schooling), which led to him not realizing the significance or gravity of his confession. Also playing a major part was what an Army lawyer called the woman's 'remarkable conduct in going out with the accused at midnight [which] cast doubt on her credibility'. Padmore noted that one English newspaper editorialized: 'It is scarcely conceivable that a British jury would have convicted the defendant on such evidence'.[34]

As the war wound down in late 1944, Padmore also wrote of the problem surrounding several hundred babies fathered by U.S. black soldiers with white British women, some of whom were single and others who were married with husbands out of the country in the military. In some cases, this resulted in babies being sold desperately on the 'black market'. 'These unfortunate married women have to surrender their children, especially if the child happens to be colored, to a "baby farmer" so as to get the child out of the way before the husband returns', he wrote. 'In cases where the illegitimate child is by a white soldier, the husband is prepared to forgive the wife and adopt the child, as the family could move to another town and start life anew. This cannot be done if the child is colored'.[35]

By the time that the war ended in Europe, Padmore had written 129 stories about Americans and the U.S., with the two largest categories being ninety-three articles about blacks in the military and another ten about the American Red Cross in Great Britain.[36] While those numbers were substantial, the striking thing was how small they were in comparison to his output about non-Americans and countries other than the U.S. As Table 1 shows, only 22.4 per cent of his 575 bylined articles in the *Pittsburgh Courier* and the *Chicago Defender* from December 1941 to May 1945 were about Americans and the U.S. Thus, even though he was writing for two U.S. black newspapers and was constantly around a rapidly growing number of black American troops from the summer of 1942 onward, slightly more than three-quarters of his articles did not focus on them and the U.S. Equally notable are the figures on his stories that ran on the front pages of the two papers. Of 113 front-page stories (19.7 per cent of the total number that he wrote during the war), only forty-seven of them (41.6 per cent) focused on Americans and the U.S. Thus, almost six of every ten of his stories that appeared on the front pages, where the editors placed what they felt was the most important news and where they tried to set the agenda for their black readers, were about non-Americans and countries other than the U.S.

Table 1: George Padmore's World War II Stories

Pittsburgh Courier

Number of Stories	*Front-Page Stories*
1941 2 (none about Americans and/or U.S.)	none
1942 49 (20 about Americans and/or U.S.)	14 (11 about Americans and/or U.S.)
1943 83 (18 about Americans and/or U.S.)	11 (6 about Americans and/or U.S.)
1944 73 (14 about Americans and/or U.S.)	14 (4 about Americans and/or U.S.)
1945 37 (3 about Americans and/or U.S.)	7 (none about Americans and/or U.S.)

Total Number of Stories: 244
Number of Stories about Americans and/or U.S.: 55 (22.5% of total stories)
Number of Front-Page Stories: 46 (18.9% of total stories)
Number of Front-Page Stories about Americans and/or U.S.: 21 (45.7% of total front-page stories)

Chicago Defender

Number of Stories	*Front-Page Stories*
1941 none	none
1942 28 (14 about Americans and/or U.S.)	13 (9 about Americans and/or U.S.)
1943 137 (29 about Americans and/or U.S.)	25 (10 about Americans and/or U.S.)
1944 123 (27 about Americans and/or U.S.)	21 (7 about Americans and/or U.S.)
1945 43 (4 about Americans and/or U.S.)	8 (none about Americans and/or U.S.)

Total Number of Stories: 331
Number of Stories about Americans and/or U.S.: 74 (22.4% of total stories)
Number of Front-Page Stories: 67 (20.2% of total stories)
Number of Front-Page Stories about Americans and/or U.S.: 26 (38.8% of total front-page stories)

Total Number of Stories for the Two Papers: 575
Total Number of Stories for the Two Papers about Americans and/or U.S.: 129 (22.4% of total stories)
Total Number of Front-Page Stories for the Two Papers: 113 (19.7% of total stories)
Total Number of Front-Page Stories about Americans and/or U.S.: 47 (41.6% of total front-page stories)

Intense interest in Ethiopia

In focusing on other countries (not including England), Padmore wrote more about Ethiopia than anywhere else, which was not surprising because of the heightened interest in the black press in the country in 1935 when it was invaded by Italy. Emperor Selassie was forced to flee into exile in England a year later but he returned to Ethiopia in 1941 when British forces, with the help of Ethiopian resistance fighters, captured the capital, Addis Ababa.[37] In his seventy-one stories on the country, Padmore ranged widely, apparently feeling that the readers of the *Courier* and the *Defender*, as well as the editors, had an insatiable interest in everything that happened there. Thus, he discussed such things as: Ethiopia's recovery from the Italian occupation, including a reorganization of the government into a constitutional, democratic monarchy; its attempt to decrease illiteracy while becoming more modern; its training of troops to fight under the Free French in Europe; its desire after the war to have the Italian colony of Eritrea, which would give it an outlet to the Red Sea; and its growing friendliness with Russia.[38]

Not surprisingly because of his background, Padmore's articles continually promoted uniting the world's blacks. In 1942, for example, he pointed out to Ayela Gabre, the Ethiopian minister to Great Britain, that Italian fascists 'and their black stooges in America' were telling U.S. blacks that Ethiopians did not think of themselves as black and wanted nothing to do with American blacks. 'Professor Gabre emphatically denied the canards, [which were] seeking to divide and undermine the solidarity between the peoples of Africa and their descendents in the Western Hemisphere', wrote Padmore. 'Please convey to the colored people of America my greetings and let them know that Emperor Haile Selassie and his people appreciate all they have done for Abyssinia'. And then, in a demonstration of how the black press sometimes abruptly shifted into an editorial mode in news stories, Padmore continued, 'When the war is over and the colored races settle down to rebuilding a new world order from Nazism and fascist imperialism, American Negroes desiring to settle in Africa will find a warm welcome in Ethiopia.'³⁹ It was just one of numerous times that he used the word 'imperialism'.

Besides Ethiopia, Padmore wrote extensively about blacks from other countries, many of whom were in Africa. Those countries, which had ten or more of his articles focused on them, included: South Africa (thirty-one stories); India (twenty-seven stories); Liberia (twelve stories); Russia (eleven stories); and French Equatorial Africa, the Gold Coast and Nigeria (ten stories apiece). In addition, he occasionally wrote about Algeria, the Belgian Congo, British Guiana, Canada, China, Kenya, New Zealand, Senegal, Sierra Leone, Tunisia and Uganda. Finally, he frequently wrote about the countries that made up the West Indies, treating them usually as a group in his sixty-one stories about that region.

Depending on the country that Padmore was writing about, the tone of the articles could differ radically. Those about the British colony of South Africa, for example, were frequently critical. In August 1942, following heavy losses by white South African troops in the fighting in Libya, he noted in the *Pittsburgh Courier* that there was a demand to end the long-standing ban against arming native non-Europeans in the country. He speculated that if such 'prejudice' could be overcome, an army of 500,000 Zulus and Bantus could be raised quickly.⁴⁰

Towards the end of the war, Padmore covered the escalation of problems between whites and blacks in racially tense South Africa. In November 1944, after a black was hit and killed by a streetcar driven by a white man, a riot erupted in Johannesburg with 2,000 blacks throwing stones, which stopped traffic, and 700 whites beating up blacks, destroying property and burning down the offices of the *Bantu World*, the largest black newspaper in Africa. Several hundred white police finally restored order but the riot resulted in $50,000 of damage and the death of more than 100 people. Padmore noted in the *Defender* that the incident involving the streetcar killing the black, along with bus fares that recently had been substantially increased for blacks, making them pay more than whites, resulted in a boycott of the city's bus system by more than 500,000 blacks in December. Thus, rather than walk as much as eighteen miles to work each day, many simply stayed home. This, in turn, led to complaints from numerous white housewives, who now had to do their own shopping, cooking and housework, and white industrialists, who were alarmed by a sharp drop in their cheap black workforce. Then, in January 1945, 10,000 blacks in Johannesburg staged a sit-down strike against all of the municipal transport lines, resulting in even further losses of workers in war plants and more complaints to the government from the plant owners. Finally in February, the blacks ended their strike when the government agreed to meet their demands for reduced fares. Padmore noted the *Johannesburg Daily Mail* ran an editorial headlined 'Common Sense *Wins*'.[41]

In contrast to his numerous articles that criticized South Africa and its treatment of blacks, he was far more positive – and clearly naïve – about the treatment of blacks in Russia, which was particularly interesting because of his expulsion from the Communist Party. In October 1942, he noted that large numbers of people of colour were serving willingly in the military.

> The explanation of this desire of the darker races to defend the Russian homeland is simple. There are no second rate citizens in the Soviet Union. The Uzebeks, Kazakhs, Tartars, and other Asiatic peoples are defending their mother, not their stepmother.
>
> Aristocracy of color obtains nowhere throughout the Soviet homeland. Racial discrimination is considered a criminal offense. The equality of the rights of citizens of the USRR [*sic*], irrespective of race or nationality in all spheres of life, is a maxim, rigorously applied.
>
> The Soviet constitution handles this problem in very direct and plain language. There is no need for long and complicated interpretations by the identical courts of the Soviet constitution to protect the rights of their racial minorities [...].
>
> The Soviet attitude on color or race is therefore a irect [*sic*] contradiction to that which exists in most Christian countries where colored people may be insulted with impunity.
>
> It is not without reason then why colored Asiatic races are fighting with so much fanaticism against Hitlerite bandits. They realize that a Nazi victory would mean enslavement.[42]

In January 1943, Padmore again praised the Russian army for having 'no racial distinctions' with everyone serving together amicably despite their race or colour or creed. Like in many of his articles, imperialism bubbled up: 'But it does demonstrate most clearly that once imperialism has been abolished and people have been granted the right of self determination with economic, political and social equality and have become integrated into the body politic, their loyalty is not only absolute but they fight with a fanaticism which can only be the mark of a free man'.[43]

Padmore constantly praised black, non-American soldiers. For example, he noted in 1943 that a Maori soldier from New Zealand had posthumously received the Victoria Cross, Great Britain's highest military honour, for his 'gallantry and leadership' while fighting in Tunisia. Lieutenant Koana Nivakiwa Ngarimu led his platoon through intense enemy fire to the top of a hill, and then, despite being wounded twice, he and his men fought off a number of counter attacks by Germans and Italians throughout the night. Finally running out of ammunition, and with only two of his platoon left, he defiantly threw rocks at the enemy as it attacked again and killed him. 'Some of the wounded enemy testified to Ngarimu's outstanding courage and fortitude', wrote Padmore.[44]

Also in 1943, he wrote about a Gurkha from India who received the Victoria Cross for successfully leading his company, despite being wounded three times, in a successful assault against a heavily fortified Japanese position in Burma. Then, in that same year, there was the Gold Coast sergeant who saw two Americans crash in their burning airplane into the ocean. He quickly gathered a black crew, paddled out to the plane in a canoe and saved the two badly burned airmen, who were taken to a hospital. Also praised were black troops from French Equatorial Africa, who were among the first to enter Paris when it was liberated in 1944 and who slogged through neck-deep snow a year later to become the first Allied troops to enter Hitler's alpine retreat at Berchtesgaden. 'To celebrate the occasion', wrote Padmore, 'Africans collected the specially gold-bound copies of *Mein Kampf* from what remained of Hitler's library, which they intend to take back to Africa to show their countrymen what the so-called "semi-apes" had done to the "superior master race"'. He said the news of their entry into Berchtesgaden caused great delight among London blacks, particularly those from Africa.[45]

Black civilians also were praised by Padmore for their contributions to the war effort. In 1943, he noted that a Royal Air Force plane had made a forced landing on the slopes of Mount Kenya in East Africa. About 150 Meru tribesmen voluntarily worked for four weeks, hacking out a mile of heather and bush as they raced frantically against the approaching rainy season. They finally were able to push the plane over the rough road to a field, where they 'stamped and danced for hours' to level an improvised runway before the plane took off only hours before torrential rains came.[46]

As the war rolled on, one thing was a constant in Padmore's articles in the *Pittsburgh Courier* and the *Chicago Defender*: change was unquestionably coming for the world's blacks. A lead of an article in February 1943 stated succinctly what he hammered home time and again: 'Africans have been asleep a long time but they are now waking. They are no longer willing to continue to bear uncomplainingly the white man's burden'.[47] Three months later, he noted that South African leaders were warning the British government that there would be trouble after the war with blacks if some of their inequities, such as segregation both in jobs and where they could live, were not abolished. 'It is pointed out that Africans now serving with the United Nations forces in North Africa and the Middle East, having come into contact with democratic elements in these places, and conscious of their contribution to the victory over the Axis, will no longer be prepared to tolerate existing economic, political and social conditions so long imposed upon them', he wrote.[48] Then, in December 1944, he said that blacks throughout the world were 'marching forward', resolutely 'determined not to be ruled by the old gang representing reactionary big business and the crypto-fascists'.[49]

Because Padmore was a British citizen from one of the colonies, it was not surprising that he particularly focused on the possibility of post-war changes for blacks in the country's colonies. As early as September 1942, he wrote an exceptionally long story in the *Chicago Defender* about how blacks in the colonies were hoping for 'emancipation'.[50] A year later, he wrote a three-part series for the paper, titled 'Africa and the Peace', with headlines that told the story: 'Imperialism Groomed for Comeback at Peace Table', 'U.S.–British Partnership in Colonies Post-War Aim' and 'Dark Continent Stirring with Upsurge for Freedom'.[51]

These types of articles became even more pronounced in 1945 as Padmore almost totally abandoned writing about Americans and the U.S. In the final four-and-a-half months of the European war, he wrote eighty articles for the *Pittsburgh Courier* and the *Chicago Defender*, and all but seven of them (8.8 per cent) were about non-Americans or other countries. Furthermore, fifteen of those stories ran on the front page and none of them were about Americans or the U.S. Instead, he was looking forward to the first United Nations' conference in April and how blacks other than in the U.S. might be affected. In March, he wrote on the front page of the *Courier*:

> The post-war status of dependent areas in Africa and Asia, largely occupied by black, brown and yellow peoples, is scheduled to become one of the most important and controversial issues with which delegates [...] will be forced to grapple.
>   Succinctly, the big, white colonial powers are going to have to invent a device which will enable them to use and exploit their colored brothers and at the same time permit these colored peoples to feel that they are 'free and equal'.[52]

By late April, however, he admitted that political officials in London believed the position of blacks in the colonies would 'remain fundamentally the same after the war' even though some reforms would take place. The headline in the *Chicago Defender* summed up his feelings perfectly: 'Future Gloomy for African Natives; Europe Wants Status Quo Unchanged'.[53]

Conclusion

In assessing the significance of Padmore's World War II articles in the *Pittsburgh Courier* and the *Chicago Defender*, it clearly was a case of him being in the right place at the right time for both himself and the newspapers.

Black papers were an advocacy press, which continuously pushed hard for more rights for blacks, while playing up injustices, and they would take victories wherever they could get them. The latter point was particularly stressed in a 1986 study which found that praise for black women workers increased substantially in the *Courier* in 1942 as they streamed into U.S. war plants and became 'Rosie the Riveter' just like white women. 'Even a cursory reading of the [*Courier*] indicates that it eagerly played up any Black gains in 1942, no matter how small, and it would have been willing to bury the myth of male dominance, at least temporarily, if this furthered the Black cause', the study concluded.[54] In looking for gains during the war, it was easy for a black paper to see that a non-U.S. black doing something praiseworthy in South Africa or in the Gold Coast or in Tunisia or in Russia or in Ethiopia, whether in the military or as a civilian, was noteworthy. A victory was a victory was a victory in the eyes of the black papers, and they were quite willing to take every one of them and play them up, knowing their readers would be interested. Furthermore, the editors looked at black injustices outside the U.S. in the same way. Mistreatment of blacks anywhere was important because it subtly hurt all people of colour worldwide, whether it was in India or in Africa or in the West Indies or in Great Britain or in the U.S. As Padmore came to believe in the latter part of the 1920s: 'All colored peoples remained down or all went up [as a group]'.[55] While the editors were clearly more concerned, as they should have been, with black Americans than blacks elsewhere because the former made up their readership, all injustices were important because it kept up the drum beat of equality.

All of this is something that historians of black newspapers have failed to realize. They have been so focused on what the U.S. black papers wrote about American blacks that they have not noticed the large number of articles about non-U.S. blacks and other countries that ran in World War II. The stories were there, often on the front pages, and yet historians have been guilty of tunnel vision. Only by broadening their focus and paying attention to everything that was written in the newspapers can mass-communication historians present an accurate picture of what the black press was really about during the war. So far, that has not happened but this chapter is a step in that direction.

As for Padmore, he was in desperate need of money before World War II and falling back on journalism, which had been his first full-time job after high school in Trinidad, was an easy way to make it. What may have surprised him was that the black newspapers were quite pleased to have him write largely about the subject that had become an obsession with him even before the war began: freeing people of colour from imperialism, particularly as it was practiced by Great Britain in its colonies. While he obviously could not totally ignore the growing numbers of U.S. black troops in Britain, an examination of his bylined stories shows that was never his major interest. On the *Pittsburgh Courier*, 40.8 per cent of his stories in 1942 were about Americans or the U.S., but in the next three years, the percentages declined to 21.7 per cent, 19.2 per cent and 8.1 per cent, respectively. The figures were similar on the *Chicago Defender*: 50 per cent in 1942, followed by 21.2 per cent, 22 per cent and 9.3 per cent, respectively.

What essentially occurred during World War II was that Padmore was gearing up for the post-war period, when he emerged as a leading figure in the Pan–Africa movement and ended up as a personal political advisor to Prime Minister Kwame Nkrumah in Ghana before dying in 1959 of hepatitis.[56] His writing in the two largest and most influential U.S. black papers during the war gave him a powerful and influential platform from which to speak – their combined circulation was more than 500,000 each week – and both he and the papers benefited greatly as they used each other to their advantage. Thus, he continued to elevate his reputation as one of the leading anti-imperialist leaders, and the papers could boast, as the *Courier* did in 1943, that it had a regular correspondent who 'strikes instant response with people who read, the world over.'[57] That was not an idle boast, at least with black readers, and it was an important one for a paper seeking avidly to increase its circulation and influence.

Therefore, the relationship between Padmore and the black press in World War II can no longer be ignored, either by mass-communication historians or African American studies historians. To do so has been a significant mistake by historians in both fields.

Notes

1   W. Randy Dixon, 'Calling: George Padmore, London Reporter', *Pittsburgh Courier*, 31 July 1943, 5.
2   For a list of the war correspondents for black newspapers see J. D. Stevens, 'From the back of the foxhole: black correspondents in World War II', *Journalism Monographs*, 27 February 1973 (1973), 10. The only white correspondent for the black press was Haskell Cohen, who covered Italy for several months for the *Pittsburgh Courier*, and the only woman was Elizabeth Murphy Phillips, who

went to London in 1945 for the *Baltimore Afro–American* but only wrote five stories before returning to the U.S. See J. D. Stevens, 13. J. C. Broussard & S. C. Cooley, 'Ebony's Era Bell Thompson Travels the World to Tell the True Story', *American Journalism*, 26 (2009), 8.

3   J. D. Stevens, 10. Homer Smith, who was a pool reporter in Moscow for black newspapers, was the only other black press war correspondent from 1941 to 1945.

4   J. R. Hooker, *Black Revolutionary: George Padmore's Path from Communism to Pan–Africanism* (New York, NY: Frederick A. Praeger, 1967), 48–49.

5   H. Adi & M. Sherwood, *Pan–African History: Political Figures from Africa and the Diaspora Since 1787* (London: Routledge, 2003), 152. P. Fryer, *Staying Power: Black People in Britain Since 1504* (Atlantic Highlands, NJ: Humanities Press, 1984), 336.

6   J. R. Hooker, 62, 85.

7   See J. D. Stevens. L. Finkle, *Forum for Protest: The Black Press During World War II* (Cranbury, NJ: Associated University Presses, 1975), 218.

8   For a discussion of the black press during World War II, see P. S. Washburn, *A Question of Sedition: The Federal Government Investigation of the Black Press during World War II* (New York, NY: Oxford University Press, 1986). and L. Finkle.

9   A. Buni, *Robert L. Vann of the Pittsburgh Courier: Politics and Black Journalism* (Pittsburgh, PA: University of Pittsburgh Press, 1974), 246.

10   J. R. Hooker, 2–4.

11   See J. R. Hooker, 4–6. and W. Randy Dixon, 31 July 1943, 5. George was his father-in-law's first name and Padmore was a friend's last name.

12   J. R. Hooker, 4–9.

13   J. R. Hooker, 14–20.

14   J. R. Hooker, 27.

15   J. R. Hooker, 30–32. and P. Fryer, 335.

16   J. R. Hooker, 42–49. W. Randy Dixon, 31 July 1943, 5. H. Adi & M. Sherwood, 153–154.

17   J. R. Hooker, 55, 57, 59.

18   J. R. Hooker, 54. H. Adi & M. Sherwood, 154.

19   W. Randy Dixon, 31 July 1943, 5.

20   J. R. Hooker, 62.

21   D. Reynolds, *Rich Relations: The American Occupation of Britain, 1942–1945* (New York, NY: Random House, 1995), 216–217, 227.

22   George Padmore, 'London Hails Arrival of American Negro Troops', *Chicago Defender*, 1 August 1942, 2.

23   George Padmore, 'Defender Man Cables Talks with Troops', *Chicago Defender*, 15 August 1942, 1.

24   George Padmore, 'London Hospitality Is Rebuke to South, Says Defender Writer', *Chicago Defender*, 22 August 1942, 1.

25   George Padmore, 'Harlem Goes to England and Staid Britons Enjoy U.S. Soldiers' Ball', *Chicago Defender*, 29 August 1942, 1.

26   George Padmore, '"Army Officers Worried, But No Problem Exists"! – Padmore', *Pittsburgh Courier*, 29 August 1942, 1, 4. See also George Padmore, 'Authorities Act to Avoid Race Friction among Troops in London', *Pittsburgh Courier*, 22 August 1942, 1.

27   George Padmore, 'Negro Troops in England Break Records as They Supply the AEF', *Pittsburgh Courier*, 19 September 1942, 1.

28   George Padmore, 'Doughboys Collect $111,516 for British War Orphans', *Chicago Defender*, 25 September 1943, 13. George Padmore, 'Hero Saves Lives as Bombs Peril British Town', *Chicago Defender*, 20 January 1945, 2. George Padmore, 'U.S. Soldiers Rescue a Britisher from Drowning', *Chicago Defender*, 31 October 1942, 3. George Padmore, 'Cited for Rescue of British Girl', *Chicago Defender*, 14 August 1943, 1. George Padmore, 'British Town Gives $2100 to Hero for Rescue', *Chicago Defender*, 16 September 1944, 1.

29   George Padmore, 'British Ack-Ack Guns Manned by Colored Troops', *Pittsburgh Courier*, 6 March 1943, 1. George Padmore, '"Negroes in Forefront of African Invasion" – Padmore', *Pittsburgh Courier*, 12 November 1942, 1. George Padmore, 'Nazi Bombs Blast Racial Prejudice in Big Convoy', *Chicago Defender*, 26 December 1942, 1.

30   George Padmore, '"Negroes in Forefront of African Invasion" – Padmore', *Pittsburgh Courier*, 12 November 1942, 1.

31   George Padmore, 'Nazi Bombs Blast Racial Prejudice in Big Convoy', *Chicago Defender*, 26 December 1942, 1.

32   George Padmore, 'Blame Army for Racial Feud Abroad', *Pittsburgh Courier*, 5 August 1944, 1. Other stories about such problems included: George Padmore, 'Padmore Told Discrimination Being Ousted', *Pittsburgh Courier*, 28 November 1942, 1. George Padmore, 'British Town Councillors Blast Dance Hall Color Bar', *Chicago Defender*, 12 February 1944, 11. George Padmore, 'Britishers Hit Jim Crow Bar on Weekly Dances', *Chicago Defender*, 5 August 1944, 11. For a discussion of the problems posed by the build up of black U.S. troops in Great Britain, see D. Reynolds, 216–230.

33   D. Reynolds, 232.

34   George Padmore, 'Soldier's Death Sentence Shock to British Public', *Pittsburgh Courier*, 17 June 1944, 1, 4. George Padmore, 'Doubt Guilt of Soldier Facing Death in England', *Chicago Defender*, 17 June 1944, 1. George Padmore, 'Eisenhower Reprieves Soldier Facing Death', *Chicago Defender*, 24 June 1944, 3. D. Reynolds, 234–237.

35   George Padmore, 'Mixed Offspring Create New Social Problem in England',
      Pittsburgh Courier, 18 November 1944, 4. George Padmore, 'Negro Babies of
      White Mothers Give Big Headache to Britons', *Chicago Defender*, 18 November
      1944, 1. George Padmore, 'British Officials Silent on Mixed Illegitimate Children',
      Pittsburgh Courier, 9 December 1944, 2.

36   For example, see George Padmore, 'American Red Cross Says "No Jim Crow in
      Britain"', *Chicago Defender*, 19 September 1942, 1. George Padmore, 'Red Cross
      Workers Win British Public', *Pittsburgh Courier*, 24 October 1942, 12. George
      Padmore, 'Red Cross Girls Oversea [*sic*] Win Hearts of Britishers', *Chicago
      Defender*, 21 November 1942, 1. George Padmore, 'Red Cross "Policy" Aimed
      at Race Troops', *Pittsburgh Courier*, 19 December 1942, 1. George Padmore, '8
      More Red Cross Men in London', *Chicago Defender*, 19 December 1942, 13.
      George Padmore, 'New London Red Cross Club Under All Race Management',
      Pittsburgh Courier, 30 January 1943, 1. George Padmore, 'Open Swank London
      Club for Negro Doughboys', *Chicago Defender*, 30 January 1943, 3. George
      Padmore, 'Archbishop Spellman at London Red Cross Club', *Chicago Defender*,
      3 April 1943, 3. George Padmore, 'Smith on Red Cross Board', *Chicago Defender*,
      27 November 1943, 20. George Padmore, 'More Red Cross Workers Arrive in
      Great Britain', *Chicago Defender*, 4 March 1944, 4.

37   'Ethiopia' and 'World War II', in L. L. Bram, W. H. Hendelson & J. L. Morse
      (Eds), *Funk & Wagnalls New Encyclopedia (1971–1972)* (New York, NY: Funk
      & Wagnalls, 1975), vol. 9, 194; vol. 25, 276.

38   George Padmore, 'Ethiopia Gets Entirely New Constitution', *Chicago Defender*,
      19 December 1942, 1. George Padmore, 'Selassie Plans "New Deal" Program for
      Abyssinia', *Chicago Defender*, 7 August 1943, 7. George Padmore, 'Haile Selassie
      Submits Reconstruction Plan', *Pittsburgh Courier*, 28 August 1943, 8. George
      Padmore, 'Ethiopians Join French for Invasion', *Pittsburgh Courier*, 3 June 1944,
      1. George Padmore, 'Ethiopia Seeks Red Aid to Get Eritrea Outlet', *Chicago
      Defender*, 5 August 1944, 1. George Padmore, 'Great Britain Calls Conference
      as Russia "Courts" Abyssinia', *Pittsburgh Courier*, 12 August 1944, 2.

39   George Padmore, 'Padmore Conveys Selassie's Greetings to Negro America'.
      Pittsburgh Courier, 17 October 1942, 8.

40   George Padmore, '"Arm Natives Against Axis" Plea Grows', *Pittsburgh Courier*,
      8 August 1942, 2.

41   George Padmore, 'Mob Burns Newspaper Office in Africa Riot', *Chicago Defender*,
      11 November 1944, 1. George Padmore, 'Half Million Join Africa Bus Boycott',
      Chicago Defender, 9 December 1944, 2. George Padmore, 'Smuts' Commission
      Proves Race Riots', *Pittsburgh Courier*, 9 December 1944, 9. George Padmore,
      'South Africans Strike Against Trolley Lines', *Chicago Defender*, 13 January 1945,

1. George Padmore, 'South Africans Win Two-Month Transit Strike', *Chicago Defender*, 3 February 1945, 18.

42 George Padmore, 'Colored Soldiers Help Russia Hold Stalingrad', *Chicago Defender*, 31 October 1942, 13.

43 George Padmore, 'Colored Soviet Armymen [*sic*] Command Assault Regiments in New Offensive', *Chicago Defender*, 16 January 1943, 5.

44 George Padmore, 'Displayed Unusual Courage in Fight', *Pittsburgh Courier*, 15 May 1943, 14.

45 George Padmore, 'Soldier Wins Highest British Award for Bravery', *Chicago Defender*, 30 October 1943, 12. George Padmore, 'May Decorate African Who Saved U.S. Airmen', *Pittsburgh Courier*, 27 February 1943, 4. George Padmore, 'Negro Troops Lead March into Paris', *Chicago Defender*, 2 September 1944, 1. George Padmore, 'Negro Troops Take Hitler's Alps Hideout', *Chicago Defender*, 12 May 1945, 1.

46 George Padmore, 'African Natives Save RAF Plane Downed in Jungle', *Chicago Defender*, 10 April 1943, 8.

47 George Padmore, 'Africans Refuse to Still Bear White Man's Burden', *Chicago Defender*, 6 February 1943, 9.

48 George Padmore, 'S. Africa Leader Sees Race Conflict If Native Don't Win Rights after War', *Chicago Defender*, 15 May 1943, 9.

49 George Padmore, 'Natives Gain Island Power', *Pittsburgh Courier*, 23 December 1944, 5.

50 George Padmore, 'The Atlantic Charter and the British Colonies', *Chicago Defender*, 29 September 1942, Sec. 3, 9.

51 George Padmore, 'Imperialism Groomed for Comeback at Peace Table', *Chicago Defender*, 18 September 1943, 13. George Padmore, 'U.S.–British Partnership in Colonies Post-War Aim', *Chicago Defender*, 25 September 1943, 13. George Padmore, 'Dark Continent Stirring with Upsurge for Freedom', *Chicago Defender*, 2 October 1943, 9.

52 George Padmore, 'Colonial Issue on 'Frisco Agenda', *Pittsburgh Courier*, 24 March 1945, 1.

53 George Padmore, 'Future Gloomy for African Natives; Europe Wants Status Quo Unchanged', *Chicago Defender*, 28 April 1945, 5.

54 P. S. Washburn, 'The *Pittsburgh Courier* and Black Workers in 1942', *Western Journal of Black Studies*, 10 (1986), 113, 115.

55 W. Randy Dixon, 31 July 1943, 5.

56 P. Fryer, 336. H. Adi & M. Sherwood, 156–157.

57 W. Randy Dixon, 31 July 1943, 5.

STEVEN M. MINER

'We Must Never Make Peace with Evil': Vasilii Grossman and a Writer's Conscience in a War of Totalitarians

In the waning days of the Soviet Union, one of Mikhail Gorbachev's advisors was asked what positive achievements remained of the Soviet era. After thinking for a moment, he answered quietly: 'we defeated the Nazis'. The Revolution, Civil War and 'War Communism' had been disastrous; the New Economic Policy (NEP) of the 1920s had simply been capitalism by another name; Stalin's crash industrialization and collectivization had cost millions of lives, and his purges and repressions many millions more; in the post-war period, Nikita Khrushchev's ideas were officially dismissed as 'hare-brained schemes'; and the Leonid Brezhnev era was labelled the period of 'stagnation'. Throughout the Soviet era, and continuing under Vladimir Putin, the victory over Hitler remains the iconic moment for modern Russia; the Red Army soldier not only saved Russia itself but also he rescued Europe and even civilization. Any attempt to question the purity of this triumph, or to pose awkward questions about the behaviour or motivation of Soviet soldiers, encounters a wall of official and even popular hostility.[1]

The myth of the noble Soviet *frontovik* (front-line soldier) grows directly out of wartime accounts and has been given new life by Western authors aware of the debt the world owes the average Red Army serviceman: at no time during World War Two did the Western Allies face more than a quarter of the Wehrmacht (unified armed forces of Germany) and it was the Red Army that, in Winston Churchill's memorable phrase, 'tore the guts out' of the Nazi invaders. In the face of such an achievement, gained at an astronomical cost of the lives of more than 8 million soldiers and almost 20 million civilians, the Red Army lost approximately 8 million

– to many it almost seems bad manners to delve too deeply into the dark side of the Soviet soldier.

Perhaps more than any other Soviet writer, Vasilii Grossman helped to create the myth of the righteous Soviet warrior, although he later regretted the myth's destructive power, tried to set the record straight and to some extent fell victim to it. Less well known to wartime Western readers than his contemporaries Ilya Ehrenburg and Alexei Tolstoi, within the Soviet Union itself and especially among servicemen, Grossman was the most admired war correspondent. Unlike others who filed their stories safely from the rear, Grossman was frequently at the front, he spoke often and easily with generals and privates, and none of his counterparts could describe more vividly and convincingly the life and thoughts of the *frontovik*. His writing continues to draw admirers: his American biographers make the extraordinary claim that 'The fiction and reports that he wrote during the war years constitute the most significant body of work by a writer on the Eastern Front, *or indeed any other front* during the war'.[2]

Although there is much to admire in Grossman's wartime reporting, Stalinist realities simply did not allow him to write the full truth even when he wanted to. Grossman laboured under a regime of police-state terror and censorship even more comprehensive than that of the Nazis and almost incomprehensible to those raised in liberal societies. The recent publication of selections from his wartime notebooks, which could never have seen print in the Union of Soviet Socialist Republics (USSR), reveals the yawning chasm between his reporting and the realities of wartime Soviet Union as he and other veterans experienced them.[3] The new availability of Soviet wartime documentation confirms this. Grossman's intentions were certainly the best, and he had more integrity than almost all his fellow Soviet writers, but if wartime reporting is judged not only by its vividness but also by its veracity, then it is hard to sustain the claim that he was a first-rate reporter of the wartime experience. Given the Stalinist context, it could not have been otherwise.

Born in 1905 to Jewish parents in the Ukrainian city of Berdichev, often called the 'Jewish capital of Ukraine', Grossman sought to escape what he saw as the confines of his background by assimilating into the Russian majority. As was commonplace among secular Jews in Ukraine, his family sided with the Bolsheviks during the Revolution and the murderous Civil War that followed, less from belief in the ostensible virtues of Communism than because most of the Bolsheviks' opponents stood for the creation of states based on ethnicity and nationality. In such regimes there would have been little opportunity for Jews, religious or secular. Grossman himself never evinced any genuine enthusiasm for Communism: he never joined the Party, even though it would have advanced his career, and in comparison with most of his contemporaries his writing is refreshingly free from ideological dogma and paeans to the Soviet leadership.

Trained at Moscow State University as a chemist, Grossman detested work in industry and drifted into what under Stalin passed as the bohemian life; soon he aspired to become a writer in the Tolstoian tradition. Like many Russian authors, Grossman viewed fiction writing as, in its essence, a deeply moral calling. Despite his intentions, he proved unable to steer the clear moral course that he set for himself; being caught between the two great totalitarian forces of the twentieth century. Nor was he able to shed his Jewish identity, which was continually thrust upon him, first by the Nazi invasion and the impact of the Holocaust, and later by the Stalinist state, which became more anti-Semitic during and after the war.

Grossman published his first novel before the war[4] and enjoyed some acclaim as a rising talent. Like so many intellectuals during the 1930s, however, he was caught up in the terror: the NKVD[5] arrested a female cousin with whom he lived in Moscow; the uncle who supported him as a child was either shot or died in the camps; his second wife's first husband was arrested, and both she and Grossman were interrogated in the fearsome NKVD headquarters, the Lubianka. During this terrible time, Grossman reacted all too humanly; he did not speak up to defend his cousin and he even put his name to a public call by writers for the execution of the members of the 'Trotskyite–Bukharin conspiracy', knowing them to be victims of a show trial.[6] His own lack of courage, although perhaps understandable, plagued him and would be a recurring theme in his later fiction.

Grossman almost welcomed the announcement of the Nazi invasion: finally, here was a genuine enemy to struggle against, rather than phantom enemies of the people; it also provided an opportunity to wash away the sins of his compromised conscience in a moral crusade that, he hoped, would once and for all unite the Soviet peoples in a genuine shared cause and create what he had always dreamed of: a society where ethnicity no longer determined one's fate. Charged with enthusiasm, Grossman tried to volunteer for the Red Army but was rejected; although only in his thirties, he was overweight, had poor eyesight and was physically unfit, even walking with a cane. His chance to serve came when David Ortenberg, the editor of *Krasnaia zvezda* (*Red Star*), the Red Army newspaper, offered him a position as a correspondent. Others objected to Ortenberg that Grossman had no journalistic experience: 'that's all right', he later recalled replying, 'He knows about people's souls'.[7]

Before heading off to the front, Grossman made a fateful decision. He allowed his second wife to convince him that they lacked sufficient room in their Moscow apartment to take in his mother, who remained in Berdichev. When the Germans captured the city on 7 July 1941, Grossman's mother perished in one of the early Nazi slaughters. Few Soviet civilians could have predicted the swiftness and depth of the Nazi invasion, and most probably Grossman never thought that his mother would fail to evacuate in time; but throughout his life Grossman was consumed by guilt for failing to act promptly. This dreadful event left a lasting mark on all his subsequent work and was one of the central themes of his great novel *Life and Fate*.[8]

Although Grossman was at the front during the great retreat of 1941, he did not publish any reports until December. The reasons for this are obscure. Some of the most memorable passages from his notebooks date from this awful time, when the Red Army was in headlong retreat and it looked as though the Nazis would triumph quickly. Perhaps the answer lies in one episode: the fall of Orel, a city south-west of Moscow. Grossman witnessed the civilian flight from the town, which he described as an 'Exodus! [a] Biblical Exodus!'.[9] His editor later asked him why he had not filed a story on the 'heroic defense' of Orel: 'because there was no defense', he replied.[10]

One thing he certainly could not report was the appalling self-inflicted carnage in the Soviet ranks. In his first wartime speech, Stalin promised 'a ruthless fight against all disorganizers of the rear, deserters, panic-mongers, [and] spreaders of rumors' and ordered all Soviet citizens to 'render [...] rapid aid in all this to our destroyer battalions'. Subsequently, with the Red

Army reeling, he issued his notorious Order no. 270, in which decreed that the families of Red Army officers who fell into German hands would themselves be treated as traitors; families of surrendering private soldiers would lose all state benefits, which, in a time of rationing and widespread starvation, often amounted to a death sentence.[11]

The carnage unleashed by these and other Orders is still not understood by most historians; the number of victims dwarfs corresponding numbers for all the belligerent powers combined and raises important questions about our understanding of the war. Between the Nazi attack and the final assault on Berlin, military tribunals convicted an astonishing 994,000 Red Army men of cowardice, desertion and unauthorized retreat; 157,000 were shot.[12] By way of comparison, the Germans executed 15,000 of their own men, the United States one.[13] As high as this figure is, it represents only a fraction of Soviet citizens put to death by their own government during the war. Many were shot in the field without any pretence of a trial; others perished at the hands of partisan tribunals; still more died from the fire of NKVD 'blocking units' set up behind the front to discourage soldiers from retreating. The NKVD also killed hundreds of thousands of civilians, as well as presiding over the vast GULag (Glavnoe Upravlenie Lagerei: Main Administration of Corrective Labour Camps), in which more than 900,000 people died during the war.[14]

Executions reached their horrific peak during 1941 and 1942, as the chart below on court-imposed death sentences shows (total executions: 236,216). Although the number of victims drops off sharply by 1945, the figures remain astronomical: by way of comparison, there have been fewer executions in American history, since English settlers first arrived in 1608, than the Soviets inflicted in 1945 alone – and the war ended mid-year.[15] Death sentences are only the most dramatic punishment meted out. Soviet society was unprecedentedly punitive: in the four years of war, special courts sentenced 16,017,854 people to prison or execution.[16] This amounts to nearly ten per cent of the pre-war population of 179,000,000; but it should be remembered that between 60 and 65 million Soviet citizens were under German occupation for much of this period and were thus beyond the reach of Soviet law.[17]

Death Sentences by Special Courts

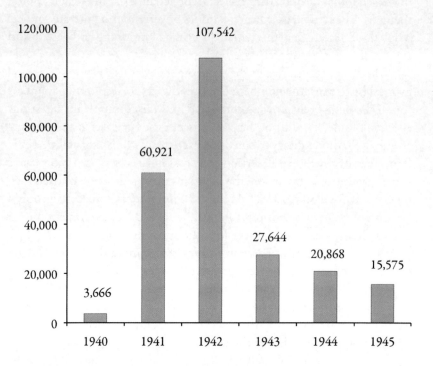

Furthermore, 27 million Soviets died at the hands of the invading Nazis. In short, a vast proportion of Soviet citizens suffered repression in one form or another. Grossman could not, of course, report any of this, although as his notebooks show he saw a great deal more than he could publish. With his novelist's eye he caught the telling detail, as when he recorded how light-heartedly Soviet officers could hand down death sentences.

> After dinner, the military prosecutor arrives from 50th Army [rear] headquarters. We are all drinking tea with raspberry jam while the prosecutor reports on pending cases: cowards, deserters – among them Pochepa, an old major – [also] cases of peasants accused of [circulating] German propaganda. [General] Petrov pushes his glass aside. In the corner of the document, he approves the death sentence in red capitals

written in a small childish hand. The prosecutor reports on another case: a woman who urged peasants to greet Germans with bread and salt. 'And who is she?' Petrov asks. 'An old maid', the prosecutor laughs. Petrov laughs, too. 'Well, since she's an old maid, I'll replace it with ten years.' And he writes in the new sentence. Then they drink more tea. The prosecutor says goodbye. 'Remind them to send my samovar from headquarters,' Petrov tells him. 'I'm used to having it around'.[18]

Although he was completely devoted to the anti-Nazi cause, Grossman understood that many ordinary citizens loathed their government, given its record of mass repressions, land seizures and anti-religious campaigns. Tragically, many hoped that Hitler would improve their lives. He recounted spending a night in the home of three Ukrainian women, who clearly believed that the Germans would reopen their churches and restore their smallholdings.

'Is it true that Germans believe in God?' [one asked]. Apparently, there are many rumors about German [occupation] circulating in the village. 'Starostas are cutting strips of land', and so forth. We spent the whole evening explaining to them what Germans really are. They listened, sighed, exchanged glances, but clearly did not express their secret thoughts. The old woman said quietly: 'we've seen what's been, we'll see what comes'.[19]

In this tragic situation, Grossman continued to hope that the shared struggle against the Nazis would forge social unity and perhaps even moderate the regime following victory. He thought he had found this elusive mystical unity at Stalingrad among the *frontoviki*, whom he idealized. 'The front', he wrote, represents 'the holiness of Russian death, the rear is the sin of Russian life. At the front, there is patience and resignation, submission to unthinkable hardships. This is the patience of a strong people. This is the patience of the great Army. The greatness of the Russian soul is incredible'.[20] At Stalingrad, Grossman demonstrated genuine courage, crossing the Volga under German fire and aerial attack to interview commanders and privates, remaining in the city for a week; he did not resort to pasting together stories while safely housed east of the river as other correspondents did.[21] During this time, he promoted the stories of the sniper heroes Anatoly Chekhov and Vasily Zaitsev, whose heavily romanticized story was later made into the Hollywood movie *Enemy at the Gates*.

Grossman first established his national reputation as a correspondent in these dispatches, receiving the ultimate honour of having his work published on the front page of *Pravda*. Even at this peak, however, he could not publish anything like the full truth. He wrote that 'Faith in one another knit the entire Stalingrad front from Commander-in-Chief to soldiers in the ranks and file'. His biographers have rather uncritically accepted such claims about spontaneous cohesion in Red Army ranks during the battle, writing that the siege was 'too hot for the NKVD and their minions', who left the city 'very soon after the Germans entered the city's outskirts'.[22] In fact, the NKVD's 10th division remained on the right bank and was ground to pieces in the fighting; nor did other police units suspend their work. As the reports from the NKVD's Lavrenty Beria to Stalin show, blocking units continued to operate regularly, arresting and shooting retreating soldiers, and executing officers deemed to be *pered stroem* (cowards) in front of the ranks.[23]

Although Grossman could not write about such terrible things, he showed more integrity than some of his better-known colleagues when it came to pushing certain propaganda themes. In August 1942, during the initial phase of the Stalingrad campaign, Stalin issued another murderous decree: Order No. 227, which promised to punish troops withdrawing without orders and created *strafal'nye battaliony* (punishment battalions) to employ soldiers convicted of offences in the most deadly tasks.[24] More than 400,000 servicemen would lose their lives in these units; so lethal was service in their ranks that such men were known as *smertniki*, roughly translated as 'dead men walking'.[25] At this time, when the Kremlin was clearly pushing a hard line against waverers, Grossman's editor asked him to write a story about an evil deserter; to his credit Grossman declined. Alexei Tolstoi was less fastidious, penning a story about a deserter killing a young girl.[26]

Nor did Grossman stoop to hate propaganda; although he certainly detested the Nazis and all their works. Perhaps because of his belief in internationalism, or maybe his sensitive understanding of the compromises he himself had been forced to make under a totalitarian regime, he drew a distinction between the Nazis and ordinary Germans. Notoriously, his more famous colleague Ilya Ehrenburg drew no such line, penning strident articles entitled 'We Hate' and 'Learn to Hate', the latter published on *Pravda*'s front page.[27]

It would seem that, although he could not report everything he saw, Grossman at least tried to write only what he actually did see, not creating stories. However, his resulting stories could be as misleading as actual fabrications, like photographic images where the camera has been carefully sited to record only positive images. Thus, as the Red Army pursued the beaten Wehrmacht westwards, first into the border regions of the USSR and then into Central Europe, Soviet soldiers encountered populations which, although happy to be delivered from the Nazis, were scarcely well disposed to the new occupier. This is not the image one gets in Grossman's reporting: as he entered Poland, he penned a story entitled 'They Have Waited for Us'.[28] Polish peasants were re-emerging from the forests where they had hidden themselves and their livestock from the Germans, Grossman wrote: now they could return to normal civilian life.

> They recognise the moral and political integrity of our troops and the finality of the Red Army's military success, and they have confidence in the Soviet attitude towards the Polish people, based on the principles of respect for their property and their independence.[29]

He asked a peasant, '"Have you been waiting for us?" He answers, weeping: "Jak Boga!" As if for God'.

This probably happened, but it scarcely reported the overall nature of the Polish–Soviet encounter. The Red Army had occupied this region in collaboration with the Nazis from 1939 until 1941; they arrested, exiled and killed hundreds of thousands of Poles, and the new occupation was no less brutal. The NKVD was already conducting a running battle with the Polish Home Army as Grossman wrote this piece, which appeared the day before the Warsaw Uprising broke out.[30] Controversially, Soviet forces would halt at the very edge of the city, would not attempt to supply the insurgents for many weeks and would not allow the Western Allies to do so until most Polish insurgents had been slaughtered.[31]

Nor did the new occupiers show much respect for Polish lives or property. Looting was common, as was rape. The mass rapes Red Army personnel committed in Germany have recently been explored by historians – although Soviet veterans and military historians hotly contest this issue.[32] These outrages have been explained as the result of Soviet soldiers' anger against the people who had attacked and brutalized their own country and people.[33] Almost unknown, however, are the many instances of such crimes against Polish women.[34] Historians have yet to explore another very troubling set of crimes. As the Red Army entered Central Europe, they liberated many Soviet citizens whom the Germans had either lured or taken forcibly to the Reich as labourers, the so-called *Ostarbeiter*. Soviet officialdom viewed these people with great suspicion, imprisoning them in filtration camps and making them prove that they had not collaborated willingly. Most of these unfortunates had suffered tremendously at the hands of the Germans, but their liberators were oftentimes even harsher. More than half of these *Ostarbeiter* were women and many Soviet men regarded them as easy victims. Grossman records several hair-raising instances.

> Two hundred and fifty of our girls were working at the Focke-Wulf plant. The Germans had brought them from Voroshilovgrad, Kharkov, and Kiev. According to the chief of the Army political department, these girls have no clothes, are lice-infested and swollen from hunger. And according to what a man from the Army newspaper said, these girls had been clean and well dressed, until our soldiers came and robbed them blind and took their watches. Liberated Soviet girls often complained about being raped by our soldiers. One girl said to me, crying: 'he was an old man, older than my father'.[35]

Some of these women took refuge with Grossman's fellow war correspondents. Grossman records, 'During the night, we are woken up by screams: one of the correspondents couldn't resist the temptation'.[36]

At the very least, such crimes should cause historians to re-examine their easy assumptions that Red Army misbehaviour resulted from anger against the invader. We now know that Stalin himself was informed in detail about such things, and yet no decree ordering a halt to these outrages, or demanding the punishment of the perpetrators, has ever been uncovered.[37] The rapes and looting continued for many months without respite.

If Grossman's reporting from Poland was problematic, it was also his finest hour. The Nazis sited all their death camps in the east, directly in the path of the Red Army. Grossman was the first war correspondent to visit Treblinka, and his writings about that camp, and on the Holocaust, are among the most moving prose ever written on the subject. Here was the epicentre of Nazi evil and Grossman's writing throbs with outrage: 'in the cruel and terrible time in which our generation has been condemned to live on this earth, we must never make peace with evil. We must never become indifferent to others or undemanding of ourselves'.[38]

Grossman was one of the first people to write about the Holocaust in informed detail: at Treblinka, he interviewed the few survivors, as well as neighbouring Poles and German captives. He also became involved in his most important wartime project: a large-scale work documenting the Holocaust on Soviet territory. Albert Einstein, who was involved with the American branch of the Soviet-run Jewish Anti-Fascist Committee (JAFC), suggested that his Soviet counterparts in the JAFC should assemble first-hand testimony about the Holocaust, as well as essays concerning certain large massacres and the operation of the death camps, and that the resulting material should be published jointly in English and Russian editions. At first, the Soviet editor was Ilya Ehrenburg, whose finely tuned political antennae soon sensed that the project would bring trouble to its collaborators; he backed out, leaving Grossman as the chief editor.

The final product would become known by its shortened title *The Black Book of Soviet Jewry*. Its production did, as Ehrenburg thought, land all associated with the project in trouble.[39] There were two fundamental flaws with the book from the Soviet official point of view: first, it showed that, although all Soviet nationalities had suffered under the Germans, Jewish victimization had been unique; and, second, many non-Jewish Soviet citizens had actively collaborated with the Nazis. The first point contradicted the Soviet dictum that one must not 'divide the dead'; the second revealed the falsity of the claim that Communism had forever ended ethnic oppression in the USSR. The notorious anti-Semite Georgii Aleksandrov, the head of the Directorate of Agitation and Propaganda, reviewed the manuscript and delivered a harsh verdict. The work, he wrote, 'creates a false representation of the true nature of fascism and its organization'.

The idea that the Germans robbed and murdered only the Jews runs throughout the entire book. The reader gets the impression that the Germans went to war against the USSR with the sole purpose of annihilating the Jews. One gets the impression that the Germans simply treated the Russians, Ukrainians, Belorussians, Lithuanians, Latvians, and other nationalities condescendingly. Many reports stressed that in order to avoid death, one simply had to acquire a 'Russian passport' so as not to look like a Jew, etc.[40]

In fact, though the Soviets could never admit this, many non-Jews had collaborated with the Nazi occupiers, either out of conviction or through fear – an option not open to Jews. Perhaps as many as 1.8 million people of Soviet origin served in the German armed forces.[41] The Nazis lacked the personnel to conduct the Holocaust without the participation of locals.[42]

Grossman and his fellow editors made every effort to downplay collaboration but in his account of the murder of Berdichev's Jews – one of them his own mother – Grossman simply could not explain how only a few hundred Germans could, unaided, manage to kill more than 20,000 Jews. He referred to the Nazis' 'henchmen' or to 'traitors'. In one passage, however, he dropped the euphemisms.

> There were shady criminal types who derived material benefit from this great misfortune; greedy for gain they got rich at the expense of the Germans' victims. Policemen, their family members, the German soldiers' mistresses, and other shady types rushed in to rob the vacated apartments. Before the eyes of the living dead they carried off dresses, pillows, and feather mattresses; some of them walked right past the guards and took scarves and knitted woollen jackets off the women and girls awaiting execution.[43]

In unforgettable prose, quite un-Stalinist in its power and pathos, Grossman described the horrific and detailed killing processes at Berdichev and the Treblinka death factory – the first, and in many ways still the most compelling, short narrative of a death-camp's operation ever written. So effective was *The Black Book*, and so uncharacteristically free of Stalinist distortions, that it was admitted into evidence at Nuremberg.

But *The Black Book* never appeared in the USSR and its heresies prevented its publication in Russian until well after the Soviet Union's collapse. Many of its contributors, including Grossman himself, came under suspicion as agents of Anglo–American or Zionist espionage; some were arrested and killed as the post-war Stalinist regime's anti-Semitism became increasingly open. Grossman continued to publish fiction but, just before the death of Stalin, a front-page article in *Pravda* denounced a novel Grossman set during the war. The Soviet press whipped up hysteria against Jews, labelling them 'rootless cosmopolitans' and accusing Jewish doctors of trying to kill the Kremlin leadership.[44] In such circumstances, Grossman feared for his life: with good reason. In January 1953, only a little over a month before Stalin's death, 'Grossman was cajoled into lending his name to a dismal letter condemning the Jewish doctors supposedly involved in the plot, and begging for Stalin's mercy.'[45]

Actually, the incident redounds even less to Grossman's credit. He signed not one but two joint letters by various Soviet authors: one condemned Zionism, which it described as a tool of Anglo–American imperialism and 'wealthy Jews and the evil enemies of the Jewish workers.'[46] The other letter, far from begging Stalin's reprieve for the accused Jewish doctors, demanded precisely the opposite.

> The group of doctor–killers has been unmasked. Yet another of the bloody gambits of Anglo–American imperialism and its Zionist agents, has been smashed. As all Soviet people, we demand the most merciless punishment of the criminals, we are confident that this demand expresses the thoughts and feelings of all laboring Jews and will be unanimously supported by them.[47]

Grossman knew the accused doctors to be innocent and, fortunately, the survivors were quickly exonerated following Stalin's death. Not every writer possessed the moral courage of Boris Pasternak who, in 1937, refused to sign a similar letter praising the execution of leading generals.[48] Grossman's signature on an open letter may have been an all-too-human action, but it fell short of his stirring vow never to collaborate with evil or to act with indifference to others' suffering. Just as in 1938 when he signed the condemnation of the Trotskyite–Bukharin accused, so in 1953, in mortal peril, he behaved little differently than the many Ukranians, Belorussians, Russians and others who had watched the Holocaust unfold in mute, impotent horror, terrified of their Nazi masters.

Grossman's situation was emblematic of the tragic condition of intellectuals under totalitarian regimes: one could either bow down and openly affirm the lies of the Party, or become a martyr, reviled by a public whipped up to a fever pitch, to be shot in some prison cellar or sent to rot in an Arctic labour camp. The martyrdom was rarely solitary: the victim's family and friends might also pay a terrible price. There was no third option: silence was insufficient; the authorities required public affirmation as the price of survival.

In the remaining eleven years of his life, Grossman returned to the war in his fiction, trying to write away the demons that haunted him. His greatest fictional work, *Life and Fate*, set in the Battle of Stalingrad, was an exploration of the terrifying dilemmas facing individuals under totalitarianism; he could also at long last detail the many dark sides of the war that he could not address as a correspondent. He made it clear in the very first pages that there was little difference between the vast slave systems of Hitler and Stalin. His last work, *Forever Flowing*, was set during the murderous collectivization of the farms of the early 1930s, which cost millions of lives.[49] In this book he committed the ultimate sin for a Soviet citizen of the Khrushchev era: he argued that Stalin and his monstrous crimes were a direct outgrowth of the system Lenin created, not some cancerous mutation. When Grossman tried to publish these works, the KGB seized the manuscripts while leaving the author at large – one cannot say free because he effectively became a non-person.

Grossman had finally reached the point occupied by Aleksandr Solzhenitsyn. There never had been a Leninist golden era; Communism had been anti-human and violent from its very inception. During the war, Grossman hoped that, in the process of defeating Hitler, the Soviet regime would moderate – that it would live up to its own humanistic rhetoric. He had helped create the image of the noble Soviet soldier, spotless and pure, rescuing civilization from fascism; he had even believed much of what he wrote, although he knew the whole truth to be much more sordid. In the end, as he tried to tell the truth, first about the Holocaust and later about the war and the man-made famines of the 1930s, he was crushed by the very myths of Soviet perfection that he had helped to foster. He died in 1964, certain that his greatest work would never be published and equally convinced that the system he had served was little better than the one he had helped to vanquish.[50]

Notes

1   See, for example, how the Russian government, and much of popular opinion, objected when the Estonians moved a statue of the 'Soviet Liberator' from the centre of Tallinn; or how Russians (official and private) have responded to the complaints of Poles about the Katyn massacres with charges that Soviet soldiers were also mistreated by Poles during the Russo–Polish War of 1920.

2   J. Garrard & C. Garrard, *The Bones of Berdichev: The Life and Fate of Vasily Grossman* (New York, NY: The Free Press, 1996), 136. [Emphasis added.]

3   A. J. Beevor & L. Vinogradova (Eds and translators), *A Writer at War: Vasily Grossman with the Red Army, 1941–1945* (New York, NY: Random House, Inc., 2005).

4   *Glück auf!* published in Moscow in 1934.

5   Narodnyy Komissariat Vnutrennikh Del: the public and secret police organization.

6   J. Garrard & C. Garrard, 135.

7   A. J. Beevor & L. Vinogradova, 5.

8   V. Grossman, *Life and Fate* (New York, NY: Collins Harvill, 1985).

9   A. J. Beevor & L. Vinogradova, 48.

10 A. J. Beevor & L. Vinogradova, 56.

11 I. V. Stalin, Vystuplenie po radio, 3 July 1941, in *O Velikoi Otechestvennoi voine Sovetskogo Soiuza* (Moscow: Fond 'Kovcheg', 2002), 11–16. I. V. Stalin, 19–22.

12 This figure was first published in English by D. Volkogonov, *The Rise and Fall of the Soviet Empire: Political Leaders from Lenin to Gorbachev* (London: HarperCollins, 1998). Figures later confirmed by A. Iakovlev, *Istoriia I sovremennost: Voina so 'svoiei' armiei. Grazhdanin* No. 2 (2003).

13 W. Wette, *The Wehrmacht: History, Myth, Reality* (Cambridge, MA: Harvard University Press, 2006), 165.

14 The mortality figure for the years 1941–45 is 941,268. This includes the months of both 1941 and 1945 when the USSR was not at war. However, it does not include the numbers of those who were under 'special exile' and other forms of imprisonment not under Gulag administration. A. I. Kokurin & N. V. Petrov (Eds), *GULAG: glavnoe upravlenie lagerei, 1917–1960* (Moscow: Materik, 2002), 441–442. This is half again as high a figure cited by Russian nationalist historians and repeated by Western authors. See R. Overy, *Russia's War: Blood Upon The Snow* (New York, NY: TV Books [Penguin Putnam], 1997), 276.

15 Source for graph is the report of I. Babukhin, 29 December 1955, in I. A. Afanas'ev et al. (Eds), *Istoriia stalinskogo gulaga, konets 1920-kh-pervaia polovina 1950-kh*

godov: Sobranie dokumentov v semi tomakh. 1. Massovye repressii v SSSR (Moscow: Rosspen, 2004), 610. The number of executions in the United States between 1608 and 2002, including colonial times and military sentences, is 15,269. M. W. Espy & J. O. Smykla, *Executions in the U.S. 1608–2002: The Espy File* (Washington, DC: Death Penalty Information Center, 2010), http://www.deathpenaltyinfo. org/executions-us-1608-2002-espy-file

16   I. A. Afanas'ev *et al.*, 619–620.

17   A. Poliakov (Ed.), *Vsesoiuznaia perepis naseleniia 1939 goda: osnovnye itogi* (Moscow: Rossiiskaia akademiia nauk, 1992), 57.

18   A. J. Beevor & L. Vinogradova, 48–49.

19   A. J. Beevor & L. Vinogradova, 38.

20   A. J. Beevor & L. Vinogradova, 95–96.

21   Later, one of the key commanders at Stalingrad, General Vasily Chuikov, accused the press of cowardice for this practice. See A. Werth, *Russia at War, 1941–1945* (London: Barrie & Rockliff, 1964).

22   J. Garrard & C. Garrard, 160.

23   Beria to Stalin, 23 September 1942, in V. N. Khaustov, V. P. Naumov & N. S. Plotnikova (Eds), *Lubianka Stalin I KNVD-NKGB-GUKP "Smersh", 1939–Mart 1946* (Moscow: Fond Demokratiia, 2006).

24   V. V. Katinov, *Ocherki o Velikoi otechestvennoi voine, 1941–1945* (Moscow: Politizdat, 1975), 45–50.

25   A. J. Beevor & L. Vinogradova, 73. A memoir of a commander of one of these battalions exists: N. I. Obryn'ba, *Red Partisan: The Memoirs of a Soviet Resistance Fighter on the Eastern Front* (Barnsley: Pen & Sword Military, 2006).

26   A. J. Beevor & L. Vinogradova, 117.

27   'We Hate', *Soviet War News*, No. 255, 13 May 1942. 'Learn to Hate', *Soviet War News*, No. 262, 21 May 1942.

28   'They Have Waited for Us', *Soviet War News*, No. 923, 21 July 1944.

29   'They Have Waited for Us', *Soviet War News*, No. 923, 21 July 1944.

30   The reports to Stalin about this conflict are contained in A. F. Noskova (Ed.), *NKVD I pol'skoe podpol'e 1944–1945: Po 'Osobym papkam' I. V. Stalina* (Moscow: Institute of Slavic and Balkan Studies, Russian Academy of Sciences, 1994).

31   Historians continue to argue whether Stalin deliberately halted his forces to enable the Nazis to exterminate the Polish nationalists. Richard Overy and Geoffrey Roberts argue that he did not [R. Overy (1997). G. Roberts, *Stalin's Wars: From World War to Cold War, 1939–1953* (New Haven, CT: Yale University Press, 2007)]. Norman Davies makes a passionate and compelling case to the contrary: N. Davies, *Rising '44: The Battle for Warsaw* (New York, NY: Macmillan, 2003).

32 N. Naimark, *The Russians in Germany. A History of the Soviet Zone of Occupation, 1945–1949* (Cambridge, MA: Harvard University Press, 1995).

33 C. Merridale, *Ivan's War: Life and Death in the Red Army, 1939–1945* (New York, NY: Metropolitan Books, 2006).

34 I am grateful to my colleague David Curp for sharing with me the documentary evidence of such crimes.

35 A. J. Beevor & L. Vinogradova, 321.

36 A. J. Beevor & L. Vinogradova, 327.

37 See, for example, Beria to Stalin and Molotov, 17 March 1945, in V. N. Khaustov, V. P. Naumov & N. S. Plotnikova, 502–503.

38 J. Garrard & C. Garrard, 171.

39 The English version published at war's end was incomplete; recently a full English-language version has been published. I. Ehrenburg & V. Grossman (Eds), *The Complete Black Book of Russian Jewry* (New Brunswick, NJ: Transaction Publishers, 2003). [David Patterson, translation and editing.]

40 G. Aleksandrove to A. A. Zhdanov, 3 February 1947, in G. V. Kostrychenko (Ed.), *Gosudarstvennyi antisemitizm v SSSR. Ot nachala do kul'minatsii 1938–1953* (Moscow: MFD–Materik, 2005).

41 General Eisenhower reported shortly after the Battle of the Bulge that five per cent of prisoners in American and British custody were Soviet citizens. The National Archives, Great Britain, 12 January 1945 (wrongly dated 1944), from SHAEF MAIN-1 to AGWAR for combined Chiefs of Staff, signed by Eisenhower. FO 371/50606. The figure is from K. M. Aleksandrov, *Armiia General-Leitenanta A. A. Vlasova, 1944–1945: Materialy K. Istorii Vooruzhennykh Sil KONR* (Saint Petersburg: SPbGU, 2004). A Khrushchev era secret study suggested a lower figure of 800,000. The discrepancy can probably be explained by the latter number not including police units or uniformed logistical personnel.

42 M. Dean, *Collaboration in the Holocaust: Crimes of the Local Police in Belorussia and Ukraine, 1941–1944* (New York, NY: St Martin's Press, 2000).

43 V. Grossman, 'The Murder of the Jews of Berdichev', in I. Ehrenburg & V. Grossman, 16.

44 J. Brent & V. P. Naumov, *Stalin's Last Crime: The Plot Against the Jewish Doctors, 1948–1953* (New York, NY: HarperCollins, 2003). A. Lustiger, *Stalin and the Jews. The Red Book: The Tragedy of the Jewish Anti-Fascist Committee and the Soviet Jews* (New York, NY: Enigma Books, 2002). J. Rubenstein & V. P. Naumov (Eds), *Stalin's Secret Pogrom: The Postwar Inquisition of the Jewish Anti-Fascist Committee* (New Haven, CT: Yale University Press, 2001).

45 Keith Gessen, 'Under Siege: A Beloved Soviet Writer's Path to Dissent', *The New Yorker*, 6 March 2006.

46   Draft letter to the editors of *Pravda*, 20 February 1953, in G. V. Kostrychenko, 474–478.
47   Joint letter to G. Malenkov, 29 January 1953, in G. V. Kostrychenko, 470–473.
48   R. Conquest, *The Great Terror: A Reassessment* (New York, NY: Oxford University Press, 1990), 252.
49   V. Grossman, *Forever Flowing* (New York, NY: Harper & Row, 1972).
50   *Life and Fate* was finally first published in Switzerland in 1980.

PHYLOMENA H. BADSEY

Vera Brittain: War Reporter 1939–1945

Vera Brittain (1893–1970) is best known as the author of the bestselling *Testament of Youth*, a very personal account published in 1933 of her experiences as a nurse with the British Army in the First World War, serving as a Voluntary Aid Detachment (VAD) nurse on the Western Front, in Great Britain and in other countries. In fact she had a long and important career after the First World War, first as a journalist and novelist (*Testament of Youth* was her sixth book to be published), and increasingly from the 1930s onwards as an influential equality feminist and as a Christian pacifist, including her little-recognized role after the Second World War in the early Campaign for Nuclear Disarmament (CND) and the Anti-Apartheid Movement. By the time of her death in 1970 she was internationally recognized as one of the most important British women political activists of her generation.[1]

Between 1923 and 1925, shortly after she came down from Oxford University where she had read first English and then changed to modern history with international relations after her First World War experience, Vera Brittain earned much of her living based in London as a professional journalist, writing articles for a variety of newspapers and magazines. The skills that she learned as a journalist stayed with her throughout her long and prolific writing career, and she never abandoned the practice of writing short articles for newspapers and magazines, both British and overseas, as well as writing full-length books of reportage. By the Second World War she was a well-established popular author and to a large extent financially independent, but the circumstances of the war deprived her of several outlets for her writing talents, leading her to concentrate on reporting the events of the war as she saw them. In particular, she wrote about her own experiences and perceptions as a middle-aged, middle-class mother living in England, who also happened to be an accomplished writer and speaker, and also by then a devout pacifist, something that she had not been in the First World War. Throughout the war, although kept under the occasional notice of the authorities, Vera Brittain was judged to be neither a spy nor a security risk and, although she was forbidden to travel overseas after 1940 (meaning that she did not see her children from July 1940 when they were taken to the United States for safety until October 1943 when they returned), no attempt was made to prevent her writing or publishing. Although Vera Brittain's additional career as a writer and reporter during the Second World War has been almost entirely eclipsed by the fame brought to her by *Testament of Youth* and her nursing career in the First World War, her writing in the Second World War was both insightful and valuable, recording especially the experience of ordinary people on the home front in detail and from a unique perspective. As she wrote in 1941:

> The Front is no distant battlefield to which a small contingent of men and women go forth, leaving family and friends with the sense that they have departed to some remote unimaginable adventure. Today the front line is part of our daily lives; its dugouts and First Aid posts are in every street; its trenches and encampments occupy sections of every city park and every village green. Not only regiments, air squadrons and the crews of ships are holding that line, but the whole nation, its families, households and workers, whether they like it or not. Neither their talents nor their preferences have been consulted by the fate which is upon them.[2]

Vera Brittain's role as a journalist, reporter and pamphleteer during the war also brought her into correspondence and public debate with commentators much better known than her for their views on warfare, including George Orwell and the military critic Basil Liddell Hart.

Vera Brittain became a convinced Christian pacifist relatively late in her life, in her middle forties. In 1936 she fell under the influence of the charismatic Anglican Canon H. R. L. 'Dick' Sheppard, of St-Martin's-in-the-Fields Church in central London (she would later describe herself as 'a Quaker-inclined Anglican married to a Catholic').[3] The different Christian doctrines of Quakerism and Catholicism share much, but in particular the belief that faith is not enough and must be supported by good works, which can be defined as individual actions or conduct carried out as a part of a person's religious faith. Her Christian beliefs took a very distinct and personal form in relation to the outbreak of the Second World War. Unlike many convinced pacifists she had travelled to Germany before the war, including a trip in 1936 as a journalist, and had seen and written about Nazism at first hand. However, her experience of the First World War (including being bombed by German aircraft while on active service at Etaples field hospital in April 1918), together with her understanding of history and political science gained at Oxford, had led her to the belief that a cycle of wars had come into existence in her lifetime: suspicion and hatred between nations bred war, the violence of war led to an unjust peace (such as the Peace of Versailles, of which she was very critical), and this in turn led to another war for the next generation. Vera Brittain saw the only hope for humankind in breaking this cycle of violence through pacifism. On 7 August 1940 she wrote to her close friend and fellow author (Margaret) Storm Jameson, who was extremely critical of her pacifist stance:

> I hate Nazism and *all* forms of totalitarianism as much as you do. The difference between us, I think, is that I have never believed that Nazism could be effectively beaten *by force*, since it is on force that it thrives. I always believed that to fight Nazism by war would simply cause it to spread, first to Europe, then to this country, then America. And so far everything that I expected to happen has happened.[4]

This was the start of a tempestuous correspondence between the two women, which was to end their friendship. In one of her last letters, dated 5 September 1941, Vera Brittain summarized her own pacifist position:

> I fully agree with you that pacifists are mentally dishonest *if* they think Hitler's victory would be a worse blow to humanity than war itself. But I am not mentally dishonest because I *don't* think Hitler's victory would be worse for humanity in the long run (though it might be for this generation) than recurrent war. Basically, though I am not a good Christian, I accept the fundamental Christian belief that the road to spiritual victory is more likely to lie through suffering and defeat than through the victory of material force. And politically I think that we are so unfit for victory as a nation that our victory would merely mean yet again a divided Europe, a forcibly disarmed Germany [and] war all over again in twenty years. I am literally putting my fate in your hands by telling you this, for I know that these views, if publicly expressed with the frankness I have uttered them here, would put me in prison. But they don't

– heaven help me – mean that I *want* to see England defeated and Hitler win [...]
All I *can* do is try to further wartime experiments in Christian living: to endeavour
to 'build Jerusalem' even in the midst of war; to achieve what Evelyn Underhill calls
'the bringing forth of eternal life in the midst of war.' Politically the best I can hope
for is a negotiated peace; but my attitude is really a religious one.[5]

Despite this, Vera Brittain was not what she called an 'absolutist'
pacifist, one who withdrew from society altogether and refused to under-
take any activity that might be connected with the war effort. Her own
Christian pacifism was closely tied up with the idea of 'good works' and
the need to supplement her intense faith with practical action, very often
of a political nature. Either alone or together with her husband, the political scientist George Catlin (known in all her writings as 'G'), she had
visited the United States several times, including her most recent visit in
January 1940 to promote her book *Testament of Friendship*, a memorial
to her late friend Winifred Holtby. At the end of June 1940, after the fall
of France, she and her husband paid for their two children to be sent for
safety to the United States and, like other prominent British intellectuals,
she could easily have followed them. Instead, although largely ostracized
by professional friends and colleagues for most of the war because of her
pacifist stance, she chose to remain in London, working for the Children's
Overseas Reception Board (CORB), a government charity that evacuated
children to the United States, Canada and Australia, joining a Society of
Friends (Quakers) Ambulance Unit as a nurse, working in a mobile canteen
in Bermondsey, and even leading community singing in a shelter in Bow,
another poor district of East London.

As well as her many practical works, Vera Brittain continued to write
and publish on a formidable scale. From October 1939 onwards she wrote,
because of public demand, a weekly private-subscription broadsheet *Letter
to Peace-Lovers*, which lasted until December 1946. In her travels and lectures around the country she wrote about the people and the scenes that she
encountered, either for overseas newspapers or for collection into books,
such as her *England's Hour* about the Battle of Britain and the London
Blitz, published in 1941. The fact that as a pacifist she was allowed to publish her writings without official oversight is a reflection both of the light

touch with which British government control of the press was exercised, and also her own undoubted patriotism and recognition of the nature of the war. In *England's Hour* she described the response to the Blitz.

> In the shelter, a few of the girls hide their faces as they wait. They are not afraid; they are probably thinking of young men, whose lives were before them, falling from the sky and crashing in flames on the ground. The young men of both sides. These orators and broadcasters who treat war as though it were a blood sport and describe it in terms of a cup-tie final, do not represent the spirit of ordinary British men and women who offer cups of tea to crashed German pilots or go out to rescue them in small boats when they fall into the Channel. We stay below the ground for over an hour. The air conditioning plant which is supposed to operate has failed. At the end of half the period, the danger of asphyxiation appears at least as great as the risk of damage by bombs. Silence gradually descends upon the waiting crowds of workers. Fortunately my reports are finished, for the heavy atmosphere has completely obliterated my powers of concentration. Dimly I begin to understand the preliminary sufferings of sailors, English or German, who dive to their death in submarines. The air raid wardens and their Red Cross assistants walk around the basement squirting disinfectant into the air. Just as some of the frailer inhabitants of the shelter begin to look like requiring their assistance, a shrill whistle blows through the building. 'It's the All Clear at last! Come on! Come on!'[6]

England's Hour was very well reviewed in the United States and sold well, but it received a hostile reception in Great Britain, in particular for its message that if the country could not forgive Germany for the war 'then it has already lost the peace; and if it loses yet another peace, the war of 1965 will annihilate our children and our London'.[7]

Vera Brittain recognized the bravery and heroism both of the armed forces and of ordinary civilians in the face of the Blitz. In 1942, her article 'England's Bombed Cities' was published in the *Toronto Star*, in which she detailed many individual acts of courage and bravery that she had recounted to her on her travels.[8] She was particularly concerned in her writings about the aircrew of all sides, not only because of the risk to their lives but also because she believed that the kind of war that they were being required to fight by their commanders, including bombing attacks on civilian targets, would have a long-term moral effect on them as human beings. In *England's Hour* she wrote that:

> Some day peace will return, though many of this country's citizens will not live to see it, and a few of us believe that, in preparation for the distant hour, we must endeavour to keep alive the peacetime values of charity, truth and compassion. Not least we must preserve with determination those minority rights which are an essential part of the liberties that our young pilots are ready to defend with their lives.[9]

As the war continued Vera Brittain became a highly vocal critic of British military strategy, especially the area bombing of Germany and the refusal to make exceptions to the blockade of occupied Europe for humanitarian reasons, including the delivery of vitamins and powdered milk to children in occupied Europe. She wrote articles and pamphlets, the most important of these being: *One of These Little Ones ... A Plea to Parents and Others for Europe's Children* (1943), which sold over 30,000 copies and which argued that food should never be used as a weapon of war, and *Seed of Chaos: What Mass Bombing Really Means* (1944), in which she criticized Air Marshal Sir Arthur Harris (later Air Chief Marshal) and his Bomber Command for the area bombing strategy.[10]

The clearest expression of Vera Brittain's pacifist beliefs came in her book *Humiliation with Honour*, written in 1942 in the form of a series of letters to her son John, who was then in the United States.

> War begins first in the human soul. When a man has learned how to wrest honour from humiliation, his mastery of his own soul has begun, and by just that much he has brought the war against war nearer to victory. He no longer looks to the men on the heights to supply him with evidence that God exists. Instead he himself, from the depths, becomes part of that evidence. He has proved that power itself is powerless against the authority of love.[11]

These beliefs were also central to her decision to write a pamphlet in 1942 entitled *The Higher Retribution*, which sought to counter the anti-German views prevailing at that time in British Establishment circles, particularly those of the former diplomat and politician Lord Vansittart and his supporters. She was vehemently opposed to Vansittart's belief in draconian actions to be taken against the German population. In 1941 he had written, 'The *German* is often a moral creature; the *Germans* never; and it is the *Germans* who count. You will always think of *Germans* in the plural, if you are wise. That is their misfortune and their fault'.[12] She replied that given Great Britain's behaviour in India and Africa over many years the British were not in a position to be 'judge and executioner', and further:

> For ourselves retribution has followed, not only the punishment and humiliation of Germany by the Treaty of Versailles, but the blindness and pride of our Far Eastern 'pukka sahibs' who habitually treated black, brown and yellow races as 'lesser breeds without law', and were guilty of racial superiority little different in essentials from that of the Nazis [...] We can safely leave the war's criminals – whether nations or individuals – to the Almighty who has claimed vengeance as his, and to the working out of his moral law as demonstrated by history.[13]

But Vera Brittain's strongest condemnation was reserved for Allied bombing of German cities, which she saw as an act of barbarity.[14] This led to her most controversial publication, the pamphlet *Seed of Chaos: What Mass Bombing Really Means*, which appeared in Great Britain in April 1944, the same month that the Pope spoke out against the Allied bombing campaign; the pamphlet was also published in the United States in an amended version as *Massacre by Bombing*. In this pamphlet she wrote not only about the appalling loss of life but also the moral and spiritual damage that was being done to human civilization, quoting frequently from the Bible, and using religious as well as pacifist arguments against the policy. She also quoted her Quaker friend Corder Catchpool, the head of the Bombing Restrictions Committee, repeatedly in the pamphlet, and criticized the refusal of the Archbishop of Canterbury to debate the issue. Writing in 1963 she summarized the experience and the efforts of the British government to silence the protests of the Bombing Restrictions Committee.

> I was their scribe, incorporating in articles and booklets the facts patiently collected by Corder Catchpool from foreign newspapers. One of our pamphlets, the American version of *Seed of Chaos*, renamed *Massacre by Bombing* and published by the New York Fellowship of Reconciliation, was shouted down in the United States by over 200 journalistic blasts. In Britain the original was so quietly and effectively suppressed that today the younger writers even on such leading pacifist publications as *Peace News* are unaware that the protest was made.[15]

Seed of Chaos was not suppressed by the British government in any official sense. It was reprinted together with another of her wartime works

Humiliation with Honour (1942) as *One Voice: Pacifist Writings from the Second World War* by Continuum Press in 2005.

In *Seed of Chaos* Vera Brittain repeated her anger at the deaths of children, and the destruction of historic towns and cities. She challenged the notion that even the people of Coventry, badly bombed by the Germans on 14 November 1940, would want revenge enacted on another city, and used evidence from Mass Observation to support her argument. She also criticized Prime Minister Winston Churchill's description, in *The Times* of 7 June 1943, of the mass bombing as an 'experiment'. She concluded that:

> If the nations of the world cannot agree, when peace returns, to refrain from the use of the bombing aeroplane as they have refrained from using poison gas, then mankind itself deserves to perish from the epidemic of moral insanity which today afflicts our civilisation.[16]

The pamphlet argued for a negotiated peace to end the war as soon as possible, and ended with a call for at least the abandonment of the policy of area bombing before further escalation took place, including the possible use of bombing with poison gas.

As a political pamphlet, *Seed of Chaos* appealed to a wide range of mainstream opinions beyond pacifism. Perhaps surprisingly, one of the few letters of support that *Seed of Chaos* received came from Basil Liddell Hart, the distinguished military commentator and certainly no pacifist, who wrote to Vera Britain on 25 July:

> I have read your 'Seed of Chaos' with profound respect for your courage in upholding the claims for human decency in a time when war fever is raging [...] In such times as these, those who have an understanding should not only avoid fanning the flames of hatred, but ought to do what they can to check the spread – which endangers the prospects of future peace [...] Since you are likely to have abundant evidence of the resentment you create, you may like to have some evidence of the respect you inspire.[17]

Liddell Hart opposed area bombing on military grounds as a poor use of resources and ineffective as a weapon of terror, arguing for precision bombing on targets such as German communications and industrial sites. But he also regarded area bombing as incompatible with the stated Allied aim of unconditional surrender, given at the Casablanca Conference of

January 1943; and, in keeping with his wider theories about warfare, he believed that the war should be fought with restraint, and with the aim of a negotiated peace.[18] Many years later Vera Brittain read and favourably reviewed Liddell Hart's memoirs, writing that even without a knowledge of military history the intelligent reader, 'will have a unique understanding of our epoch from the end of the last century to the present day' from Liddell Hart's book.[19]

The most extreme attack on *Massacre by Bombing/Seed of Chaos* came from the United States in a review by the journalist and later historian William L. Shirer, who claimed that 'Dr. Goebbels, with whose writings and tricks and lies I have certain familiarity, would hardly have written it differently'.[20] Even President Franklin D. Roosevelt responded with a public letter, reported in the *News Chronicle* of 27 April:

> It is a mis-statement, Mr. Roosevelt said, to describe the bombings as revenge. Bombing, he declared, is shortening the war in the opinion of an overwhelming percentage of military authorities 'You cannot talk conciliation,' the letter concluded. 'You can be pro-German and pro-Japanese and look forward to a new "dark ages," attended by world-wide death and destruction – or a continuance of the philosophy of peace and the maintenance of civilisation. You cannot effect a compromise between these two views'.[21]

Vera Brittain's response was an article in June entitled 'Not Made in Germany – a reply to William L. Shirer and the President', in which she argued a political case against area bombing and the Allied policy of unconditional surrender, rather than an ethical or moral case based on pacifism.

> Mr. Shirer argues that the only alternative to fighting Hitler with bombs is 'slavery to the Nazis.' This is not the case. One alternative to fighting Hitler with bombs is fighting him with intelligence; with constructive political proposals, the lack of which the Bishop of Chichester lamented in the House of Lords protest against mass bombing. If the United Nations sincerely desired to shorten the war, they would long ago have abandoned the obtuse demand for unconditional surrender and offered the German people some better incentive for abandoning Hitler than the dismemberment of their country and prolonged occupation by Allied troops. Offered no prospect better than this, the German people have no alternative to putting up with Hitler and enduring mass raids, which increase their resistance just as their smaller onslaught on us in Britain increased ours.[22]

She also challenged what she claimed as President Roosevelt's position that in the circumstances of the war individual conscience should give way to the demands of patriotism.

> If that State is indeed all, and those who criticise its policy must be ranked with its enemies, for what are we fighting the Nazis? Could we not merely have adopted their doctrines, without the trouble and expense of going to war? Is it not to demonstrate their belief in a higher Authority than the State, that thousands of American and British boys are offering their lives?[23]

The most savage criticism of *Seed of Chaos* in the British press appeared on 19 May 1944 in an opinion column written by George Orwell, who was also far from being either a militarist or a pacifist.

> She is willing and anxious to win the war apparently. She merely wishes us to stick to 'legitimate' methods of war and abandon civilian bombing, which she fears will blacken our reputation in the eyes of posterity [...] Now, no one in his senses regards bombing, or any other operation of war, with anything but disgust. On the other hand, no decent person cares tuppence for the opinion of posterity. And there is something very distasteful in accepting war as an instrument and at the same time wanting to dodge responsibility for its more obviously barbarous features. Pacifism is a tenable position, provided that you are willing to take the consequences. But all talk of 'limiting' or 'humanising' war is sheer humbug [...] The immunity of the civilian, one of the things that has made war possible, has been shattered. Unlike Miss Brittain, I don't regret that.[24]

In response, Vera Brittain defended her position in a letter, published alongside a reply from Orwell, on 23 June, writing that 'My chief concern is with the moral deterioration to which a nation condemns itself by the unrestrained infliction of cruelty; and with the setback of European civilisation which obliteration bombing must cause in addition to blockade and invasion'.[25] Orwell's reply set out his own view of war and of pacifism, rejecting her moral and political arguments: 'As to war, you can not at present avoid it, nor can you genuinely humanise it. You can only, like the pacifists set up a moral alibi for yourself while continuing to accept the fruits of violence. I would sooner be Air-Marshal Harris than Miss Brittain, because he at least knows what he is doing'.[26] In a later column on 14 July, Orwell dismissed the idea of condemning the killing of women in warfare as 'sheer sentimentality'.[27] Vera Brittain confronted this challenge directly, although not by writing again to Orwell's column. In a short letter to *The Friend* dated 3 June, and an article 'Should We Humanise War?' in the July 1944 issue of *Christian Pacifist*, she explored historical examples of the humanizing influence on war and its possibilities, developing her argument that those with direct experience of the worst aspects of warfare, in particular being bombed, had more pity and toleration for their enemies. She concluded her moral and political analysis by quoting Kant: 'But if we proceed by gradual reform, and are guided by certain clear and fixed principles, we may lead by continuous approximation to the highest political good; we may lead to Perpetual Peace'.[28] She maintained this position in a further article in July 1944, arguing that the highly indiscriminate German V-1 'buzz bomb' pilotless aircraft were, as a further escalation in the barbarization of war, a response to Allied area bombing as part of the cycle of violence. She saw the mechanisation and depersonalization of war, from blockade to bombing to 'robot planes', as inherently dehumanizing.[29] Her worst fears about the policy of saturation bombing and the effects of total war were realized with the Allied bombing of Dresden on Shrove Tuesday, 13–14 February 1945, for which she collected newspaper reports, writing in the margin of one clipping, 'The evil that men do'.[30] It gave her little comfort that this woeful collection of press cuttings now included an article by George Orwell, dated 8 April 1945, in which he shared many of her earlier concerns about British bombing policy.[31]

From late 1940 onwards, Vera Brittain's writings show an increasingly marked religious imagery, particularly when discussing the war and what she believed to be the correct response to it. In October 1941 she wrote an 'Open Letter' to the workers in the Christian Pacifist Forestry and Land Units, which were composed of conscientious objectors, in which she stressed the importance of their work both in itself and as a practical expression of their convictions: 'As pacifists you and I are attempting to cultivate more than the land; we are trying to sow the seed of the Kingdom of Heaven in the minds and hearts of men and women'.[32] After the Japanese attack on Pearl Harbor on 7 December 1941, she wrote her own definition of what she believed a true Christian Pacifist should aspire to, following the attack: 'He must point ceaselessly to the ideals of a nobler community even though he knows it is far away and that he is unlikely ever to see it'.[33] In an unpublished and undated article that comes from this period, entitled 'Loving Our Enemies', she stressed the importance of the Sermon on the Mount and how it offers 'not only religious values but sound practical politics, offering clarity to both the general public and politicians when discussing international treaties and accords'. She called for Christian Pacifists to use faith, hope and charity in particular in their work with international refugees, and for no bitterness or revenge, even for the crimes against the Jewish population, to enter into the political process with the German people when the war was over, concluding that 'Our hate recoils upon us and destroys us. It is only our love that survives and is immortal'.[34] This was also the reason why she published *Above All Nations*, a collection of first-hand reports of acts of humanity and kindness, carried out by all sides and often at great personal risk, during the Second World War. This appeared in late April 1945, only a few days before inconvertible evidence of the final solution and the death camps became public knowledge in Great Britain, and in May was distributed by the Friends Committee to German prisoners of war.[35] In reviewing the book, John Betjeman wrote of the German entries that there were 'hundreds of instances where Germans acted, for a moment, as humans instead of Germans, where they obeyed their consciences instead of their State'.[36]

For Vera Brittain war was the ultimate evil, in her work as a war reporter she sought constantly to remind her readers of this view, and force them to consider and reflect that their democratic government and Allies were carrying out certain actions in their name. For her once the war was won it would be too late to voice concerns about how the war had been fought, and how or why certain principals had been lost in the process. She wanted people to question and think about the consequences for a post-war society. This is the very essence of her reporting, and why even today her writings during the Second World War are both still controversial and relevant to wars fought in the twenty-first century. In her own words, reflecting on the reaction to *Seed of Chaos* in 1944: 'When you are putting forward unpopular views, the thing that really creates despair is to be ignored; when people take notice, abuse you & defend themselves, you know you have got under their skin & uncovered a bad conscience!'.[37]

Notes

1   This chapter is derived largely from work carried out by the author for her doctoral thesis P. H. Badsey, *The Political Thought of Vera Brittain* (Kingston University, UK, 2006). See also P. Berry & M. Bostridge, *Vera Brittain: A Life* (London: Chatto & Windus, 1995).

2   V. Brittain, *England's Hour: An Autobiography 1939–1941* (London: Futura, 1941 reprinted 1981), 38.

3   Quoted in P. Berry & A. Bishop (Eds), *Testament of a Generation: The Journalism of Vera Brittain and Winifred Holtby* (London: Virago Press, 1985), 337.

4   Vera Brittain Archive, McMaster University, Hamilton, Canada (hereafter VBA): Letter from Vera Brittain to Margaret Storm Jameson, 7 August 1940.

5   VBA: Letter from Vera Brittain to Margaret Storm Jameson, 5 September 1941.

6   V. Brittain (1941 reprinted 1981), 102–103.

7   V. Brittain (1941 reprinted 1981), 286. VBA: Letter from Vera Brittain to Margaret Storm Jameson, 12 April 1941.

8   VBA: 'England's Bombed Cities', *Toronto Star*, 2 January 1942.

9   V. Brittain (1941 reprinted 1981), 100.

10   V. Brittain, *One of These Little Ones ... A Plea to Parents and Others for Europe Children* (London: Dakers, 1943). V. Brittain, *Seed of Chaos: What Mass Bombing Really Means* (London: Bombing Restrictions Committee, 1944a).

11   V. Brittain, *Humiliation with Honour* (London: Andrew Dakers, 1942b), 114.

12   R. Vansittart, *Black Record: Germans Past and Present* (London: Hamish Hamilton, 1941), 18.

13   VBA: Vera Brittain, 'The Higher Retribution', pamphlet for The Peace Pledge Union, 1942: G581.

14   VBA: Anglican Pacifist Fellowship Deputation to Archbishop of Canterbury undated, but *c.* 1948.

15   VBA: Vera Brittain, 'The Annihilation of Dresden', book review, *The Friend*, 5 July 1963: G840.

16   VBA: V. Brittain, *Seed of Chaos – What Mass Bombing Really Means* (London: Brock & Co. Ltd., 1944b), Spec. Coll. D 786, B72, cop. 1.

17   VBA: Letter from Basil Liddell Hart to Vera Brittain, 25 July 1944; see also letter from Vera Brittain to Basil Liddell Hart, 28 July 1944.

18   For Liddell Hart's view of the importance of restraint in warfare see B. Bond, *Liddell Hart: A Study of His Military Thought* (Aldershot: Ashgate, 2001). A. Danchev, *Alchemist of War – The Life of Basil Liddell Hart* (London: Weidenfeld

& Nicolson, 1998). A. Danchev, 'Liddell Hart's Big Idea', *Review of International Studies* 25(1) (1999), 29–48.

19   VBA: Vera Brittain, 'A Revolutionary Historian', unpublished (11 January 1966): I26.

20   VBA: William L. Shirer, 'Claim U.S Pacifists' Cry Against Bombings Based on Nazi Texts', *The Pasadena Post*, 12 March 1944.

21   VBA: 'F.D.R. [Franklin D. Roosevelt] Defends Mass Raids', *News Chronicle*, 27 April 1944.

22   VBA: Vera Brittain, 'Not Made in Germany', *Fellowship*, June 1944: G594. An extract of this article was also published in *The New York Herald Tribune*, 29 May 1944.

23   VBA: Vera Brittain, 'Not Made in Germany', *Fellowship*, June 1944: G594.

24   VBA: George Orwell, 'As I Please', *Tribune*, 19 May 1944.

25   VBA: Letter from Vera Brittain, 'Humanising War?' to *Tribune*, dated 22 May 1944, published 23 June 1944: G593.

26   VBA: Comment on Letter from Vera Brittain by George Orwell, *Tribune*, 23 June 1944: G593.

27   VBA: George Orwell, 'As I Please', *Tribune*, 14 July 1944.

28   VBA: Vera Brittain, 'Seed of Chaos', letter to *The Friend*, 3 June 1944. Vera Brittain, 'Should We Humanise War?', *Christian Pacifist*, July 1944: G596. The quotation appears to come from a translation of Immanuel Kant, *A Philosophical Essay on Perpetual Peace* (London: Swan Sonnenschein, 1795).

29   VBA: Vera Brittain, 'The Human Factor and World Peace', *The Friend*, 21 July 1944: G595.

30   VBA: See 'Another Great Attack On Hamburg', no date or place of publication. 'The Street Called Broad-Lubeck', 'Bride Buried on Wedding Day', *Sunday Express*, 19 April 1942. 'The Roofless City', *The Times*, 25 April 1942, is annotated by Vera Brittain. 'Have a look at Lubeck', *Daily Herald*, 25 April 1942.

31   George Orwell Archive, University College London, UK. 'Future of a Ruined Germany', *The Observer*, 8 April 1945. See also V. Brittain, *Testament of Experience: An Autobiographical Story of the Years 1925–1950* (London: Gollancz, 1957), 358–359.

32   VBA: Vera Brittain, 'The Land and Peace', *C.P. Newsletter*, October 1941: G561.

33   P. Berry & M. Bostridge, 424.

34   VBA: Vera Brittain, 'Loving Our Enemies', undated and unpublished: H349.

35   VBA: Letter to Vera Brittain from Victor Gollancz's office, 14 May 1945.

36   Quoted in P. Berry & M. Bostridge, 445.

37   Quoted in P. Berry & M. Bostridge, 441.

BRIAN P. D. HANNON

Richard Dimbleby:
The BBC's Original War Reporter

Television viewers from the late 1940s to the 1960s knew him as an elec-
tion-night anchorman, commentator at state events and the host of the
acclaimed news programme *Panorama*. Yet before becoming a regular
presence on the small screen, Richard Dimbleby was the 'original' war
reporter for the British Broadcasting Corporation (BBC) and one of the
most prominent voices to bring the Second World War to millions of
radio listeners.

Dimbleby was the first BBC journalist to cover conflict in the field
and continued to be the first to report many of its most important stories
throughout the war. He was also original in the sense of being an innovator
who helped to usher in a new era of radio journalism at the BBC, bringing
war news to people in a more direct and emotive manner than ever before
experienced. Yet his career was not flawless and his work raises questions
about Second World War reporting in terms of journalistic objectivity
and propaganda.

A pioneer

A one-page internal BBC document, dated 12 January 1946, sums up the
basics of Dimbleby's career with the Corporation – date of joining, date of
leaving, positions held, salary grade – and carries a single-paragraph assessment by administrator A. E. Barker stating that Dimbleby's work with the
News Services was 'a field in which he was really a pioneer'. Barker notes

that there were also 'little weaknesses'. It was a combination of pioneering and weaknesses that marked Dimbleby's career, especially in the early days.[1]

Born in 1913 in Richmond, Surrey, Dimbleby's family owned the local newspaper, the *Richmond and Twickenham Times*; his father, Fred, served as its Editor in Chief while his uncle ran the business side. Fred also worked on London's Fleet Street and later on publicity campaigns in Whitehall during the First World War, becoming the government's Director of Publicity and a confidant of Prime Minister David Lloyd George, 'sometimes accompanying him on speaking tours and frequently being summoned to Downing Street'. Lloyd George's wife told Fred's wife, Gwen, that he was 'such a reassuring presence – when he's around we know everything is going to be all right'. After the fall of the Liberal government Fred Dimbleby departed Whitehall and wrote for the *Daily Mail*, but its support of the rising Fascist movement abroad prompted him to leave the newspaper in 1931, scuttling Richard's plans to work for the paper in Paris when he graduated from Mill Hill public school or attend university. Instead, he moved back to Richmond and worked on the family newspaper, composing pages and working on the printing press before graduating to reporting. Here he met his future wife, Dilys (a fellow aspiring journalist), and remained until 1934. After leaving for a stint on sister papers the *Southern Echo* and the *Bournemouth Echo*, covering a district of approximately one hundred square miles, Richard followed in his father's footsteps and in late 1935 gained employment on Fleet Street with the trade magazine *Advertisers Weekly*, first as a £4 per-week reporter and then, at age twenty-three, as the journalistic boulevard's youngest news editor.[2]

In spring 1936 Dimbleby contacted the BBC seeking work at Broadcasting House, the organization's London headquarters. In a letter to Chief News Editor John Coatman, Dimbleby boldly offered suggestions for livening up radio news.

> I suggest that a member or members of your staff – they could be called 'BBC reporters, or BBC correspondents' – should be held in readiness, just as are the evening paper men, to cover unexpected News for that day. In the event of a big fire, strikes, civil commotion, railway accidents, pit accidents, or any of the other major catastrophes in which the public, I fear, is deeply interested, a reporter could be sent from Broadcasting House to cover the event for the bulletin. At the scene, it would be

his job, in addition to writing his own account of the event, to secure an eye-witness (the man or woman who saw it start, one of the survivors, a girl 'rescued from the building') and to give a short eye-witness account of the part he or she played that day. In this way, I really believe that News could be presented in a gripping manner, and, at the same time, remain authentic.[3]

This was during a period when BBC news consisted largely of staid announcers reading tightly scripted 'Talks' and short bulletins from its own staff as well as from press agencies, such as Reuters, bulletins which Dimbleby deemed 'a trifle flat'. His use of the word 'gripping' suggested news as much for entertainment as information. He also saw the BBC's civic and historical value: 'It does seem to me that in the future and particularly in the event of national emergency, the BBC will play a vital part. Recorded news bulletins of the type I suggest would also prove valuable libraries of this century, for the next'. The BBC rejected Dimbleby's initial application for employment as a sub-editor in June 1936 in a letter simply stating he had not been chosen for the job, although they would keep his name in their files.[4]

When he finally arrived at the BBC in mid-September 1936, as a Topical Talks Assistant on £350 per year, Dimbleby did not immediately impress. His newsroom boss, Sir Ralph Murray, said that Dimbleby initially reaped 'the role of stooge, junior reporter, dogsbody, help'. His colleagues were university graduates while Dimbleby did not have a degree, and his workmates gave him the nickname 'Bumble' because, as Murray said, 'he was fat and buzzed'.[5]

In the 1975 biography of his father, Jonathan Dimbleby – also a renowned television and radio presenter, and author – describes his father's first BBC reporting assignment in October 1936: 'It was not a strike, or a hunger march, or a political rally in the East End, but the annual conference of the Council for the Preservation of Rural England. Though his report [...] revealed heroic attempts to inject some life into the bucolic ruminations of the assembled delegates, England must have rattled to the sound of turning-off switches in living rooms throughout the land'. Afterwards, the BBC's esteemed Deputy Director-General, Sir Cecil Graves, decreed that Dimbleby was not to broadcast again because he had used an inverted sentence. The newsroom editor was more forgiving, however, and after a brief hiatus Dimbleby was on air with his next big story: the record milk production of a cow named Cherry.[6]

Dimbleby overcame this slow start, and earned a reputation for doggedness and originality. By 1939 he had been awarded three raises of his salary bringing him to £542 per annum. He was one of the news department's first practitioners of the technique of 'actuality' – background sounds from the scene of a story, such as a mooing cow, incorporated into a verbal news report – that later became a hallmark of the BBC's Second World War reporting. He also suggested attaching a microphone and amplifier to a public phone box, which enabled reporters for the first time to broadcast directly into the studio from remote locations.[7]

Dimbleby and BBC engineer David Howarth were on hand on 30 September 1938 at West London's Heston Airport to observe Chamberlain waving the Munich Agreement and later, at Downing Street, they recorded for radio and television the Prime Minister's naïve belief that this promised 'peace for our time'. An opponent of 'appeasement', Dimbleby commented, 'I wish that were true'. Dimbleby and Howarth then headed to the continent to report on the handover of the Sudetenland to Germany. The Nazis made them wait in Germany for two weeks and never fulfilled their promise of accompanying the international force that was to oversee – but never did – the annexation of the border regions of western Czechoslovakia. Howarth wrote, 'I specially recollect that journey because the pomposity and false dignity of Nazi officials set a spark to the boyish naughtiness in Richard's character'. When they first arrived, the German Ministry of Propaganda met the BBC recording car at the German–Franco border and escorted them in a motorcade of Mercedes to nearby Aachen, but Goebbels' men were unprepared for the show Dimbleby planned. Dimbleby greeted the contingent with his arm extended in the Nazi salute, saying 'Heil Hitler' and clicking his heels. They later drove to the hotel in Godesberg where Hitler had met the British prime minister on 23 September. Hitler was gone, but the Nazi officials showed them where he stayed in the hotel, which included a green water closet the proprietor had installed specially for Hitler. Howarth recalled, 'Richard wrote a broadcast, tongue in cheek, about the Fuhrer's taste in plumbing'.[8]

In early 1939, Dimbleby got a wholly different experience of foreign coverage during the politically charged Spanish Civil War. Dimbleby deployed to the Pyrenees as an 'observer', where he related stories of thousands of exhausted and starving Spanish refugees streaming into France, and gained the dubious honour of being the first radio reporter to make a live broadcast of the sounds of battle, gunfire cracking and shells exploding in the background of his report.

> Since early today [...] there have been crowds, masses, lines of wretched, torn and tattered soldiers going by, throwing down their guns, their rifles and their pistols at the guards on the frontier [...] There are machine guns by the dozen stacked up just behind me [...] Now here comes another procession of lorries. I'm going to stop for a moment and let you hear it go by. The first one is a Russian lorry piled high with soldiers [...] The second carries a heavy gun [...] and behind it is another lorry with two soldiers in it, four or five sheep and a cow piled up in the back of the lorry. This would be almost comic if it weren't such an appalling tragedy to watch down here [...].[9]

One internal memo to him in February 1939 stated, '[Your] effort on Wednesday night, for instance, in taking a microphone right down to a frontier road showed great enterprise and resulted in a very successful broadcast. I expect you had a strenuous time, but the results did you credit'.[10]

A *Daily Mail* critic said the Spanish Civil War reports were 'inextricably linked with the growth of radio news, with the fear, relief, and shame of the Munich settlement, with the curious change of mood in the ensuing twelve months, and with one of Hitler's speeches relayed from a Nazi gathering in the Berlin Sportpalast [...] young Dimbleby's broadcast from Spain, carefully neutral because the BBC news had to be neutral, nevertheless aroused something to which its hearers had to respond: the stirrings of dread, disgust, anger and determination'. This time in Spain, 'produced reporting from him of a kind that had never been heard before on radio'.[11]

Milestones and controversy

When Germany threatened war in 1939, Dimbleby and his engineering team (David Howarth and Harvey Samey) took a car with recording equipment on the ferry across to France without the BBC's permission or knowledge. Covering the vehicle in camouflage paint and mud, they hid it in an underground car park in Paris and returned to London. After the declaration of war a short time later, the trio embarked for Paris, decked out in new official war-correspondent uniforms, collected the car and drove to the British Expeditionary Force (BEF) headquarters in Arras. Dimbleby and his team spent months with the BEF but at the time there was little war reporting to do. Howarth said they drove along the Rhine 'begging the French to fire a gun so that we could record it; but they never would, in case the Germans fired one back at them'. Instead they spent much of their airtime broadcasting quiz shows and spelling bees with soldiers. The heavy censorship in France meant they could not go anywhere outside BEF headquarters without a 'conducting officer' to police their actions, while stories went through rigid and sometimes nonsensical vetting. On a temporary detachment with the French army, one of its officers informed Dimbleby he could not divulge their location. The correspondent explained he would only say the report was from France. Still, he was rebuffed. 'But everyone knows we are in France', he said, 'and everyone knows that the French Army is in France'. Refused again, Dimbleby shouted, 'What shall I say then, that we're on the front line in the middle of Switzerland!'.[12]

Dimbleby, however, took the assignment very seriously. 'In his own estimation he was no mere reporter [...] he was the representative of the largest broadcasting organisation in the world: in France at least, he was the BBC.'[13] This attitude did not endear him to the administrators back in London. Jonathan Dimbleby writes, 'In France, even more than in London he became a law unto himself, jealous of his territory: he was BBC representative, features producer, quiz-master, public relations officer, policy-maker and impresario – and he wanted to do all this alone. To the growing irritation of the News Department in London he refused simply to be what they thought he should have been – their "observer".[14]

By March 1940, Dimbleby was keen for action and decided to leave the Phoney War for the theatres of North Africa, the Middle East and the Mediterranean, during which time he became the BBC's most experienced and skilled war correspondent. Reporting from places such as Cairo, Khartoum, Alamein, Istanbul, Damascus, Athens, Albania and Eritrea, he travelled more than 50,000 miles in fourteen countries. He became the first Allied reporter to broadcast from Tehran and it was there he witnessed the earliest meeting between British and Soviet troops. He learned to deal with rough roads, privations and oversensitive army censors. He cajoled and charmed his way into situations where he could get the latest story, and for his efforts was nearly killed on more than one occasion; in Eritrea, when he looked over a ridge at a nearby Italian position, a bullet struck a rock near his head, prompting a soldier to remark that the enemy normally did not shoot at that hour, adding, 'It must be your size, thought you were a general I expect'. He even collapsed after contracting diphtheria and spent a month in bed.[15]

In 1942, the BBC recalled Dimbleby to London following repeated accusations that he was frivolous with the Corporation's money, partly because he had lived comfortably on a houseboat in the Nile, where he frequently entertained military and government officials. Dimbleby said that this was a manner of gaining access to newsmakers and he was quite frugal in his personal habits. BBC executives also claimed that such associations influenced him to file unduly optimistic stories about the army's progress.[16]

Dimbleby had indeed spent money far beyond the expectations of the BBC administrators. In early 1940, Dimbleby took a trip to Paris to smooth over a BBC transmissions problem with French authorities; his conducting officer was an aristocrat and the pair placated the French officials with 'a little expensive entertaining' while they lodged at the Ritz. In the Middle East, he answered one of the frequent complaints from the accounting department by noting it was necessary to stay in a certain expensive hotel with other reporters so he did not miss any important news but that in order to keep expenses low he had taken 'a very ordinary [room], placed on the hot side of the hotel'.[17]

In an internal memo dated 21 April 1944 – the year in which Dimbleby's annual salary reached £1,000 – News Administrative Officer G. J. B. Allport explains that he looked back at Dimbleby's expenses and calculated that he owed the Corporation £291 as a result of overspending: 'There is little doubt that Dimbleby was both extravagant and careless with his accounts, and the total amount expended, approximately £4,500 by him alone in just over two years exclusive of all salary, is obviously extremely high and far away in excess of anything that we allow for war correspondents at the present time'. Allport, however, had retroactively approved some of Dimbleby's Middle East expenses, including a car, the houseboat and servants who tended it, and suits for travel to Turkey where he could not wear a uniform, in a memo in November 1943.[18]

The withdrawal of Dimbleby was about more than money. The new top editor, A. P. Ryan, was caught in an argument with Whitehall (which expected the full support of the state broadcaster) that was worsened by some of Dimbleby's reporting. In one example, Dimbleby provided first-hand accounts of Greek men taking to the mountains and fighting a desperate, bloody struggle to defend their homeland. He called them 'our new ally', which went against official government policy lest they be called upon to provide military or material aid; Dimbleby's Greek reports never aired.[19]

He also endured accusations of unrealistic sanguinity. His colleague in the western desert, Frank Gillard, explained that Dimbleby suffered from both the process of reporting and the immediacy of radio. Dimbleby and Gillard traded off reporting positions, one out in the desert while the other remained back at headquarters. When reporting from the rear, 'he was wholly dependent on second-hand information. He had no means of checking the accuracy of what he was told. There were times when some of the information filtering back to these headquarters was sadly over-optimistic if not misleading'. Newspapers would often take six weeks to get back to the front line and, therefore, could be put into better perspective by the army personnel. The BBC reports were usually heard just 24 hours later. At times this angered soldiers, especially when Dimbleby recorded an optimistic report on their progress and then the situation changed by the time it was broadcast. Gillard said, 'if in those intervening twenty-four hours things had gone badly, with fortunes perhaps reversed, there was little understanding on the spot for the unhappy BBC reporter. With some in the Army he became discredited, and sometimes confused and dispirited fighting men tended to find an outlet for their own understandable dejection in voicing harsh judgments against him'. Gillard defended Dimbleby as always having been professional and objective: 'His reporting throughout was totally conscientious and honest. He never spared himself in his efforts to give as faithful a picture as his own very shrewd and experienced observation, and his sources of information, would permit'.[20]

Godfrey Talbot, the reporter sent to replace him in Egypt, agreed Dimbleby 'had been getting a raw deal' owing to his circumstances and the nature of the war.

> As our soldiers in the desert fell back, and optimistic official reports were followed by disillusioning admissions of inadequacies and reverses, Richard – perforce back at base in Cairo more than he wished to be – was for some time persistently given information and 'guidance' by army public relations spokesmen which did not correspond with the position at the front; and his broadcast messages, heard by the desert fighting troops as well as Supreme Command and the listeners at home, caused complaints, and the B.B.C. was accused of peddling the official view. Dimbleby was a scapegoat.[21]

As he had in France, Dimbleby came to regard himself as the personification of the BBC in the Middle East. Talbot said 'he was more rajah than reporter, proud of being "the BBC" but seeing himself as a roving British diplomat'. The army commanders felt the same and treated him with a deference not shown to most other reporters, even objecting to the War Office upon hearing the BBC had recalled its senior correspondent. For a time they, and Dimbleby, got their way; when his replacement arrived he dragged out his exit. Talbot said, 'Richard greeted me briefly but with cordiality. There was little time for professional handing-over because his farewells all round the town and Army GHQ were keeping him busy. There were several postponements of his departure for London. He didn't *want* to leave. One day, when I was told he had really gone, it turned out that he was only visiting Palestine: he had flown to Jerusalem to collect, of all things, a bottle of Jordan water to take home for a christening'.[22]

The rumours he was living high on Corporation funds and the perception he 'had become a law unto himself' unanswerable to Broadcasting House fuelled the decision to withdraw him, but these were partly the fault of Corporation executives who were slow to define the rules of being a war correspondent, or even understand what it meant to be the BBC's delegate in the field. Allport admitted as much in his 1944 memo about Dimbleby's expenses when he said, 'In his favour, it can be said that there was no one authority who made it his business to keep in touch with Dimbleby over his allowances and keep him on the right path'. Dimbleby defended himself using a similar argument in a letter to London while he was still in the Middle East, expressing the weight of working as 'the official envoy of a very great and powerful national organisation' and how he felt that responsibility was misunderstood by the Corporation.[23]

> When one represents the BBC one is not in the same category as a correspondent of a newspaper of which the country visited knows little or nothing. You are representing something that the foreign people as well as one's own diplomatic representatives regard as part of their lives. Therefore as the representative of the BBC, you are the BBC, and your arrival is quite an event [...] I don't think anyone working at Broadcasting House in London who has not represented the BBC (and how few have) realises fully the important part played by the Corporation in the lives of other nations [...] I cannot help the fact that the BBC enjoys much fame abroad; nor can I avoid appearing as the living embodiment of the BBC wherever I go.[24]

His vanity was somewhat justified. By the time of his recall, Dimbleby had become so well known that Talbot said, 'I was a journalist succeeding a personality. There were war correspondents and there was Richard Dimbleby'. Head editor Ryan saw this as the reporter's ego trumping the Corporation's news mission and took to referring to Dimbleby as 'Master Richard'.[25]

Jonathan Dimbleby said in 2007, 'I doubt that my father's spat with the BBC in London while he was in Cairo had any effect on his attitudes. He was young, forward-looking and passionately committed to victory. He was merely perplexed by the row going on in London over his head and which related to issues that he was not aware of '.[26]

Spartan and the RAF

In March 1943, Dimbleby participated in Operation Spartan, a British army exercise along the Thames that was vital to future BBC war coverage. Two teams covered the event as if it was a real battle between British and German forces, proving through more than ninety recordings, played afterwards for the Secretary of State for War and high-ranking staff officers, that the BBC could successfully handle the anticipated invasion of France with its nascent War Reporting Unit (WRU) – a group of reporters and engineers it was putting together to cover the remainder of the conflict. Beginning on D-Day, the programme *War Report* broadcast the unit's stories to an estimated 10–15 million British listeners every day.[27]

Dimbleby provided the BBC with crucial feedback on the Spartan exercise, describing problems encountered by the teams and making various suggestions based on his experiences in the field. These ranged from very small amendments, such as reducing the requisite number of script copies to save paper, to more involved upgrades including using motorcycle dispatch riders to deliver recordings and jeeps rather than less-durable saloon cars.[28] Most important, he strongly warned against deploying personnel who did not understand the responsibility their correspondent badges and status as honorary officers carried:[29] 'At present they do not seem to realise that by donning the uniform, the correspondent is assuming automatically the status and most of the privileges of an officer, a status for which any soldier or officer-cadet must work and train'. He explained that during the 'Spartan exercise, I was continually meeting officers of Field and General rank who were friends of mine in France and the Middle East. But it is not enough to be on friendly terms with these men; to win their full confidence you must show a sense of military discipline and bearing'. Dimbleby singled out the engineer with whom he was paired during Spartan as an example. The young technician wore his cap 'at a rakish angle' and kept a cigarette dangling from his lip even while talking to a War Office general, whom he did not salute and had hailed by calling, 'I say'. The engineer also 'addressed private soldiers, military policemen and sentries, as "old boy"'. Dimbleby advised his superiors that there had to be a strong military bearing among WRU staff: 'I am interested only in doing the war-reporting job efficiently, and I know from experience that we cannot succeed in our job if any one of us behaves grotesquely in a purely military area. Such people as that engineer will only be looked upon as oddities that should be better employed in an infantry battalion. We simply must fit ourselves into the landscape and conduct ourselves in accordance with the rank whose privileges we enjoy'.[30]

The BBC smoothed the wrinkles of Spartan and deployed its team with the invasion force. D-Day and the weeks immediately following marked the official debut of the WRU and produced some of its most memorable broadcasts, including Dimbleby reporting live as he flew over the Normandy beachhead in a Mosquito aircraft.

> A very lovely sight the Spitfires are on our port side ranged in their ranks of three. Now as we fly closer in to the coast of France, we're pulling away to starboard and overtaking the formation of Spitfires, hanging there so perfect, almost motionless in the wonderful clear air. Down below us on the surface of the glistening sea, the everlasting procession of ships going to France. There they are in a line with their silver wakes coming up behind them, so stately [...] And there, in the distance, and all around us as though in a great semicircle, is the battlefront. I can see the whole of it from east to west. Fires are burning in every direction, there's smoke going up in clouds. We've seen the guns firing and the ships firing in shore. And we're flying so low now that I can see individual people on the ground. There are antiaircraft guns, there are some cows sitting in a field. I'm describing them all as they go past the port-side window of this Mosquito cockpit. More guns, and there, transport on the roads. And at that road junction just below us, there's a military policeman waving them on. And you know I can even see his red cap from here; he's wearing that and not his tin hat. The roads are full of our transport, all our chaps driving on the right-hand side in the continental style.[31]

Dimbleby had been up in the air long before D-Day. Although called back to Britain he had not stopped reporting, becoming a Royal Air Force correspondent who stayed close to the action. In January 1943, Dimbleby was among the first group of journalists to climb aboard RAF Lancasters for a bombing run over Berlin; he eventually flew on twenty bombing missions. By comparison, that is only five fewer than the number of missions originally required of American B-24 pilots in Europe.[32] Dimbleby took a huge risk by going on so many flights with the RAF: Bomber Command flew over 300,000 sorties during which 57,000 airmen lost their lives, 18,000 were wounded or became prisoners of war (POW), while 13,000 aircraft were destroyed; Fighter Command lost 5,300 men.[33] The risks he took became even more obvious with the deaths of two of his BBC colleagues during bombing missions over Germany.[34]

However, these dangerous forays into the sky produced some of Dimbleby's best descriptive reporting, including one on 1 November 1944 about dropping flare markers for bombers.

> The first cluster went down as we were approaching, red and green lights hanging from their parachutes, just on top of the great white cloudbank that hid Cologne. This was 'skymarking': the bombs of the main force, now streaming in above and below us, jet black in the brilliant light of the full moon, had to pass down by the flares. They vanished into the cloud, and soon the underside of it was lit by a suffused white glow, the light of incendiaries burning on the ground and the baffled searchlights. The flares seemed to be motionless, but round them and just under us as we drove steadily over in a dead level straight line, the German flak was winking and flashing [...] We circled round the flares, watching the light under the cloud going pink with the reflection of fire and, silhouetted against it, the Lancasters and Halifaxes making off in the all-revealing light of the moon.[35]

Another notable broadcast from the air came on 24 March 1945.

> The Rhine lies left and right across our path below us, shining in the sunlight – wide and with sweeping curves; and the whole of this mighty airborne army is now crossing and filling the whole sky. We haven't come as far as this without some loss; on our right-hand side a Dakota has just gone down in flames. We watched it go to the ground, and I've just seen the parachutes of it blossoming and floating down towards the river. Above us and below us, collecting close round us now, are the tugs as they take their gliders in. Down there is the smoke of battle. There is the smoke-screen laid by the army lying right across the far bank of the river; dense clouds of brown and grey smoke coming up [...] Ahead of us, another pillar of black smoke marks the spot where an aircraft has gone down, and – yet another one; it's a Stirling – a British Stirling; it's going down with flames coming out from under its belly – four parachutes are coming out – one, two, three, four – four parachutes have come out of the Stirling; it goes on its way to the ground.[36]

Despite his flying record, Dimbleby was not the type who scoffed at danger. 'At the best of times he was frightened of flying; he always felt ill and was frequently sick', Jonathan Dimbleby wrote, adding that his father felt it necessary to share in the peril of the men upon whom he reported, air crews who endured nightly, nerve-wracking ordeals of which he believed the British people were not well enough aware.[37]

Passion and empathy

One of the reasons for his success was Dimbleby's ability to forge relationships. During the Phoney War, engineer David Howarth commented to a brigadier on the reporter's knack for connecting with a variety of people, to which the officer responded, 'Of course, we all adore him'.[38] This closeness to the military, while at times drawing the ire of his editors, continued through Dimbleby's war-reporting years, especially when he worked with the RAF. Dimbleby expressed this in a two-page memo to BBC editors, on 6 January 1945, complaining that his story summarizing the deeds of Bomber Command in 1944, 'its greatest year', was not aired.

> Up to long after 'D' Day, the Command's casualties were higher than all the British Armies put together, and the list of young men whose nerves and morale have been shattered by the strain of the work runs into thousands. The Command is the only branch of our Services based entirely on Britain and using a great preponderance of British made instruments of war. The facts of the damage it has inflicted on Germany are extraordinary. In these circumstances we must surely not allow ourselves to believe that people are 'tired' of hearing about Bomber Command. I cannot imagine a more cynical or callous suggestion, nor, in my opinion, does it hold water.[39]

Dimbleby's passion for Bomber Command was also on display in his broadcasts, as in a November 1944 report about the bombing of Cologne.

> Once before, this same fate befell a German city, when Bomber Command laid Hamburg waste in a series of concentrated attacks. And now Cologne has gone, and with it a most important forward base and collecting point for the German

Army in the field. The enemy did not choose to learn the lesson of Hamburg, but he must now realize that any city that lies just behind the battlefront and serves the German Army may have to be destroyed. He knows, too, that we can do it for with last night's culminating attack on Cologne, Bomber Command has shown that, led by its Pathfinders, it can go on its tremendous errands by night, by day, in darkness, or in the light of the full moon.[40]

While enthusiastic about the British war effort, Dimbleby also proved through his humanity that war journalism was essentially about people. He may have presented a stoic facade but part of what made Dimbleby's wartime broadcasts compelling is that he was clearly moved by what he observed.

The first example of this was the Spanish Civil War, on which three decades later he wrote: 'It was my first experience of war, and a pretty shattering one. The sky was lit up with gunfire and bursting bombs [...] But I don't think that I was so much moved by the proximity of war as by the awful appearance of these desperate people [...] It was the first time that I had seen the innocent victims who suffer so terribly in war'.[41]

In the ensuing years he never lost that empathy, with another of the best examples coming from his book, *The Frontiers Are Green*,[42] in which he described watching a desert field surgeon's operation on a South African soldier.

> I moved up to the table. The anaesthetist at the man's head was adjusting the controls of his machine. I tried to look bright and confident. I said to the black boy, 'You're all right now. You'll soon be better.' He smiled faintly and gave a little groan. Then he said in a very low voice, almost a whisper: 'My mother – she'll be crying for me.' He looked at me once again as the mask was put over his nose. It was the look of a dumb, frightened creature. I wanted to take his hand and say something to comfort him, but it was the anaesthetist who spoke. 'Breathe', he said [...] 'breathe'.[43]

The greatest exhibition of his compassion, and the seminal moment of his war-reporting career, was Dimbleby's account of the horrors he found upon being one of the first people, and the first reporter, to enter the liberated Belsen concentration camp on 15 April 1945. Fellow BBC correspondent, Wynford Vaughan-Thomas, said that when he saw Dimbleby as he returned from Belsen, his colleague was a 'changed man'. Vaughan-Thomas wrote, 'Richard got out and said to me at once, "It's horrible; human beings have no right to do this to each other. You must go and see it, but you'll never wash the smell of it off your hands, never get the filth of it out of your mind [...] I must tell the exact truth, every detail of it, even if people don't believe me, even if they feel these things should not be told. This is an outrage [...] an outrage".'[44]

Dimbleby later recalled the approach to Belsen with a medical officer to investigate a report of a camp infected with typhoid. His colleagues declined to go, assuming it would be no different than the POW camps they had already seen. They 'drove like fools' down the tree-lined road for fear of snipers and even before reaching the camp he said they encountered a stench that war had made sadly familiar. 'I remember turning to him and saying, "That's the smell of death". But even that didn't prepare us for what we saw.'[45]

His account of Belsen is reminiscent of Dante's *Inferno* as Dimbleby describes entering another city of woe where all hope has been abandoned.

I passed through the barrier and found myself in the world of a nightmare. Dead bodies, some of them in decay, lay strewn about the road and along the rutted track. On each side of the road were brown wooden huts. There were faces at the windows, the bony emaciated faces of starving women too weak to come outside, propping themselves against the glass to see the light before they died. And they were dying, every hour, every minute. I saw a man, wandering dazedly along the road, stagger and fall. Someone else looked down at him, took him by the heels and dragged him to the side of the road to join the other bodies lying unburied there. No-one else took the slightest notice – they didn't even trouble to turn their heads. Behind the hut two youths and two girls who had found a morsel of food were sitting together in the grass in picnic fashion, sharing it. They were not six feet from a pile of decomposing bodies. Inside the huts it was even worse. I have seen many terrible sights in the last five years, but nothing, nothing approaching the dreadful interior of this hut at Belsen. The dead and dying lay close together. I picked my way over corpse after corpse in the gloom, until I heard one voice that rose above the undulating moaning. I found a girl – she was a living skeleton – impossible to gauge her age, for she had practically no hair left on her head and her face was only a yellow parchment sheet with two holes in it for eyes. She was stretching out her stick of an arm and gasping something. It was 'Englisch – Englisch – medicine – medicine' and she was trying to cry, but had not enough strength.[46]

Dimbleby continued with his heart-rending descriptions: over an acre of bodies dead or on the edge of death, 'you could not see which was which except by a convulsive movement or the last quiver of a sigh from a living skeleton too weak to move'; piles of naked corpses who had 'yellow skin [that] glistened like stretched rubber on their bones' and others he thought looked like 'polished skeletons'; survivors heating soup over fire fuelled by the clothes of the dead; women who 'stood and squatted stark naked in the dust, trying to wash themselves and catch the lice on their bodies'; evidence of prisoners eating the livers and kidneys of campmates to stay alive. He said babies had been born in the camp, but some were 'tiny wizen things that could not live, because their mothers could not feed them'. An example of this is one of the more disturbing stories he tells: a female prisoner 'distraught to the point of madness' accosted a British soldier and 'begged him to give her some milk for the tiny baby she held in her arms. She laid the mite on the ground and threw herself at the sentry's feet and kissed his boots. And when, in his distress, he asked her to get up, she put the baby in his arms and ran off crying that she would find milk for it because there was no milk in her breast. And when the soldier opened the bundle of rags to look at the child, he found that it had been dead for days'.[47]

Astonished by the report, BBC editors wanted to wait for confirmation from newspapers. Dimbleby angrily told London that if it was not aired immediately he would never broadcast again. The British public heard his account, albeit heavily edited, on 19 April 1945. Years later people still stopped Dimbleby on the street to express the shock and anger they felt while listening to the report. On the same day as the broadcast, BBC Director of European News, D. E. Ritchie, sent a directive to his staff stating, 'There has never been a greater opportunity than there is now to reveal to the world the essential truth about Nazism – Buchenwald and Belsen'. He said all editors should put commentators on to the story because 'it is something which has to be understood by everybody and which the European Service must talk about in every language that it uses'.[48]

Broadcasting weeks later, Dimbleby said doctors and hardened army personnel were 'nauseated, literally horrified' by the sight of 'human beings who had been deliberately degraded to the level of animals. In Belsen there were peasants, factory workers, and musicians, artists, and the whole range of professional people, who fought for dirty scraps of food and, in the last stages of typhus, dragged themselves towards the heaps of bodies to lie there and die'. He admonished his audience, 'There is one other thing that you must do – something without which all the measures of relief and succour would be but temporary remedies – and that is to vow with all your heart that such things will never happen again'.[49]

Vaughan-Thomas said that he had always considered Dimbleby a journalist who did not let his emotions show through his on-air professional veneer, but that his experience at Belsen not only affected him personally but also his later commentary work in that he had 'a feeling for the suffering and anxiety of others which was instantly perceived by the viewer'.[50]

In the original broadcast Dimbleby stated, 'This day at Belsen was the most horrible of my life'. In 1957 on *Panorama* he said that after twenty-one years of broadcasting, Belsen was still one of his five most personally significant broadcasts out of thousands and 'something so horrible I'll never forget it'. He returned to Belsen for the first time in the summer of 1959 and after sitting in silence for fifteen minutes in his car with a colleague, looking at the grounds of the camp that had been burned down by British troops and where signs marked the location of mass graves, he remarked, 'Do you know what's strange about this place? There isn't a single bird singing here'. When he returned again in 1965, the same year of his own death from cancer, he recalled that he broke down five times while making the Belsen recording.[51]

An imperfect original

While most will agree that no one at the time expected Allied reporters to be impartial about the fight against a marauding Germany and the atrocities of the Nazis, the question that might be debated is whether the nationalistic enthusiasm of reporters during the Second World War was acceptable in journalistic terms? Do journalists (then and now) have a responsibility to maintain the professional neutrality of the observer or can they discard that standard when their country is at war?

While Gillard defended Dimbleby's reporting as 'conscientious and honest', Dimbleby almost certainly crossed the line of journalistic neutrality; for instance, when he agreed to carry diplomatic bags with sensitive documents between the British embassies in Cairo and Ankara using a courier's passport. His biographer writes, 'He set off with glee and a forgivable air of restrained self-importance'. The original reason for Dimbleby's trip was to set up BBC communications between Turkey and Britain, but he felt no compunction about combining his work as a reporter with a direct role in the British government's war effort.[52]

Yet Dimbleby was not alone among Allied journalists in taking an 'us and them' attitude. Many correspondents went along with government and military influence over their work not only because they were patriots but also because not to do so was a professional, tactical error. As Trevor Royle has explained, 'Eisenhower clinched the issue by adding that he regarded a mass of copy covered with [a censor's] blue pencil marks as failure. Stay on our side, tell our story, he seemed to be saying, and we'll treat you well. Give your own version, and you're out on your own'. The threat was largely unnecessary. In August 1943, when General George Patton infamously slapped one of his infirm soldiers for alleged cowardice, journalists were on hand but did not report the story; instead a group of American correspondents presented Eisenhower with a petition demanding Patton privately apologize. Eisenhower noted there was no military security censorship in the matter and that the journalists 'have got [themselves] good stories'. Apparently concerned about public morale and the continued fighting status of one of their nation's best generals, the reporters declined and said, 'we're Americans first and correspondents second'. Phillip Knightley, in his seminal 1975 history of war correspondents, *The First Casualty: The War Correspondent as Hero, Propagandist and Myth-Maker from the Crimea to Iraq*, noted that American correspondents had a pro-British bias fuelled by fears of what a German victory might mean for the United States.[53]

Knightley expounded on the idea of journalistic nationalism in June 2009: 'There are basically two types of war as far as journalists are concerned – other people's wars, and our wars. You can hope to get a reasonably accurate and objective report of other people's wars (although idealism might interfere) but it's naive to expect objectivity from journalists covering their own country's war. They are pulled into line by their own patriotic instincts, pressure of public opinion and the military which puts them into uniform, censors them and only grants access in return for propaganda. It was called accreditation. Now it's called embedding. It hasn't changed over the years'.[54]

Emotional patriotism aside, Dimbleby considered the correspondent's role during war to be one of great public service, saying it was 'a link between the men fighting at the front and the men and women working in the factories and at home throughout the Empire [...] It is useless [...] to ask for greater effort from the factory workers unless they have a direct connection with their husbands, sons and sweethearts abroad [...] only the war correspondent could bridge the gap between them'.[55]

Many will agree that Dimbleby succeeded in closing the divide between the war zone and the home front, and much more. Knightley believes Dimbleby made a real impact on journalism during the Second World War. 'He contributed to making radio reporting both respectable and important. Radio came into its own in WW2. It developed an immediacy and a drama of its own. Dimbleby, [Chester] Wilmot, Talbot all helped it gain this reputation. *War Report* was the best source for real news during the war', Knightley said, adding that Dimbleby is still considered an important figure in journalism. 'Fathering two such sons alone [Jonathan and television presenter David Dimbleby] is a pretty impressive contribution to journalism [...] He brought gravitas [to what] up until his arrival was a fairly louche sort of job'.[56]

Glasgow *Evening Citizen* writer, George Blake, in 1944 singled out Dimbleby's reporting during the D-Day operation, encapsulating his innate qualities: 'He brought back a picture of Normandy that I, for one, shall always count as one of the best bits of descriptive reporting in this war [...] Probably a faculty like this is inborn and unaccountable. You can do something with any cub reporter but no amount of teaching and experience will turn the wrong sort of man into the right sort of reporter'.[57]

Dimbleby provided memorable reporting long after D-Day. In addition to the Belsen report, in July 1945 he reached another physical and professional landmark as the first Allied reporter to enter a fallen Berlin, where he broadcast from Hitler's chair in the Chancellery. Throughout the war, whether having colourful adventures or detailing the stark horror of the concentration camps, Dimbleby proved he was the right sort of reporter.[58]

Richard Dimbleby was far from perfect. He was professional but not always objective. At times he had an exaggerated sense of self-importance and got too close to his official sources. Yet he was a broadcaster of exceptional skill who had an ability to paint vivid images with his words. His extraordinary career as the BBC's first war reporter was filled with milestones, and his innovations and compelling belief in its mission helped to bring the BBC, and radio as a whole, into a new era. He could broadcast with factual clarity without divorcing his reporting from his passion and empathy. The job of a BBC war correspondent would later be described as 'the simple, human, honest account of what one man had seen and heard'.[59] In this regard, even among that select group of broadcasters, Richard Dimbleby was an original.

Notes

1   BBC Written Archives Centre (hereafter BBC WAC), Reading, UK: BBC personnel document, *Richard Dimbleby*, 12 January 1946: Dimbleby-L1.131.1.

2   BBC WAC: Richard Dimbleby to the BBC General Establishment Officer, 7 May 1936, and Dimbleby to Coatman, 26 March 1936: Dimbleby-L1.131.1. J. Dimbleby, *Richard Dimbleby: A Biography* (London: Hodder and Stoughton, 1975), 35–36, 42–43, 50–52, 58. See also L. Miall (Ed.), *Richard Dimbleby: Broadcaster* (London: British Broadcasting Corporation, 1966), 4–5.

3   BBC WAC: Dimbleby to Coatman, undated: Dimbleby-L1.131.1. See also J. Dimbleby, 35–36, 60–63. L. Miall, 1–5.

4   BBC WAC: General Establishment Officer to Dimbleby, 26 June 1936, and Dimbleby to Coatman, undated: Dimbleby-L1.131.1. See also J. Dimbleby, 35–36, 60–63. Miall, L. (1966): 1–5.

5   BBC WAC: Mr R. Dimbleby, Topical Talks Assistant, News Dept, 27 August 1936, and B. E. Nicolls to Dimbleby, 13 August 1936: Dimbleby-L1.131.1. L. Miall,

7–8. See also R. Havers, *Here Is The News: The BBC and the Second World War* (Stroud, Gloucestershire: Sutton Publishing, 2007), 31.

6   J. Dimbleby, 72–73.

7   BBC WAC: 'To Mr. F. R. Dimbleby', 22 March 1937, 'Annual Revision of Salaries', 1 April 1938, and From Director of Staff to Dimbleby, 'Annual Revision of Salaries', undated: Dimbleby-L1.131.1. J. Dimbleby, 63, 74–75.

8   J. Dimbleby, 88–89. L. Miall, 20–21.

9   J. Dimbleby, 86.

10 BBC WAC: BBC to Dimbleby, 10 February 1939: Dimbleby-L1.131.1.

11 J. Dimbleby, 84.

12 J. Dimbleby, 94. L. Miall, 22–23.

13 J. Dimbleby, 89–94, 102.

14 J. Dimbleby, 99.

15 J. Dimbleby, 109–113, 123–131, 166–169, 190–194. L. Miall, 23–24.

16 J. Dimbleby, 136–137, 146–147, 154–157.

17 J. Dimbleby, 100–101, 109.

18 BBC WAC: G. J. B. Allport, 'Richard Dimbleby', 21 April 1944: Dimbleby-L1.131.1. BBC WAC: Allport to Dimbleby, 24 August 1944: Dimbleby-L1.131.1. BBC WAC: G. J. B. Allport, 'R. Dimbleby', 4 November 1943: Dimbleby-L1.131.1.

19 J. Dimbleby, 112–119.

20 L. Miall, 29–30.

21 G. Talbot, *Ten Seconds From Now: A Broadcaster's Story* (London: Hutchinson, 1973), 66.

22 G. Talbot, *Permission to Speak* (London: Hutchinson, 1976), 41–42. J. Dimbleby, 115–119.

23 BBC WAC: G. J. B. Allport, 'Richard Dimbleby', 21 April 1944: Dimbleby-L1.131.1. J. Dimbleby, 136–137, 146–147, 156–157, 163.

24 J. Dimbleby, 146–147.

25 J. Dimbleby, 115–119, 159.

26 Jonathan Dimbleby, 'Re: Richard Dimbleby', personal email to Brian Hannon, 30 April 2007.

27 BBC WAC: R28/280/2 and R28/280/3. D. Hawkins (Ed.), *War Report: A Record of Dispatches Broadcast by the BBC's War Correspondents with the Allied Expeditionary Force 6 June 1944–5 May 1945* (London: Oxford University Press, 1946), 9.

28 BBC WAC: Dimbleby to Ryan, 'Report on Spartan Exercise', 15 March 1943: R28/280/2.

29 All correspondents and engineers received the rank of captain, although engineers' pay grade was that of first lieutenant.

30 BBC WAC: Dimbleby to Ryan, 'Report on Spartan Exercise', 15 March 1943: R28/280/2.

31 W. Grierson, M. Jones & H. Waiwyn (Producers), *D-Day Despatches: Original Recordings from the BBC Sound Archives June 1944* (London: BBC Radio Collection, BBC Audiobooks Ltd, 2004). See also T. Hickman, *What Did You Do In The War, Auntie?: The BBC at War 1939–1945* (London: BBC Books, 1995), 180.

32 R. Havers, 203–204. See also J. Dimbleby, 184. S. E. Ambrose, *The Wild Blue: The Men and Boys Who Flew the B-24s Over Germany 1944–45* (New York, NY: Touchstone, 2001), 87n.

33 W. R. Chorley, *RAF Roll of Honour, Bomber Command Losses* (Hinckley, UK: Midland Publishing, 2007). Y. T. McEwen, '"Their Ancient Valour": Irish Volunteer Deaths in Ireland in the Second World War', in G. Morgan & G. Hughes (Eds), *Southern Ireland and the Liberation of France: New Perspectives* (Oxford: Peter Lang, 2011), 177–204. N. L. Franks, *Fighter Command Losses of the Second World War* Vols I, II & III. (Hinckley, UK: Midland Publishing, 1997, 1998, 2000).

34 Kent Stevenson went down in an RAF Lancaster on 22 June 1944; Guy Byam died flying with the U.S. Air Force on 3 February 1945. D. Hawkins, 58.

35 D. Hawkins, 281–282.

36 D. Hawkins, 326–327.

37 J. Dimbleby, 169, 184–185. See also R. Havers, 204.

38 L. Miall, 23.

39 BBC WAC: R. Dimbleby, 'My Despatch of January 5th', 6 January 1945: Dimbleby-L1.131.1.

40 D. Hawkins, 282.

41 J. Dimbleby, 85.

42 R. Dimbleby, *The Frontiers Are Green* (London: Hodder & Stoughton, 1944).

43 As quoted in L. Miall, 26–27.

44 L. Miall, 42–43.

45 L. Miall, 47.

46 J. Dimbleby, 190.

47 BBC, 'Audio Slideshow: Liberation of Belsen', http://news.bbc.co.uk/1/hi/in_depth/4445811.stm (accessed 9 June 2009). D. Hawkins, 401–402. J. Dimbleby, 190–193. See also L. Miall, 44–46.

48 D. E. Ritchie, 'News Directive on Reporting the Concentration Camps', 19 April 1945, BBC online archive, http://www.bbc.co.uk/archive/holocaust/5133.shtml (accessed 10 June 2009). J. Dimbleby, 193–194. L. Miall, 45–46.

49 J. Dimbleby, 193–194. L. Miall, 45–47.

50   L. Miall, 42–43.
51   BBC, 'Audio Slideshow: Liberation of Belsen', http://news.bbc.co.uk/1/hi/
     in_depth/4445811.stm (accessed 9 June 2009). L. Miall, 46–47, 108–109.
52   J. Dimbleby, 111.
53   T. Royle, *War Report: The War Correspondent's View of Battle from the Crimea
     to the Falklands* (Worcester, England: Mainstream Publishing, 1987), 149.
     R. Collier, *Fighting Words: The Correspondents of World War II* (New York,
     NY: St Martin's Press, 1989): 146. P. Knightley, *The First Casualty: The War
     Correspondent as Hero, Propagandist and Myth-Maker from the Crimea to Iraq*
     (London: Andre Deutsch, 2003), 256–257.
54   Phillip Knightley, 'Re: Richard Dimbleby questions', personal email to Brian
     Hannon, 6 June 2009.
55   J. Dimbleby, 163.
56   Phillip Knightley, 'Re: Richard Dimbleby questions', personal email to Brian
     Hannon, 6 June 2009.
57   As quoted in J. Dimbleby, 182.
58   L. Miall, 49–50. J. Dimbleby, 194–195.
59   D. Hawkins, 9.

JILL STEPHENSON

Shooting the War: Hans Ertl, Film Cameraman, and German Newsreels during the Second World War

'During the war, I shot thousands of people [...] with my camera, not with a weapon in my hand! [...] I didn't kill anyone'. Towards the end of his long life, Hans Ertl (1908–2000) reflected on his career as a film cameraman in Nazi Germany – as the leading member of Leni Riefenstahl's team for the 1936 Olympic Games, as a film-maker in his own right and as a film reporter on several fronts during the Second World War. He had been a mountaineer, sportsman and traveller, but his lasting fame derived from his skill and innovatory techniques as a film cameraman. Certainly, he served Hitler's Germany and its propaganda purposes, saying with some pride, 'I hold to the English view: "Right or wrong, my country"'.[1] Ertl's obsession was, however, with perfection as an artist.

Ertl very nearly managed to avoid involvement in the war altogether. He was in Berlin in early October 1939, preparing to leave for Chile in order to make a film, when he and his long-time collaborator, Robert Dahlmeier, had a chance encounter with a Nazi Propaganda Ministry functionary, Eberhard Fangauf, whom they had met a few years earlier. Two days later, they received a summons to present themselves at the Adolf Hitler barracks in Potsdam for basic military training. They considered absconding, via the ship moored at Hamburg on which they were booked to travel, but, with families in Bavaria and after weighing the probable consequences of flight, they complied with the summons. In the army, according to Ertl, 'it didn't matter that you had travelled the world, had meals with famous stars and made films'; they were under the authority of men whom they despised and at times they behaved in a subversive manner. At least once, Ertl ended up on guard duty for his pains. He and Dahlmeier did, however, win respect as expert sharp shooters, having grown up in the Bavarian countryside – unlike the rest of their 'fellow sufferers', who came from editing suites, film laboratories and radio studios. After three months, their military training was complete and, in mid-January 1940, Ertl and Dahlmeier were sent to join infantry regiment 501 at Trier. Here they met a group of war correspondents and photographers who would form the nucleus of a propaganda company – *Propagandakompanie* (PK).[2]

Ertl's career in film-making began in 1932. As a keen photographer and highly skilled mountaineer, he had already been commissioned to write articles about his exploits for newspapers, including *Frankfurter Zeitung*, while he somewhat reluctantly pursued his studies in commerce at Munich Technical College. Aware of his articles, Dr Arnold Fanck, the renowned film-maker, contacted Ertl to fill the vacancy on his expedition to Greenland left by the Swiss mountaineer, Otto Furrer, who had fallen ill. The purpose of the expedition was to make the film *SOS Eisberg*, starring Leni Riefenstahl. Ertl leapt at this chance to develop a career in film-making.[3] After several months in Greenland, Ertl was hired for further film work with Fanck. In 1934, before he set off on a mountaineering and filming expedition to the Himalayas, Ertl bought a Bell and Howell 'Eyemo' camera with which he made a trial promotional film for Garmisch-Partenkirchen, the venue for the 1936 Winter Olympic Games.[4] In this, he adopted innovative techniques; for example, he secured a camera, facing backwards, to his ski stick and shot atmospheric film as he – himself a champion skier – took to the slopes with Dahlmeier and others skiing behind him. He also strapped a camera to his chest before setting off on a ski-jump.[5] During the games, film that he shot at the top of the ski-jump run and below it, from the ground, provided unusual and highly effective footage of ski jumpers in motion. As part of Leni Riefenstahl's team on *Olympia*, the film of the 1936 games, he filmed divers in flight from the diving board and also under water after their entry into the pool, using a camera with a waterproof housing.[6] His particular aim was to capture the sense of movement and to transmit its energy to cinema audiences. The techniques that he developed at this time would serve him well as a film-maker on various fronts during the war.

Ertl judged people and events by the contribution that they made – positively or through obstruction – to his activity and career as a film-maker.

He clearly despised Nazi functionaries, not least because they sometimes tried to obstruct him, but he was not an opponent of Hitler's regime, whose policies he seems to have accepted mostly uncritically – before the war, at least. This was evident in, for example, the short propaganda film that he made for the Nationalsozialistische Deutsche Arbeiterpartei (NSDAP) in 1939, *Glaube und Schönheit* ('Faith and Beauty'), about the eponymous section of the *Bund Deutscher Mädel* (BDM: League of German Girls) for young women aged between eighteen and twenty-one. The activities that he portrayed in this were entirely in keeping with the Nazis' theoretical conception of women's roles in German society, of which he appears to have approved. In 1935, he had been a leading member of Riefenstahl's team for *Day of Freedom*, a film about Germany's celebration of its defiance of the clauses of the Treaty of Versailles of 1919 that banned German rearmament and conscription.[7] Ertl was not, however, a member of the Nazi Party, as he believed 'that one could be a good German and a patriot without carrying a party card'.[8] He had been disgusted, in 1934, when 'a nit-picking Nazi snooper' had branded the son of Professor G. O. Dyhrenfurth, team leader of the Himalayas' expedition, as 'not entirely of "Aryan" lineage', leading the young man to flee to Switzerland.[9]

As a proud Bavarian, Ertl disliked the tone and mannerisms of the Prussian officer class. Of General Model, he said that 'this prototype of a Prussian "er, um" officer', would not have felt fully dressed without his monocle in place. Ertl was not impressed when Model enlisted him as an interpreter for the general's visit to a rifle division from Munich, 'because he could hardly understand these old Bavarians'. By contrast, Field Marshal Erwin Rommel was a Württemberger (a south German like Ertl) and was far from pompous, and it is clear that Ertl liked and admired him. According to Ertl, Rommel viewed monocle-wearing 'er, um' Prussian officers with horror, as 'comic-book figures from a bygone age', and in return they looked down their noses at him. The easy access to himself that Rommel allowed PK reporters made him a favourite with them, even if the results of that brought him into disfavour with staff officers in Berlin.[10]

Ertl reserved his deepest disdain for 'the Browns', NSDAP functionaries, in particular those at the Propaganda Ministry, including Fangauf, who tended to treat him as a lowly technician rather than the artist that

he, justifiably, believed himself to be. In December 1941, having returned
to Berlin from a tour of duty in the Russian winter with German troops
on the outskirts of Leningrad, Ertl was asked by two Propaganda Ministry
'Browns' about troop morale. When he expressed the doubts he had heard
from soldiers, about the order to halt before Leningrad rather than taking
it, and about the value and distribution of clothing, skis and other items
collected for the troops from patriotic citizens at home, they brushed them
aside.[11] Doubtless the 'Browns' were well aware of the propaganda effort
made in the newsreels to persuade ordinary Germans to contribute to the
clothing collections, and further to persuade them that warm clothing
was reaching the troops they had seen shivering in inappropriate apparel
in previous newsreels. The SD (*Sicherheitsdienst* – Security Service of the
SS) reported that there was popular demand for scenes of German soldiers
actually wearing the clothes that had been collected.[12] Ertl commented
that there was little point in sending women's ski equipment to help the
troops, and that most of the warm clothing that had been collected ended
up not with soldiers engaged in combat but with members of the pay and
catering corps.[13]

Ertl evinced few feelings of guilt about the violence and depreda-
tion inflicted on much of Europe by the German forces whose activities
he was reporting. There is but one brief passage in his war memoirs that
appears to recognize what the *Wehrmacht* (armed forces) had wrought.[14]
It is, however, unlikely that he had no knowledge of, and indeed had not
witnessed, *Wehrmacht* atrocities against Soviet soldiers and/or civilians. On
the other hand, he was censorious about British bombing.[15] He dealt with
the issues arising from knowledge of the Holocaust by using a stock tactic
among Germans wishing to assert their personal ignorance: he related a tale
about an alleged chance encounter. Travelling by train from the Crimea to
Posen in early 1943, he was, he said, joined by a young SS lieutenant from
the South Tyrol, where Ertl's wife, Relly, had been born. After much remi-
niscence, and after Ertl had told tales about his time on the Eastern Front,
he asked his companion about his own experience. The young man gave a
nervous laugh and said: 'My "service at the front" so far was in concentration camps – in Maidanek and in Auschwitz – and the unarmed enemies
were Jews, Gypsies and so-called "asocials and racially worthless elements"'.

According to Ertl, he was struck dumb by the 'hair-raising stories' that his companion related. As they neared Warsaw at dawn, the young man told Ertl to try to forget what he had told him and not to breathe a word of it until the war was over.[16] Ertl did not refer to this episode again in his war memoirs, which may well have been more invention than truth. He clearly felt that recounting it had served the purpose of absolving him of complicity in the regime's crimes. Nor did he refer to film that appears to have been shot by him – although this is not certain – of Jewish families being loaded onto rail trucks under guard by *Waffen-SS* men.[17]

By 1939, there was nothing new about war correspondents using visual aids to illustrate their reports from the field to the home front. In the twentieth century, a newer medium of visual reportage was available: already used in conflicts, such as the First World War (as silent footage), the Abyssinian War and the Spanish Civil War, film was an important vector bringing the experience of combat home to civilians. For the overwhelming majority, this involved visiting a cinema to view newsreels; very few people were able to watch footage of the Second World War in the comfort of their own home.[18] 'World War II was a cinematic war', in which 'the armed forces of every major nation employed photographers who used lightweight 16mm cameras [...] to provide usable images for military and civilian purposes'.[19]

In Nazi Germany, these photographers were obliged to belong to the Reich Film Chamber, a subdivision of the Reich Chamber of Culture, a department of Joseph Goebbels' Reich Ministry for Propaganda and Popular Enlightenment, which ensured that they were 'racially valuable' and 'politically reliable'.[20] It did not necessarily mean that the photographers were diehard Nazis, although some of them were.[21] This ensured that their function was propagandistic – hence the name *'Propagandakompanien'* for the units to which photographers, correspondents, radio reporters and cameramen belonged.[22] The PKs were destined to accompany military units on campaign and to be a part of these units. Goebbels accepted the view of the military High Command that reporters accompanying troops and relating their deeds should have some appreciation of the discipline and rigours of military life. Thus, PK members underwent basic military training, wore military uniform and were under the authority of the *Wehrmacht*'s leadership.[23]

Preparation for war reporting began in the mid-1930s and by 1938 the PKs were formed. The cameraman Georg Schmidt-Scheeder relates how, in early March 1936, he and other print and photo journalists were transported to Cologne and its environs to report on the remilitarization of the Rhineland by German troops, in breach of the Treaty of Versailles. According to Schmidt-Scheeder, the success of the publicity surrounding this event convinced Goebbels that he should create his own corps of reporters responsible to his Propaganda Ministry.[24] Although this brought Goebbels into conflict with the War Ministry, his newly formed civilian 'Propaganda Units' were permitted to report on the *Wehrmacht*'s autumn manoeuvres in 1936 and 1937, while film-makers accompanied the Condor Legion in the Spanish Civil War. They also accompanied the forces that absorbed Austria into the Reich in the *Anschluss* in March 1938 and newsreels showed film of Hitler's triumphal entry into Vienna. In October 1938, a group of reporters and cameramen was sent to record the assimilation by Germany of the Sudetenland, after the Munich Agreement of 30 September 1938. This was judged to be a success, although it was said that the PK men had insufficient military training.[25]

By the time German forces invaded Poland on 1 September 1939 there were eleven PKs and by 1942 there were forty, attached to units in the three services of the *Wehrmacht* and to the *Waffen-SS*. By 1942, there were 219 film cameramen in the PKs: eighty-five with the army, forty-six with the air force, forty-two with the navy and forty-six with the *Waffen-SS*. By that time, sixty-two film cameramen had lost their lives in the conflict or were 'missing', fifty-seven were wounded and four had been taken prisoner.[26] Goebbels tinkered with the composition and structure of the PKs throughout the war and in September 1944 he recorded that the total number of reporters was being reduced from 15,000 to around 3,000, although he wondered if even that was too many, given 'the current state of the war'.[27] This was doubtless partly because of Germany's desperate shortage of manpower: PK members with military training could better be deployed in combat. In addition, however, there were few successes to report by this time, which meant that there was less for the PKs to do.

Film was explicitly regarded by Goebbels as a propagandistic weapon of war.[28] As part of the ethos of 'total war', the close involvement of those on the home front was essential in stiffening resolve and motivating civilians to strain every sinew to support the war effort.[29] Any recurrence of the 'stab-in-the-back' myth, which Hitler and his close associates believed had sabotaged the efforts of the fighting front in the First World War, had to be avoided at all costs.[30] Cheerleading for Germany was a major function of the films of the army's exploits that were made, edited and shown in newsreels throughout the war, not only in Germany but also in occupied, allied and neutral countries. The PKs' initial training included a spell with officials of the Propaganda Ministry to ensure that correspondents, broadcasters, cameramen and photographers were imbued with the message and manner of reportage that was expected of them.[31]

Goebbels was more than satisfied with provisos that he should have the final decision on who was chosen for membership of the PKs, and that his Ministry should decide on precisely which material was put in the public domain, after the military censors had approved it.[32] In wartime Goebbels spent two evenings a week supervising both the editing of the vast amounts of film sent home from the front and the scripting of the commentary to accompany newsreel film.[33] The chief editor of the newsreels was Dr Fritz Hippler, head of the film section in Goebbels' Ministry and director of the notorious propaganda film *Der ewige Jude* ('The Eternal Jew': 1940). It took at least a fortnight to edit and prepare the film, and to add both music and commentary. Then, between 1,700 and 2,400 copies were made to be distributed to cinemas across the country and to the mobile units that served smaller communities.[34]

The scope for selectivity of material for the newsreels was enormous. By September 1944, PK cameramen had sent back from the front more than 5 million metres of film to the Propaganda Ministry in Berlin. That amounted to a weekly total of 20,000–30,000 metres. This provided some twelve to eighteen hours of playing time, of which only about 6 per cent was actually used in newsreels. The most that was ever shown in a weekly newsreel was forty minutes, covering the invasion of France, with that declining to thirty minutes for even as major an event as the invasion of the Union of Soviet Socialist Republics (USSR) in June 1941. As there

was less of propaganda value to show with German forces in retreat, and
as camera film became less available and communications were disrupted,
newsreels from the front were reduced to some ten minutes' duration in
1944–45. From June 1942, film from the front was eked out by film from
various domestic events. While some interest was shown in these domestic
scenes, audiences made it clear that they were more concerned about seeing
footage from the fighting fronts.[35] The Nazi regime did not allow scenes
of defeat or retreat, or of wounded German servicemen, to be reported or
shown in the newsreels, although film from military hospitals was permitted.[36] Yet male members of audiences in Württemberg repeatedly asserted
that there should be 'far more realistic scenes' from the Eastern Front,
including 'even German casualties and disabled German tanks'. Their view
was that 'we can surely take the truth'.[37]

At first, there was great popular enthusiasm for the newsreels. In
October 1939, the SD reported 'once again, an extraordinarily high level
of attendance at cinemas'.[38] In March 1942, some people were said to have
been so impressed that they sat through the newsreel twice.[39] Cinemas in
small towns had previously received out-of-date newsreels but the prolif-
eration of copies in wartime enabled the most up-to-date newsreels to be
shown in virtually any cinema, until bombing took its toll and fuel became
scarce, with the result that many cinemas ceased to receive a copy of the
newsreel. At first, the massive demand in rural communities for news about
the progress of the war led many country dwellers to travel for the first time
into town to visit a cinema. As Bernd Kleinhans says, 'There was a particular psychological effect with the newsreel that made it peerless among the
media'. Cinema goers felt that they were virtually present at the dramatic
events that unfolded in the newsreels, with cameras on the move imparting
immediacy and intimacy, which were often carefully staged, and far from
as authentic and spontaneous as they tended to appear to the viewer.[40] As
early as 9 February 1940, the SD reported that scenes of German soldiers
on manoeuvres were regarded by cinema goers as 'completely unrealistic'
and as clearly having been staged.[41]

As Gerhard Stahr shows, doubts about the veracity of the information portrayed in newsreels developed largely independently of Germany's
fortunes in the war. It was said that soldiers home on leave noticed the

gulf between portrayal and reality, and there were rumours that, because of this, soldiers were being prohibited from viewing the newsreels.[42] The SD sent mixed messages, at times – as on 17 September 1942 – reporting soldiers' scepticism but at other times stressing that soldiers home on leave confirmed that the footage shown was a fair representation of reality.[43] Nevertheless, the SD's view was that the newsreels were 'one of the strongest propagandistic leadership tools', not least because audiences were amazed by the technical feats performed by PK cameramen.[44] As victory turned into defeat, Goebbels resorted to hiring claques of supporters to give a positive response in cinemas. However, the audience knew very well – from letters from the front, soldiers home on leave and listening to forbidden foreign radio – that, with 'German losses and wounded [...] not mentioned or shown', the camera could certainly lie.[45] Nevertheless, the SD continued to report that various sections of newsreels were being well received by audiences, and that newsreel footage was regarded by viewers as far more convincing than press or radio reports.[46]

There were, however, clear indications that the regime was becoming dissatisfied with the popular response to newsreels. In the middle of November 1941, the normal format of reporting opinion from named cities was abandoned and the formula 'from the whole area of the Reich' was adopted, making it difficult to track opinion on a local level.[47] During 1941, the SD reported frequently on responses to newsreels, during 1942 it reported on them less often and in September 1943 the last such report was made.[48] The last newsreel appeared on 27 March 1945 but, by this time, distribution was very limited and few people outside Berlin saw it.[49] The SD increasingly reported that attendance at newsreels had diminished. In September 1942 there was talk of 'newsreel weariness' and on 4 March 1943, the SD reported that, in Vienna on a Sunday, 40 per cent of the audience left the cinema at the end of the feature film and before the newsreel. In Stuttgart, at special showings of the newsreel on 1 and 2 March 1943, only twenty-five to thirty people had paid for admission.[50]

Probably nothing prepared Hans Ertl better for his role as a war reporter than his experience as Leni Riefenstahl's leading cameraman at the 1936

Olympic Games. The techniques that he developed for making evocative and realistic – as well as sometimes carefully staged – film of wartime events derived from his innovations at that time. Ertl's recruitment directly into military training evidently spared him from having to attend a training course in the Propaganda Ministry, whose functionaries he despised. Of the vice-president of the Reich Film Chamber, Hans Wiedemann, an *alter Kämpfer* ('old fighter') of the NSDAP, Ertl commented that he 'was not burdened by any professional knowledge, above all any relating to techniques of filmmaking'.[51] The less-than-talented cameraman, an NSDAP member, whom Ertl displaced for the Garmisch-Partenkirchen film, was dismissed by him as typical of the kind of person who had found a safe berth in the Propaganda Ministry.[52] In spite of his somewhat subversive attitude – which included dubbing Goebbels 'Mahatma Propagandi' – during the French campaign in 1940, Ertl was promoted to the rank of lieutenant and Dahlmeier became a non-commissioned officer in PK 501. As they were civilian professionals with only basic military training, these were not full military ranks with appropriate insignia, but they carried the pay and status of their respective ranks. Eventually, on 1 July 1942, after undergoing further military training, Ertl became a full lieutenant.[53]

In the absence of any official issue of camera equipment, Ertl was permitted to retrieve his own cameras from his home in Munich and, throughout the war, he submitted expenses chits for their use and was reimbursed. Armed with these cameras, his first assignment – in February 1940, during the 'phoney war' – was to film troops stationed in western Germany in order to show cinema audiences how well they were provisioned and accommodated. After filming troops on manoeuvres, Ertl's baptism of fire came with the invasion of the Low Countries and France in May 1940. Filming some German corpses, and the retrieval of identification marks and valuables from them, he had to choke back feelings of nausea at the stench of what he surmised was the beginning of decomposition. His commanding officer told him that his film 'will never be shown in public', to which Ertl replied that at least it could be deposited in an archive.

Shaken by the sight of German corpses mutilated by machine-gun fire, in May 1940, Ertl commented in his memoirs that he and Dahlmeier would become so habituated to this kind of sight that later they would be able to view piles of corpses with sangfroid, grateful only that they were not among them.[54] Nevertheless, on the Eastern Front in 1942 it took him much willpower to film 'gruesome scenes' of slaughtered Soviet soldiers half buried in the snow. His only wish was that he could send back to his masters in Berlin not only the sight of these but also the stench that accompanied them.[55] Ertl was particularly shocked when confronted with the fresh graves of General Lanz's first *Gebirgsjäger* ('mountain troop') division after a very bloody battle at Bereka (Ukraine) in May 1942. The names of many of the dead were well known to him, as former mountaineering or skiing companions.[56]

In France in 1940, Ertl and Dahlmeier were able to keep up with the troops at the front and film their activities because they had acquired a motorcycle with sidecar, which enabled them to travel faster, with handheld cameras, than the wagon carrying their more sophisticated film equipment. Close to Sedan, German troops came under attack from low-flying French aircraft. Finding cover behind a wall, Ertl filmed the French bombers and fighters with enthusiasm, regretting that he had only the handheld cameras and not his large tripod-mounted camera with a 300mm telephoto lens. Dahlmeier, crouching in a brick oven, replaced the film magazines in turn to enable Ertl to shoot virtually continuously.

Afterwards, Ertl mused on how his propaganda masters would not want to use this film of a damaging French attack but how his French counterparts would have coveted it, opining that war reporters should really be neutral, or have Red Cross status, and be able to exchange their acquisitions. Ertl and Dahlmeier were able to film the *Wehrmacht*'s march down the Champs Elysées in June 1940 with their large camera 'in complete peace', using a handheld camera only for short sequences. This, along with 'thousands of metres of celluloid' from recent campaigns, was used to make the documentary film *Sieg im Westen* ('Victory in the West'). The balance of what was to be included was controversial: Ertl wanted to record the successes – albeit limited – of French, Belgian and Dutch troops as well as of German forces, but caution was required because Hermann Göring had already complained that the cameramen who had filmed paratroopers during the invasion of the west had not shown them in a sufficiently flattering light. Accordingly, new scenes of paratroopers in western Europe were staged and shot especially for the documentary.[57] After Hitler had given his approval, the film had its premier in Berlin on 31 January 1941 and was then shown in cinemas all over Germany, to great acclaim.[58]

It was on the Western Front that Ertl met General Erwin Rommel and they renewed their acquaintance in the North African desert when Ertl was sent to join the German Afrika-Korps in March 1941, as a 'special war reporter', freed from the constraints of membership of a PK, and the only German film cameraman in North Africa at that time. He had requested that Dahlmeier join him but Fangauf at the Propaganda Ministry turned him down and Ertl had to reload his own cameras. Nevertheless, as a member of a three-man team, with photographer Erich Borchert and reporter Hans Gert von Esebeck, and with the mobility and independence that his own Volkswagen (VW) off-road vehicle afforded, he shot a considerable amount of film in the desert during his seven-month sojourn there. Using the VW enabled him to transport heavier-duty cameras, including an Askania 'Z' which took a 120-metre film magazine.[59] From March to June 1941, the SD reported the warm reception given by cinema audiences to film of the North African campaign, although it recognized in June 1941 that the scenes shown were becoming very familiar. Mention was made of the appreciation shown for the 'technically especially impressive and successful' film footage from Africa.[60] Film of Rommel's exploits was particularly welcomed, making him a popular hero at home.[61] In May 1941, film of the bombing of Tobruk aroused great interest, especially for its demonstration that 'not every bomb hits its target', and for its depiction of the troops' equipment for tropical conditions, including the provision of medical care for those who had contracted tropical diseases.[62]

After the invasion of the USSR, however, SD reports show that the majority of newsreel film was coming from the Eastern Front, with audiences eventually growing weary of seeing the same kind of sequences repeatedly. There was constant demand, especially in August 1941, for footage from other fronts and particularly from North Africa.[63] In September 1941, the weekly newsreel showed film from there that generated a very positive response, including 'resounding merriment' when Ertl's subsequently famous scene of soldiers frying eggs on the steel plate under a tank's gun was shown.[64] Yet even this was carefully staged, with someone – who, in popular legend but erroneously, became Rommel himself – holding a blowlamp under the steel plate to intensify the heat so that the filming session could be completed in much less than the fifteen minutes that Ertl estimated it would otherwise have taken. The purpose of the sequence was to give a graphic representation of the kind of heat with which the Afrika-Korps was having to contend. To the amusement of Rommel's staff, it emerged from letters to members of the tank corps from their wives and girlfriends that it had caused great anxiety about the hazards of this 'barbaric heat' and its presumed 'danger to male potency'.[65]

Senior officers of the High Command, including Franz Halder, resented the image and publicity that Rommel had acquired as a result of his exploits in the desert. The solution, they thought, was to deprive Rommel of the cameraman recording these exploits. Twice letters were sent to Rommel's headquarters recalling Ertl to Berlin. On both occasions, Rommel disposed of them and ordered Ertl to remain with him. When a third letter arrived, Rommel was in Rome and those left in command at his headquarters despatched Ertl to Berlin, where he was told that he had 'rommeled' too much, meaning that he was responsible for 'exaggerated propaganda about the general of the tank corps, Erwin Rommel, that was out of proportion to his achievements and especially to those of other army leaders, particularly those in the Russian campaign'. Ertl was asked to confirm that he had shot film on expeditions to Greenland, the Himalayas, the Andes and the Alps, and that he had experienced Arctic conditions. He was told, 'we are now giving you the opportunity to go to the Russian front in winter'. One reason for Ertl's transfer to the Eastern Front was, it transpired, that much less film was being shot there because the cameras being used would not operate in the freezing conditions of a Russian winter. His view was that the cameramen had been issued with the wrong kind of cameras for the conditions.[66] Having persuaded Fangauf that traipsing round all the PKs in Russia to advise cameramen to use a smear of petroleum jelly on the mechanism of their cameras would be a waste of his time, Ertl was assigned as special reporter to the front at Leningrad to shoot film on the theme of 'Christmas among our soldiers in the front line'.

Armed with new Agfa colour film, with which he had already experimented in North Africa, Ertl set off for the east with Dahlmeier. He marvelled at the beautiful countryside in Estonia. It could, he said, have been a scene from somewhere in Bavaria. On the outskirts of Leningrad, he and Dahlmeier lodged with an elderly couple who spoke German and lived in 'appalling poverty'. Ertl watched as the man carefully collected sawdust for his wife to use to eke out flour supplies for bread making and as the woman removed from a samovar tea leaves, which she then dried in order to reuse them. Because of this – and grateful for the warm hospitality they had received – he and Dahlmeier left their full army rations with their hosts on their departure.

With scenes of winter on the outskirts of Leningrad filmed, they returned to Berlin. Ertl did not regard these scenes as particularly noteworthy but Boese, the PK chief in Berlin, marvelled at the subtlety of his pictures, compared with the 'chalky, brutal black and white' film taken by others. Ertl's reply was that it was 'purely a question of filters [...] and above all a matter of experience'.[67] His film was not always as well received. In spring 1942, the military censor in Berlin reprimanded him for having filmed in colour – and somewhat sympathetically – particularly bloody scenes of dead Soviet soldiers and civilians, and then going on to shoot film of devout Russians in the gilded cathedral at Smolensk, which had been reclaimed from use as a 'museum of the godless' under the Soviets. 'First you film these filthy scenes with the corpses, and then you go on to make propaganda for the church!'[68] There was, however, legitimate concern about scenes that were particularly gruesome. The SD had reported from early in the Russian campaign that women cinema goers expressed strong dislike of them and sometimes sat with their hands over their eyes until a shocking scene had passed.[69]

In order to keep him under control, Ertl's next assignment was to film officers in their quarters at Chudajarovo, near Kharkov. He regarded filming a commander with his staff at a map table, where 'the only movement was that of a finger pointing out to some men the target of an attack', as unproductive. Although he learned a lot from consorting with these officers, the arrival of Dahlmeier by car, with the heavy camera equipment, afforded Ertl the mobility he craved, and he left to film soldiers of the fourteenth and twenty-second tank divisions on campaign in the Voroshilovgrad area. His adventures included a close encounter with Red Army soldiers and

airmen, and drinking wine in a cellar in Rostov-on-Don while two dead
Russian soldiers floated in the overflow from the burst barrel. Then Ertl ran
the gauntlet of Soviet snipers and grenade-throwers in Rostov, as he tried
to capture on film the house-to-house fighting there. On one occasion, he
and Dahlmeier exited their sleeping quarters through the window, driven
out by a plague of insects, just as Soviet soldiers burst into the building.
On 27 July 1942, they used the last of their film and set off for Schachty,
where the first tank corps was located, to send home their film and replen-
ish their empty canisters with new film.

Then they set off into the Kuban, in the Caucasus.[70] Assigned to a
Gebirgsjäger company in the Kuban as leader of its PK platoon, Ertl admired
both the beauty of the scenery and the determination and tenacity of
the Red Army soldiers. The *Wehrmacht* was still in a position to provide
splendid fare – including goose and French red wine – for the troops'
Christmas celebration in 1942, but by now Ertl had run out of film. He
had sent his last completed film to Berlin by courier but had received no
new film in return. He assumed that, as he was now unable to fulfil his
role as a war cameraman, he would have to become a full-time soldier.[71]
Nevertheless, the film that Ertl had sent back to Berlin was well received
when sequences were shown in newsreels. According to the SD, his scenes
of the burning oil wells at Maykop were watched with particular interest.[72]
Little did cinema goers know that Ertl had again staged these scenes. Film
of German soldiers climbing to the summit of Mount Elbrus was, however,
genuine. Cinema audiences were clearly impressed by this September 1942
newsreel, especially the closing scenes which showed the snow-covered
peaks of the Caucasus.[73]

Ertl's personal luck held but only for a short time: his unit was recalled
to Posen and he left the Caucasus in an airplane that he described as 'a
museum piece from the First World War', piloted by a seventeen-year-old.
After an attack by Russian fighters, the pilot brought the plane down in a
snowy field not far from their destination in the Crimea and the platoon
continued its journey by train. After three weeks' leave, Ertl and Dahlmeier
worked in a studio in Berlin-Spandau editing the colour film taken in the
Caucasus, for a documentary entitled *Alert at the Pass*. At the end of June
1943, Goebbels, who praised the quality of the film, prohibited its release

to the public on the grounds that German troops were no longer in the Caucasus region and had no prospect of returning there.[74] In Normandy, in May 1944, Ertl was able to show the film to two generals and other senior officers who had not previously seen colour film of German campaigns. In the lecture that preceded the viewing, he stated that film of the war should not merely be material for the newsreels but should also serve as an authentic historical record. Although he was not above doctoring his scenes at times, this was undoubtedly why he was bitter about the 'web of deceit' spun by Goebbels' Ministry and which enveloped war reporters: 'Truth was not sought, was even forbidden, and if one took film that showed how the war really was, one was immediately suspected of being a defeatist'.[75]

Ertl spent the rest of the war in either Germany or western Europe, where German forces were – as in the east – on the defensive. Following a tour of duty in northern Italy, he was allocated leave but, while he was at home in Munich, his house was bombed. The family was at the time sheltering in a three-metre-deep bunker that had recently been built in the garden by six Russian prisoners of war (POW) with materials supplied by a Nazi relief organization. Ertl's attempts to rescue his equipment from the cutting room that he had established in the house were to no avail. The family had to move out to stay with his parents in the countryside while the roof was being repaired. The neck wound that Ertl had sustained in the bombed house festered and eventually consigned him to hospital. While he was in hospital, his youngest daughter, Marlene, experienced breathing difficulties, from which she subsequently died.[76]

In March 1944, once his wound had healed, Ertl's PK platoon was sent to join Field Marshal Rommel in France. 'Don Erwin', as they now dubbed him, was delighted to see Ertl again and promptly took him on a tour of inspection of the coastal defences in Normandy. While Ertl once again marvelled at the beauty of the scenery, Rommel checked the placing of mines and gave instructions on how soldiers were to respond to any landing attempted by the enemy. Ertl and Fred Rieder, a photographer, filmed the Atlantic Wall and its defenders, for the newsreel and for an illustrated magazine, respectively. Rommel then embarked on an exhausting series of tours of defences around France, with Ertl in attendance and taking so much footage in different settings that even Rommel told him that he should be more sparing with the film.[77]

Thereafter, Ertl and Dahlmeier took advantage of Rommel's absence at a briefing with Hitler in Berchtesgaden to make a sightseeing trip along the French coast to Honfleur, Deauville and Caen, filming defensive installations. They made a detour to Camembert where lived the wife and family of a French POW who was working on a farm in Bavaria, whom Ertl had met and with whom his father-in-law was well acquainted. Ertl had brought with him an uncensored letter and a photograph for Madame Thérèse from her husband, Georges Charlais. A parcel and photographs of the family were taken in return and Dahlmeier was able, a fortnight later, to deliver these to Georges when he returned to Bavaria on holiday and to collect Ertl's spare camera. A few months later, they had the opportunity to revisit Camembert, with Dahlmeier once again leaving with a parcel for Georges, which he delivered when on a visit to Munich to have his camera repaired. Finally, in July 1944, Ertl and Dahlmeier helped the family to dig a pit in a barn to accommodate their small car, pram, bicycles and boxes of valuables, so that they would not be seized by retreating German troops. They left with another parcel for Georges. At the end of the war, French soldiers who were part of the occupation force in southern Germany formally thanked Ertl for his kindness to the Charlais family.[78]

While he was in France, Ertl's off-road VW was at long last returned from eastern Europe, along with a sound film camera in its trailer and a sound engineer, Heini Glieman. In mid-May 1944, together with Dahlmeier, they accompanied Rommel on an inspection tour in the Pas-de-Calais, making a sound film of his major speech at Le Touquet to soldiers and construction workers. A fortnight later, Ertl and Glieman filmed the twenty-first tank division on manoeuvres and, a week after that, the D-Day landings kept the entire platoon busy, filming, photographing and writing reports in circumstances that were often extremely dangerous. When the press reporter, Clemens Graf Podewils, returned from working with Rommel and related how enemy air power and paratroopers had destroyed the twenty-first tank division, Rieder said 'What film shots that would have made!'. Ertl, however, recognized that such a film would never have been shown. Propaganda masters did not expect them to report about heavy German losses in the Cotentin peninsula. Regretting that he did not have his 1000mm telephoto lens with him, but merely a 650mm lens, Ertl filmed the invasion fleet and noted the inability of German artillery to destroy it: 'I have never felt, as a war reporter, our powerlessness so acutely as in these moments'. When he saw his own film on a newsreel for the first time, he was horrified that the commentary claimed that it showed German military successes when the contrary was the case. By now, travelling by road was hazardous, with enemy fighters having superiority in the air and strafing moving traffic at will. Rommel would be injured by this kind of attack on 17 July 1944. Returning safely to their base at Tripleval, Ertl learned from Glieman that some friends sent to the front to film had been killed, and their sound camera and other equipment destroyed. Among other close colleagues of Ertl who were already dead were Gustav von Etzdorf, formerly of PK 501, who was killed in Russia, and Erich Borchert, Ertl's companion in North Africa in 1941.[79]

Under pressure from Berlin to produce film about the fighting in and around Caen, Ertl, Dahlmeier, Rieder and Glieman, with their driver Vandenhövel, set off for the area on 6 July. Ertl and Dahlmeier filmed, from a gravel pit in the lea of a hill, 'chaotic scenes' caused by bombing of the city. Anxious to leave the area before the British renewed their attack, on the grounds that 'only a cameraman who is alive can deliver war reports', they encountered Glieman and Rieder, who had witnessed the American attack on St Lô. Glieman commented, 'This isn't war any more – it's sheer madness!'. By now, Ertl and other war reporters despaired of the conduct of the war, but knew that they had to follow orders from Berlin about where and what to report – if they wanted to remain reporters rather than become soldiers in combat. Ertl was also aware that Rommel, angry at being denied additional troops to counter the invasion, because Hitler was keeping them in reserve, favoured an armistice in the west because, he believed, every success he had in delaying the enemy's advance meant an advantage for the Red Army as it advanced in the east.[80]

Ertl and his platoon spent much of August 1944 preparing to retreat, which they eventually did dispiritedly along with German troops, periodically taking cover from enemy fighters and reaching Holland in early

September. Ertl had an extremely narrow escape when an enemy para-
trooper's gun that was aimed at him jammed. At another time, while hiding
from the invaders, he was unable to warn seven German soldiers carrying
plates of soup that they were in the enemy's sights and they were gunned
down. Ertl and his team fled towards Germany, leaving his trusty Bell and
Howell handheld camera and other belongings in his Dutch lodgings. The
lodgings were later raided by an SS troop looking for enemy soldiers and the
SS officer in possession of Ertl's belongings refused to return the camera.

After filming the British assault on Arnhem, with his equipment heavily camouflaged, Ertl was at last able to fulfil his desire and leave for Italy
with Dahlmeier and Rieder. Back in the mountains, near the Swiss border,
he began filming (in colour) the *Alpenfestung* ('Alpine Fortress') – with
enemy bombers above – that was planned by *Gauleiter* Franz Hofer as a final
Nazi redoubt.[81] In November 1944, Ertl was summoned to Berlin where
Fangauf ordered him to the Courland bridgehead in the east. However,
Ertl regarded this as a suicide mission and he did not go. It is possible that
it was assumed that Ertl had been killed in the heavy air raid on Berlin
on the night following his meeting with Fangauf because he was never
punished for his disobedience. Instead, he returned to the Alps for the
remainder of the war, working on the film of the *Alpenfestung*. Although
the Alpine area was constantly bombed, Ertl regarded it as much safer
and more congenial than either the Western or Eastern Fronts. There is an
aura of unreality about the way in which he and his colleagues continued
working as normal on their film, listening to news of the death throes of
Germany's war effort on German and Swiss radio, until American forces
arrived in April 1945.[82]

Hans Ertl was a maverick who fitted no stereotype, whether of a German
or a photographer. He was completely obsessed by his involvement in
film-making, before, during and after the war, until much of his camera
equipment was destroyed in an accident in Bolivia in 1962. After that, he
gave up photography and filming altogether and lived as a farmer.[83] He
had emigrated from Germany after being stripped by the interior ministry
in Bonn – without being told the reason – of the national film prize that

was to be awarded to him at the Berlin Film Festival in 1954 for his film *Nanga Parbat 1953*, about Hermann Buhl's successful ascent. 'The twelve-year Nazi regime had not succeeded in driving me from my beautiful south German home', he said, 'in spite of much humiliation and harassment', but the democratic Bonn government did.[84] By his own account, Ertl was arrested by the Americans at the end of the war but was able to escape. In the chaos of Germany after 1945, he was a photographer for *Quick* magazine, capturing everyday scenes with a camera attached to his head and hidden under a hat.[85] He also returned to mountaineering, participating in the German expedition to Bolivia in 1950, climbing several mountains there before tackling Nanga Parbat.[86]

Hans Ertl was a contradictory figure. In so many ways a non-conformist, he was politically highly conservative. He was a German patriot who, as a Bavarian, remained hostile to and suspicious of Prussians, and remained to the end resentful that his homeland had, in his view, not valued his talents. He made films for the Nazi Party but despised most of its functionaries and was not himself a party member. He accepted German aggression during the war but condemned the British for bombing French towns in 1944. Yet he was by no means xenophobic. He manifested genuine fellow feeling for Russian and French civilians whom he encountered, as his part in the illicit traffic between Georges Charlais and his family, in particular, demonstrates. Yet Ertl could be distinctly disingenuous. According to him, the inhabitants of the areas in which he worked were 'nice', 'friendly', even though they were under German occupation. He waxed lyrical about this in Normandy, without explaining how he had obtained the use of a French motor manufacturer's country villa in Tripleval, much as he did not explain how he came to be lodged with – or, more probably, billeted on – Russian peasants and a Dutch family.[87] He accepted without question the use of six Russian POW in building the air-raid shelter in his garden in Munich. Yet his relationships with civilian Russians whom he encountered were apparently cordial. His aim was to shoot film of the war to serve as an historical record, yet he colluded in visual tricks and staged scenes that confirmed Senator Hiram Johnson's judgment that 'The first casualty when war comes is truth'.[88]

Ertl's complaints about his treatment by the West German government were no doubt sincerely felt but nevertheless have an aura of disingenuousness. It seems that he probably was denazified, like Leni Riefenstahl, who was classed by the tribunal in 1949 as a 'Mitläufer' (fellow traveller) but was acquitted of the charge of 'promoting the NS dictatorship'.[89] Some sources say that Ertl was not only denazified but also was banned from film-making for two years.[90] Being a cameraman with PKs was not of itself a disqualification from employment after 1945, as the cases of other PK men demonstrate.[91] Yet Ertl must have been aware that some of his activities in the Third Reich made him suspect after the war, even if he repetitively claimed that he had merely made a record of events and had not been a participant in them. Membership of Riefenstahl's team for the 1935 film about German rearmament was perhaps not decisive, and probably few people had watched – or remembered having watched – *Glaube und Schönheit*, about the BDM. However, it all amounted to having worked on commissions for the NSDAP. Whether or not that is what led to the rather clumsy last-minute withdrawal of his film prize in 1954, and his disqualification from eligibility for government grants for his work, is unclear. What cannot be doubted is that, as a film-maker, he was an inspired, creative and original artist.

Notes

1   Regisseur: Hans Ertl 2/3: http://www.youtube.com/watch?v=2swjEtGfICo &feature=related. I am grateful to Dr R. W. Bingham, ARPS, EFIAP, of the Edinburgh Photographic Society, for expert advice on technical matters.

2   H. Ertl, *Als Kriegsberichter 1939–1945* (Innsbruck: Steiger, 1985), 7–12. For Ertl's earlier encounter with Fangauf, see H. Ertl, *Meine wilden dreissiger Jahre: Bergsteiger, Filmpionier, Weltenbummler* (Munich and Berlin: Herbig, 1982), 190–191. On Fangauf himself, see D. Uziel, *The Propaganda Warriors: The Wehrmacht and the Consolidation of the German Home Front* (Bern: Peter Lang, 2008), 74, 76, 78, 162. On the organization of the *Propagandakompanien*, see D. Uziel, 106–181.

3   H. Ertl (1982), 11–20, 45–46, 48, 63.

4   H. Ertl (1982), 47–187.

5   H. Ertl (1982), 187–190.

6   Regisseur: Hans Ertl 2/3.

7   Regisseur: Hans Ertl 2/3.

8   H. Ertl (1985), 200.

9   H. Ertl (1982), 185.

10   H. Ertl (1985), 52–53, 57, 193, 251. G. Schmidt-Scheeder, *Reporter der Hölle: Kriegsberichterstatter im 2. Weltkrieg* (Stuttgart: Pietsch Verlag, 2003), 398–399. Regisseur: Hans Ertl 3/3: http://www.youtube.com/watch?v=2pe2_LuDRSA& feature=related

11   H. Ertl (1985), 118.

12   H. Boberach (Ed.), *Meldungen aus dem Reich 1938–1945* (Herrsching: Pawlak, 1977), Vol. 9 [Nr. 249 (8 Jan 1942)], 3138; [Nr. 251 (15 Jan 1942)], 3167.

13   H. Ertl (1985), 118–119.

14   H. Ertl (1985), 153.

15   H. Ertl (1985), 260.

16   H. Ertl (1985), 168, 173–174.

17   Regisseur: Hans Ertl 2/3.

18   The war on German television, see G. Paul, *Bilder des Krieges, Krieg der Bilder: Die Visualisierung des modernen Krieges* (Paderborn: Ferdinand Schöningh, 2004), 244–247.

19   J. W. Chambers II & D. Culbert (Eds), 'Introduction', in *World War II, Film and History* (New York, NY: Oxford University Press, 1996), 4. See also D. Uziel, 9–10.

20   G. Paul, 226. J. F. Bruns, *Nazi Cinema's New Women* (New York, NY: Cambridge University Press, 2009), 16–17, 20–23. H. A. Winkler, *Germany: The Long Road West, 1922–1990* (Oxford: Oxford University Press, 2007), 28.

21   H. Ertl (1985), 175.

22   D. Uziel, 87–91.

23   H. Barkhausen, *Filmpropaganda für Deutschland im Ersten und Zweiten Weltkrieg* (Hildesheim: Olms Presse, 1932), 202–205. G. Schmidt-Scheeder, 35–36.

24   G. Schmidt-Scheeder, 24–36. On the events of March 1936, see also: R. G. Reuth (Ed.), *Joseph Goebbels Tagebücher*. Band 3: *1935–1939* (Munich and Zürich: Piper Verlag, 1999), 933–934 (footnote 14). H. Hoffmann, *The Triumph of Propaganda: Film and National Socialism, 1933–1945*, J. A. Broadwin & V. R. Berghahn (trans.), (Providence, RI, and Oxford: Berghahn Books, 1996), 202–203. D. Uziel, 73.

25   H. Barkhausen, 206–207. D. Uziel, 83, 92–97.

26 G. Paul, 229. K. Hoffmann, 'Der Mythos der perfekten Propaganda: Zur Kriegs-berichterstattung der "Deutschen Wochenschau" im Zweiten Weltkrieg', In U. Daniel (Ed.), *Augenzeugen: Kriegsberichterstattung* vom 18: zum 21. *Jahrhundert* (Göttingen: Vandenhoeck & Ruprecht, 2006), 172.

27 R. G. Reuth, Band 5: *1943–1945*, 2093.

28 H. Barkhausen, 212.

29 Bundesarchiv, Berlin Document Center, Germany: 'Tätigkeitsbericht', Stichtag, 30 Oktober 1944: R55, 200. On 'total war', see P. Longerich, 'Joseph Goebbels und der totale Krieg. Ein unbekannte Denkschrift des Propagandaministers vom 18. Juli 1944', *Vierteljahrshefte für Zeitgeschichte*, 35 (1987), 290–292. R. Chickering & S. Förster, 'Are We There Yet? World War II and the Theory of Total War', in R. Chickering, S. Förster & B. Greiner (Eds), *A World at Total War. Global Conflict and the Politics of Destruction, 1937–1945* (Cambridge: Cambridge University Press, 2005), 1–14.

30 On the 'stab-in-the-back' myth, see T. Mason, *Social Policy in the Third Reich. The Working Classes and the 'National Community'*, chapter 1 (Providence, RI, and Oxford: Berg, 1993). T. Mason, 'The Legacy of 1918 for National Socialism', in A. Nichols & E. Matthias (Eds), *German Democracy and the Triumph of Hitler* (London: Allen & Unwin, 1971), 19–40. N. P. Howard, 'The Social and Political Consequences of the Allied Food Blockade of Germany, 1918–19', *German History*, 11 (1993), 161–188. U. Daniel, *Arbeiterfrauen in der Kriegsgesellschaft* (Göttingen: Vandenhoeck und Ruprecht, 1989).

31 K. Hoffmann, 172. D. Uziel, 144–149.

32 H. Barkhausen, 202–205. G. Schmidt-Scheeder, 32–36.

33 N. Frei & J. Schmitz, *Journalismus im Dritten Reich* (Munich: Beck, 1999), 92.

34 K. Hoffmann, 175–176, 180. G. Paul, 229.

35 H. Boberach, Vol. 10 [Nr. 289 (4 Jun 1942)], 3791–3792. H. Boberach, Vol. 14 [SD-Berichte zu Inlandsfragen (22 Jul 1943)], 5519–5520.

36 B. Kleinhans, *Ein Volk, ein Reich, ein Kino: Lichtspiel in der braunen Provinz* (Cologne: PapyRossa Verlag, 2003), 152.

37 Staatsarchiv Ludwigsburg, Germany: 'Betr.: Allgemeine Stimmung und Lage', 15 July 1941: K110, Bü47, 7.

38 H. Boberach, Vol. 2 [Nr. 2 (11 Oct 1939)], 342.

39 H. Boberach, Vol. 9 [Nr. 265 (5 Mar 1942)], 3411–3412.

40 B. Kleinhans, 149–151, 157. G. Stahr, *Volksgemeinschaft vor der Leinwand? Der nationalsozialistische Film und sein Publikum* (Berlin: Theissen, 2001), 176–177.

41 H. Boberach, Vol. 3 [Nr. 51 (9 Feb 1940)], 741.

42 G. Stahr, 181.

43   G. Stahr, 181–184. H. Boberach, Vol. 11 [Nr. 318 (17 Sep 1942)], 4211. H. Boberach, Vol. 14 [SD-Berichte zu Inlandsfragen (22 Jul 1943)], 5520.

44   H. Boberach, Vol. 4 [Nr. 90 (23 May 1940)], 1166; [Nr. 91 (27 May 1940)], 1180. H. Boberach, Vol. 2, Bericht zur innenpolitischen Lage [Nr. 2 (11 Oct 1939)], 342.

45   N. Frei & J. Schmitz, 93–95.

46   H. Boberach, Vol. 13 [Nr. 379 (29 Apr 1943)], 5192–5193.

47   H. Boberach, Vol. 8 [Nr. 238 (17 Nov 1941)], 3011–3013; [Nr. 240 (24 Nov 1941)], 3035–3036.

48   H. Boberach, Vol. 14 [SD-Berichte zu Inlandsfragen (9 Sep 1943)], 5726–5728.

49   H. Boberach, Vols 15, 16, 17. B. Kleinhans, 157.

50   H. Boberach, Vol. 13 [Nr. 364 (4 Mar 1943)], 4895.

51   H. Ertl (1982), 209. The *alte Kämpfer* ('old fighters') of the NSDAP were those who had joined the party before Hitler's appointment as Chancellor on 30 January 1933.

52   H. Ertl (1982), 221.

53   H. Ertl (1985), 42–43, 50, 55, 129, 141.

54   H. Ertl (1985), 29–30.

55   H. Ertl (1985), 127–128.

56   H. Ertl (1985), 132–133.

57   H. Ertl (1985), 45, 47, 49–50, 55.

58   D. Uziel, 194–195.

59   H. Ertl (1985), 59, 86.

60   H. Boberach, Vol. 7 [Nr. 180 (22 Apr 1941)], 2220; [Nr. 187 (19 May 1941)], 2318; [Nr. 189 (26 May 1941)], 2344; [Nr. 192 (9 Jun 1941)], 2397; [Nr. 197 (26 Jun 1941)], 2446; [Nr. 199 (3 Jul 1941)], 2472.

61   H. Boberach, Vol. 7 [Nr. 187 (19 May 1941)], 2318; [Nr. 197 (26 Jun 1941)], 2446. H. Boberach, Vol. 9 [Nr. 249 (8 Jan 1942)], 3139; [Nr. 265 (5 Mar 1942)], 3412; [Nr. 269 (19 Mar 1942)], 3493; [Nr. 271 (26 Mar 1942)], 3525. H. Boberach, Vol. 11 [Nr. 317 (14 Sep 1942)], 4212. H. Boberach, Vol. 13 [Nr. 364 (4 Mar 1943)], 4894.

62   H. Boberach, Vol. 7 [Nr. 192 (9 Jun 1941)], 2397.

63   H. Boberach, Vol. 7 [Nr. 211 (14 Aug 1941)], 2651. H. Boberach, Vol. 8 [Nr. 213 (21 Aug 1941)], 2674; [Nr. 215 (28 Aug 1941)], 2704; [Nr. 217 (4 Sep 1941)], 2727; [Nr. 219 (11 Sep 1941)], 2751.

64   H. Boberach, Vol. 8 [Nr. 221 (18 Sep 1941)], 2775–2776. This episode may be viewed on Regisseur: Hans Ertl 1/3: http://www.youtube.com/watch?v=LYWIgW6BfOQ

65   H. Ertl (1985), 104.

66   H. Ertl (1985), 111–113.
67   H. Ertl (1985), 116–118.
68   H. Ertl (1985), 127–128.
69   H. Boberach, Vol. 7 [Nr. 207 (31 Jul 1941)], 2596; [Nr. 209 (7 Aug 1941)], 2623–2624.
70   H. Ertl (1985), 133–134, 139–141.
71   H. Ertl (1985), 145, 149–153, 162, 165.
72   H. Boberach, Vol. 11 [Nr. 316 (10 Sep 1942)], 4192.
73   H. Boberach, Vol. 11 [Nr. 318 (17 Sep 1942)], 4213.
74   H. Ertl (1985), 165–168, 173–175.
75   H. Ertl (1985), 198, 174.
76   H. Ertl (1985), 177–183. Regisseur: Hans Ertl 3/3.
77   H. Ertl (1985), 183–196.
78   H. Ertl (1985), 187–188, 219–220.
79   H. Ertl (1985), 107, 110.
80   H. Ertl (1985), 245, 258.
81   On the *Alpenfestung*, see S. G. Fritz, *Endkampf: Soldiers, Civilians, and the Death of the Third Reich* (Lexington, KY: University Press of Kentucky, 2004), 2–6, 10–22, 221–222.
82   S. G. Fritz, 254–257, 260–268.
83   Regisseur: Hans Ertl 2/3.
84   H. Ertl (1982), 7.
85   Regisseur: Hans Ertl 3/3.
86   Herbert Huber page on Hans Ertl: http://www.sonntagshorn.de/person/ HHB07.htm
87   H. Ertl (1985), 164–165, 168, 191, 199, 230.
88   Speech to the US Senate, 1917, found in J. Simpson (Ed.), *The Oxford Dictionary of Quotations* (Oxford: Oxford University Press, 1979), 273.
89   Bundesarchiv: Leni Riefenstahl's file.
90   Herbert Huber page on Hans Ertl.
91   D. Uziel, 394–395.

Notes on Contributors

PHILLIP KNIGHTLEY was a special correspondent for *The Sunday Times* (1965–1985) and one of the leaders of its Insight investigative team. He was British Press Awards Journalist of the Year (1980 and 1988), one of only two journalists to have won this accolade twice. He is the author of ten non-fiction books, including *The First Casualty* (on war and propaganda), published in eight languages. He is the European representative of the International Consortium of Investigative Journalists, Washington. He was awarded the Order of Australia in 2005 for services to journalism and as an author. He has an Honorary Doctorate of Arts from Sydney University and the City University, London. He is currently Visiting Professor of Journalism at Lincoln University, England.

First World War

STEPHEN BADSEY is Professor of Conflict Studies at the University of Wolverhampton UK. Educated at Cambridge University, he received an MA in 1981 and a PhD in 1982, and was made a Fellow of the Royal Historical Society in 1995. He has held research positions at the Imperial War Museum in London, the British Broadcasting Corporation, and the Royal Military Academy Sandhurst, and various university posts in the UK and overseas. An internationally recognized specialist on military-media issues, he has written or edited more than 80 books and articles, including *The Media and International Security* (2000) and *The British Army in Battle and Its Image 1914–18* (2009).

JENNY MACLEOD is a Lecturer in Twentieth Century History at the University of Hull. She was a Research Fellow (2003–2006) at the Centre for the Study of the Two World Wars, The University of Edinburgh. Prior to that, she worked for King's College London, at the Joint Services Command and Staff College, and the Menzies Centre for Australian Studies. She has published on the cultural history of the Gallipoli campaign, *Reconsidering Gallipoli* (2004) and *Gallipoli: Making History* (2004). She is working on a new transnational study of the campaign to be published by Oxford University Press. She is the co-founder and treasurer of the International Society for First World War Studies, which comprises more than 300 academics and postgraduates in 24 countries.

YVONNE MCEWEN joined the Centre for the Study of the Two World Wars at the University of Edinburgh in 2005 as Honorary Fellow. In 2009 she was appointed the Official Historian to the British Army Nursing Service. In the same year she was awarded the Gloeckner Fellowship from Drexel University College of Medicine's Archives and Legacy Centre, Philadelphia. As a result of the Fellowship, she is now a Visiting Scholar at the College of Medicine and its Institute for Women's Health and Leadership. Her published works include, *'Their Ancient Valour': The Politics of Irish Volunteering and Volunteer War Deaths in the Second World War* (2011) and *It's a Long Way to Tipperary: British and Irish Nurses in The Great War* (2006).

TOM QUINN graduated from Dublin City University in 1998 with a BA in Applied Languages (French and Spanish), before embarking on doctoral research on the French novelist Louis-Ferdinand Celine's 1932 masterpiece *Voyage au bout de la nuit* (*Journey to the End of the Night*). He published *The Traumatic Memory of the Great War 1914–1918 in Louis-Ferdinand Celine's Voyage au bout de la nuit* (2005). He has lectured on World War One literature in Britain, Ireland and Continental Europe. He holds a particular affection for the history of the 16th (Irish) Division and collaborated with friend and colleague Henry Beattie, and Yvonne McEwen, to secure the Division's place in the history of the Great War.

Second World War

PHYLOMENA H. BADSEY was awarded her PhD from Kingston University on *The Political Theory of Vera Brittain* in 2005. In 2010, she was awarded her MA in Second World War Studies (with Merit) from Birmingham University. She has held administrative and lecturing posts at Kingston, Roehampton and Wolverhampton Universities. Her particular areas of research are women and warfare, first- and second-wave feminism and pacifism, strategic bombing and its critics, and France and the Channel Islands under German occupation 1940–1945. She combines both university administrative and lecturing posts, and is a member of the School of Law, Social Sciences and Communications – Research Cluster in Justice, Politics and Human Rights – University of Wolverhampton.

BRIAN P. D. HANNON is a PhD candidate in the School of History, Classics and Archaeology, The University of Edinburgh. His research focus is war correspondents of the Second World War, specifically those reporting on British and Dominion forces in the African and European theatres. In 2006 he earned a distinction from The University of Edinburgh for his MSc dissertation, *Creating the Correspondent: How the BBC Selected, Trained, and Equipped its War Reporters in WWII*. Previously he earned a bachelor's degree in English from Boston College, and worked for eight years as a newspaper reporter and editor in the eastern United States and the Czech Republic. In 2004 he gained a master's degree in Modern European History from Providence College, RI.

STEVEN M. MINER is Professor of History at Ohio University and Director of the Contemporary History Institute there. He is a recognized authority on The Great Patriotic War. His major teaching area is Russian and Soviet history. His fellowships, professional honours and teaching awards include: the Presidential Recognition Award, Rice University; two years fellowships, Rice University; Charles Septimus Longscope Award, Rice University; International Relations Fellowship, Indiana University; Dan

Armstrong Award, Russian and East European Institute, Indiana; Hoover Institution Fellowship and George Louis Beer Award, American Historical Association. He is the author of *Between Churchill and Stalin, Stalin's Holy War: Religion, Nationalism, and the Politics of Alliance, 1941–1945* and the forthcoming *The Furies Unleashed: The Soviet People at War, 1941–45.*

JILL STEPHENSON's entire academic career, apart from one year at the University of Glasgow, has been spent in History at The University of Edinburgh. Early research focused on the position of women in German society in 1918–1945. She has published widely on this subject, most recently *Women in Nazi Germany* (2001). Since the 1980s, her research focus has been 'war and society' in the twentieth century, especially the social history of Württemberg, where the population's preoccupations were family, land, community and church, regardless of Nazi propaganda and ideology. She published *Hitler's Home Front: Württemberg under the Nazis* in 2006. She retired from The University of Edinburgh in 2009 but still remains active in academic life.

PATRICK S. WASHBURN is Professor Emeritus in the E W Scripps School of Journalism at Ohio University. He has bachelor's and master's degrees in journalism, and completed a doctorate in mass communication in 1984. His doctoral dissertation, *A Question of Sedition: The Federal Government's Investigation of the Black Press during World War II*, was published by Oxford University Press in 1986. He was an advisor for a 1999 Public Broadcasting Service documentary on the history of black newspapers, *The Black Press: Soldiers Without Swords*. From 2001 to 2012, he was editor of *Journalism History*, the US's oldest mass-communication history journal. He has authored many journal articles including, 'The Office of Censorship's Attempt to Control Press Coverage of the Atomic Bomb During World War II' (1990).

FIONA ANNE FISKEN has a BSc in Biological Sciences, and enjoys a successful, twenty-six-year career in publishing. She trained as a sub-editor on journals at Blackwell Scientific Publications, Edinburgh. While at

Blackwell, she met Yvonne McEwen where they worked together editing an international journal on emergency and disaster medicine. In 1989 she joined The Zoological Society of London to work on the *International Zoo Yearbook*, an annual peer-reviewed reference book that acts as a forum for the exchange of information for professionals and others concerned with the care, conservation, biology and behaviour of wild animals. In 2003, she became Managing Editor. Furthermore, she has been a chapter contributor to books on conservation.

Index